WOMEN'S ROOTS

Status and Achievements

In Western Civilization

By
June Stephenson, Ph.D.

Diemer, Smith Publishing Company, Inc.
3377 Solano Ave., Suite 322
Napa, California 94558

The author gratefully acknowledges permission to reprint the material from the following sources:

- *The Evolution of Man and Society* by D. C. Darlington, reprinted by permission of George Allen & Unwin Inc. Copyright © 1969.
- *Man the Hunter*, Copyright © 1968 by the Wenner-Gren Foundation for Anthropological Research, Inc. Reprinted with permission from *Man the Hunter*, edited by Richard B. Lee and Irven Devore (New York: Aldine Publishing Company).
- *Daily Life in Ancient Egypt, Daily Life in the Middle Ages, Daily Life in the Renaissance, Daily Life in Ancient Rome*, Copyright © 1975 American Heritage Publishing Company, Inc., reprinted by permission from American Heritage Publishing Company, Inc.
- *Medieval Women* by Eileen Edna Power, ed. M. M. Postan, Copyright © 1975 Cambridge University Press.
- *Mothers and Amazons* by Helen Diner, reprinted by permission of Crown Publishers.
- *When God Was a Woman* by Merlin Stone. Copyright © 1976 by Merlin Stone, reprinted by permission of Doubleday and Company, Inc.
- *The Book of the Courtier* by Baldassare Castiglione, reprinted by permission of Doubleday.

Other books by June Stephenson

THE ADMINISTRATOR
HUMANITY'S SEARCH FOR THE MEANING OF LIFE
IT'S ALL RIGHT TO GET OLD
A LIE IS A DEBT

Dedicated to my father

Frederick Ortegren
who taught me freedom to choose is vital for human dignity.

Women's Roots
Status and Achievements
in Western Civilization

Table of Contents

INTRODUCTION

This short history book attempts to portray women's status and their contributions to the development of Western civilization from prehistoric times to the present. As the whole story cannot be told in a short survey, the scope of the study is focused on what seems to be the most representative of women in each historical period.

Heretofore almost all of history has been written by men, about actions which are important to men, and about the accomplishments of men. Women's lives have been virtually ignored. Throughout the United States, girls and boys for most of their 12 years in grades one through twelve in social studies or history lessons are required to learn almost exclusively about the accomplishments of men. In 1979, in spite of the women's movement, affirmative action programs, and publishers' guidelines, in the United States History texts, for example, for every 700 pages about men there were only 14 pages about women.[1]

The omission of women in history is a serious void in the education of both boys and girls. It fosters an attitude that says in effect what females did or do is unimportant, an attitude that cannot help but adversely affect human relationships. This author believes that the imbalance in the teaching of history helps to perpetuate sex discrimination and it demeans girls. This book is one small effort to help balance history so that both boys and girls can learn about the buried history of one-half of the population.

Though this is a history of women, it includes women's relationships with men. For, throughout history and before, women have lived their lives alongside men. What women could or could not accomplish, depended on what their relationship was with the men in the society. Also, women's lives are always intricately woven into the society of the historical period in which they live. So it is necessary to have some knowledge of what was going on in the society to understand the female/male relationships in each period. Because this book includes information which may not be of general knowledge, there are numerous quotations from a variety of reliable sources to substantiate history. Nothing in this book is new. It draws from scholarly books which have been written over the years. This, however, attempts to bring it together for general readership.

In some early historical periods it is almost impossible to discover the names of notable women of accomplishment.

> The zeal of masculine historians . . . in destroying even the memory of great women has rendered the pursuit of feminine historical research extremely difficult . . . yet the role of women in molding history and their influence on the events that have shaped men's destiny are incalculable.[2]

As the study moves through history, more women's names are uncovered, until, in the last periods the names of many women important to history had to be left unmentioned because of lack of space.

This book progresses from one historical period to the next. It begins with a study of the cultures of prehistoric and non-industrialized people in various places around the world, and it ends with a focus on women's lives in the United States today. The conclusion looks to the lessons of history in attempting to understand the present. The author's interest in writing this history book began in 1975 when she developed a history-of-women course at Napa High School in Napa, California. Finding material to teach the course was quite difficult. Whatever little information there was about women in history was scattered about in various libraries around the country. Because there was no book for general readership which chronologically portrayed women in the development of Western civilization, the author recognized the need for such a book.

At the end of each semester of the history-of-women course at Napa High School, both boys and girls expressed amazement at what they had learned about women's struggles and achievements. The standard comment was, "I didn't know women had done anything before." The reader of this book will learn how much women did accomplish in spite of the powerful constraints which each society throughout history has put upon them.

DEFINITIONS

In order to read without having to stop and look up words in the dictionary, it is a good idea to know the meaning of the following words:

1. *adultery*—sexual intercourse between a married woman and a man not her husband, or between a married man and a woman not his wife

2. *anthropology*—study of customs and myths

3. *archeology*—study of life and culture of ancient people

4. *canon law*—laws governing the affairs of the Christian church

5. *chastity*—abstaining from unlawful sexual activity, said especially of women

6. *concubine*—a secondary wife, wife of inferior social and legal status

7. *convent*—the building and grounds where religious women lived, prayed, worked, taught the children in the area, and carried on scholarly work

8. *courtesan*—women intellectuals, accomplished in music, or poetry, mathematics, philosophy. Their names were linked to famous men

9. *deity*—a god or goddess

10. *dowry*—the property that a woman brings with her into marriage

11. *egalitarian*—holding the belief that all people should have equal political and social rights

12. *endogamy*—marrying only within one's own tribe or group

13. *exogamy*—marrying outside the tribe or group

14. *feminism*—a theory that women should have political, economic, and social rights equal to those of men

15. *fidelity*—faithful devotion to duty or of one's obligation or vows

16. *heresy*—a religious belief opposed to the orthodox doctrines of a church

17. *heretic*—a person who holds beliefs opposed to the official church doctrines

18. *hetairae*—in ancient Greece, an educated courtesan or concubine

19. *incest*—sexual intercourse between persons too closely related to marry legally

20. *infanticide*—the killing of an infant

21. *infidel*—not believing in the prevailing religion, used by Moslems and Christians for nonbelievers

22. *kin*—a relative

23. *maternity*—the state of being a mother

24. *matriarchal*—a government, tribe, religion or other institution ruled by women

25. *matriarchy*—a form of social organization in which the mother is recognized as the head of the family or tribe, descent and kinship being traced through the mother instead of the father

26. *matrilineal*—descent and kinship derived through the mother instead of the father

27. *matrilocal*—after marriage the couple lives in the home of the bride's mother

28. *misogyny*—hatred of women

29. *monastery*—the building and grounds where religious men lived, prayed, pursued scholarly works—a base of operation for their social work in the area

30. *monk*—a man who joins a religious order, living in retirement according to a rule and under vows of poverty, obedience and chastity

31. *monogamy*—the practice of being married to only one person at a time

32. *morés*—customs and folkways of a people

33. *nun*—a woman who joins a religious order, living in retirement according to a rule and under vows of poverty, obedience and chastity

34. *paleontology*—study of prehistoric forms of life—plant and animal fossils

35. *paternity*—the state of being a father

36. *patriarchal*—a government, tribe, religion, or other institution ruled by men

37. *patriarchy*—a form of social organization in which the father is recognized as the head of the family or tribe, descent and kinship being traced through the father

38. *patrilineal*—descent and kinship derived through the father

39. *patrilocal*—after marriage the couple lives in the home of the groom's father

40. *polygamy*—the state of having two or more mates at the same time—plural marriage

41. *procreation*—producing young—beget

42. *prostitute*—to sell one's services for purpose of sexual intercourse

43. *puberty*—state of physical development when it is first possible to beget or bear children

44. *sexism*—believing one sex is better than the other

45. *sociology*—study of people living together in social groups

46. *taboo*—a sacred prohibition—something that is forbidden

47. *theology*—study of religious doctrines and matters of divinity

48. *vernacular*—using the native language of a country

49. *virgin*—a woman who has not had sexual intercourse—less commonly, a man who has not had sexual intercourse

Historical Time-Periods

It is important to know these historical periods. Other historians may disagree somewhat with these dates, but for the purposes of this study the information in the text will refer to these periods and dates. It will be a good idea to memorize this chart, differentiating between BC. and AD.

Prehistoric ....500,000 BC. to 2500 BC.

Antiquity.....................2500 BC. to 400 AD.

Medieval,
Middle Ages, Dark Ages ....400 AD. to 1400 AD.

Renaissance ....1400 AD. to 1700 AD.

Modern....................1700 AD. to the present

A historical time-line shows the distinct division between BC. and AD., dividing the time periods *before* the birth of Christ, referred to as BC., and *after* the birth of Christ, referred to as AD.

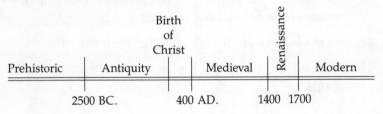

Chapter I

PREHISTORIC PEOPLES AND TODAY'S HUNTERS AND GATHERERS
Prehistoric Beginnings:
500,000–15,000 BC.

The word, "prehistoric," meaning "before history," refers to a period in time before people consciously left a record of their existence in the forms of building, writing, artifacts, and other creations. We know that the prehistoric period came to an end about 3000 BC., but we are uncertain about when human existence on earth began.

Periodically we see in the news that human fossil bones have been uncovered dating back a million years before the *last* bones were uncovered. It is difficult to keep up with the latest evidence.

It is also possible that all the scientific theories of human beginnings on earth may be overturned with a new discovery in some cave not yet found. Currently, archeological evidence supports the theory that our own species, Homo Sapiens, existed on earth at least by 40,000 BC., though the Biblical theory and its evidence date the human appearance on earth about 4000 BC. With courteous respect to everyone's right to believe as they wish,

1

this study of the beginnings of men and women on earth will refer to the scientific theory.

There may be some confusion about the words, "prehistoric," and "hunters and gatherers." Prehistoric peoples had varying degrees of culture and settlement but no written record. Tribes called hunters and gatherers are those who have chosen to stay with hunting and gathering techniques of subsistence and live much as their ancestors are believed to have lived in prehistoric times. They have complex cultures but simple technologies. They are sometimes referred to as non-technical cultures.

There are hunting and gathering tribes living in many parts of the world today, including New Guinea, Africa, South America, Indonesia, the Philippines, and Arabia, all with a life-style which anthropologists believe may retain some important characteristics of prehistoric life. For instance, some Australian Aborigines who have rejected civilization, wander nomadically, living off the land. They use stone-cutting implements and stone-pointed spears. They do not use bows and arrows. They hunt with boomerangs and spears. The women scour the land for seeds and bulb roots, edible fungus, birds' eggs, snakes, and the pupae of moths, caterpillars, beetles, flies, honey, ants and burrowing rodents.[1] They have far more sophisticated environmental knowledge than people living in industrialized societies.

The Caribou Eskimos of Northern Canada sustain themselves by methods used in the Middle Stone Age. Their implements are made of antlers and other bones. The basic social unit is the family, but that may mean a family with several wives, with an exchange of wives among friends.

Why Study Prehistoric Peoples and Today's Hunters and Gatherers?

Generally the study of history begins with the years around 2500 BC., with the beginning of civilization. Yet ninety percent of human existence on earth was in a hunt-

2

ing and gathering life-style. At least 7000 years of prehistory, about which we have fragmented information, have been largely ignored.

The history of what men and women have accomplished did not begin with civilization. There is a large body of evidence, and a great deal of scholarly writing by men and women, strongly suggesting that women's greatest achievements were made in the period *before* history. Therefore, any survey of women in history needs to include at least a brief study of the prehistoric period.

It is important to include a study of today's hunters and gatherers, as some of the subsistence customs of prehistoric tribes are replicated in the life-styles of today's tribes, such as matriliny, totems and taboos, the extended family, secondary importance of father as compared to the primary importance of mother's brother in the "family," blood taboos, and mother-in-law avoidance. All of these and more will be discussed in later sections.

There are two sources of deductive information about our buried past. We can study artifacts, graves, tools, cities, and paintings left behind from prehistory, and we can study existing tribes. Archeologists have studied evidence from caves, burial sites, and buried settlements dating back to at least 10,000 BC. In so doing they have been able to relate the drawings they have found to probable rituals and the activities in prehistoric society played by each sex. The artifacts left with the deceased have provided clues to the life-style of the group, and the buried cities have left a record of the activities and living quarters of the males, females, and the children.[2]

By assigning dates to certain articles like ceremonial bowls or weapons, by measuring the size of male and female fossil bones, archeologists, anthropologists, and paleontologists can reasonably reconstruct a culture, determine the probable diseases in prehistoric tribes, and assess the strength required of males and females in their work roles.

The customs of people who are today living in close partnership with nature, who are using stone and bone

3

tools, and governed by taboos, provide anthropologists with valuable information about probable prehistoric courtship and marriage customs, and male and female work-roles and achievements.

But studying prehistoric and today's tribal peoples does more than give us a glimpse into our own beginnings. It shows us that responses which are "natural," for one group may not be "natural" for another. In fact, what is "natural" for one group may be abhorrent to another. "The careful study of primitive societies is important today . . . for they help us to differentiate between those responses (attitudes and acts) that are specific to local culture types and those that are general to mankind."[3]

First Social Groupings—What is a Family?

Prehistoric people lived nomadically, roaming the earth's surface in search of food. The men hunted animals and the women and children gathered roots, berries, fruits, and nuts. "In 10,000 BC., on the eve of agriculture, hunters covered most of the habitable globe."[4] They did not live in houses, nor in settlements, but moved from place to place until the climate became either too hot or too cold, or when they had killed off the game and eaten all the food that grew in the area. It was not until after about 10,000 BC. that people learned to plant seeds and to remain in the planting area until the harvest.

All the people in the nomadic group were responsible for the total group for food gathering, for sharing, and for safety of the group. Life was perilous. In this period of cannibalism, human strangers were dangerous enemies. These small hordes of people needed to be constantly on the alert for animals or strangers, ready to move, to defend themselves, or to attack. "Neither large bands nor 'nuclear families' could have survived."[5] All children were protected and nourished by all women, and all women were therefore mothers to all children. Girls the same age were sisters, and boys the same age were brothers. The male who was important to a woman was her brother.[6] A male child looked to his mother's brother for guidance in learning the male skills of hunting animals and enemy people. The female child looked to her mother for learning the skills of softening hides, gathering foods, and building temporary shelters. The patriarchal family as we know it today with the father of the children as the head of the group was unknown in pre-history.

Descent was traced through the female, a matrilineal custom which persists to this day in several tribes. It was believed in prehistoric times that children came from supernatural powers, from the *mana* or magic bestowed in females, a power of fertility which men did not have, and for which women were revered.[7] Though the power of human reproduction was revered, infants were not always welcome. Because a baby was someone who had to be carried and another mouth to feed, infanticide was an accepted practice of population control. "A fifteen to twenty percent incidence of infanticide may have existed throughout the pre-agricultural history of man."[8] Girl babies who could be expected to grow up and produce other babies, who in turn would need to be fed, were more apt to be left behind or strangled than boy babies.

Infanticide is still practiced in some tribes and has been practiced throughout history in industrial societies as well as in tribal societies. A mother in the Amahuaca tribe in Peru who has just given birth, may return from her solitary trip into the jungle empty-handed if she feels she does not want the child and this will not be considered murder. ". . . for the baby is not a social being until it has grown older. Girls are less useful than boys, and are therefore more frequently strangled."[9]

Wherever they settled, if only in huts for a short time, most tribes separated the men's living quarters from the women's and children's. When a boy reached puberty he left his mother's hut and went to live in the men's hut. These characteristic patterns are still evident. Today in India, the Nayars' husbands or mates do not live with their wives, nor do they support their children.

The Pygmies who live by hunting and gathering in the African Congo Basin live in a nuclear family, "but a child will call everyone in his parents' age-group, father or

5

mother, everyone older, 'grandparent'."[10] Among the Herero in Southwest Africa, the principal property, cattle, is inherited through the mother and a child is part of his mother's matriclan, not his father's.[11] In the Trobriand Islands, New Guinea, "legally speaking a father is not a kinsman to his children . . . he is just their mother's husband following the view that all inheritance of blood, property, power and spirit pass from the mother. The children's real guardian is their mother's brother. Trobrianders actually deny the father's role in procreation. Whether or not the Trobrianders are ignorant of biological paternity is much debated."[12] Though the Trobriand Islander children receive guidance and discipline from their mother's brothers, they grow up in a loving relationship with their biological father, referring to him as the one who helped to care for them when they were young.

Among the Xikrin in Brazil, all family members, grandmothers, granddaughters, husbands, sons, brothers live together in one hut, under female authority.[13] The children call their mother's sisters, "mother," and when the mother wants her young son to obey, she tells him she will call his uncle.[14]

It would seem that each group, whether a small horde, a related family, a clan, or a tribe would be overrun with children in the absence of scientific knowledge about contraception and with relative sexual freedom. But an over-abundance of children was and is not the case. Infanticide was a socially accepted way of limiting population. But probably more important as a reason for the small number of children by tribal women was and is the taboo or restriction which prohibits sexual intercourse with a mother until she has weaned her child, which may take several years.[15] This sexual taboo during the long nursing or lactation period may be one of the reasons why so many tribes practice polygamy. Polygamy in tribal life is not likened to a man with a harem. The tribesmen provide separate huts for each wife and her children, and it is she, not he, who decides when she will have sexual intercourse with him.[16] Rather than jealousy among wives, women in polygamous tribes encourage their husbands to take another wife, for each wife reduces the total work load.

In summary, a prehistoric "family" was at first a group of people who traveled together for mutual protection, production, and survival.

Since it was the mother who fulfilled most of the parental functions, the family was first (so far as we can pierce the mists of history) organized on the assumption that the position of the man in the family was superficial and incidental while that of the woman was fundamental and supreme. In some existing tribes, and probably in the earliest human groups the physiological role of the male in reproduction appears to have escaped notice . . .[17]

When nomadic tribes settled down to live continuously in one place, the "family" was a mother and her children who lived in her own hut, while the men lived in the men's house. The relics of prehistoric "family" structure which exist in today's tribes are the matrilineal qualities of tracing descent and inheritance in some tribes, the separation in many tribes of men's and women's eating and sleeping quarters, and the importance of the mother's brother instead of the father in the upbringing of children.

Gender Roles

In any society the work to be done is divided into man's work and woman's work. Whether this should or should not be is not an issue in this stage of this study. In hunting and gathering societies men hunt during the day, and women and children roam in search of edibles such as roots, berries, nuts, and grains. In prehistoric times when the men returned with an animal, they turned it over to the women for skinning, hanging, and for any other preparation, including tanning the hides to later sew into clothing or boots.

Looking at the remains of buried living areas, archeologists have surmised the work-roles of females around their area, and the work-roles of the males around the men's hut. Though there are some exceptions where women participated in the hunt, as for instance among the tribes of New Spain, Nicaragua, Terre del Fuego, Tibet, West Africa, and Tasmania, or as with the traditional Eskimos where it is a cooperative enterprise for the entire family group, hunting is considered primarily a male domain. ". . . hunting is so universal and so consistently a male activity that it must have been a basic part of the early cultural adaptation, even if it provided only a modest proportion of the food supplies."[18]

Prehistoric man was essentially an idler who hunted and that was all. The women gathered food, built and repaired the huts, and did all the other chores.[19]

Because the hunt is an unreliable source for food and men often came home empty-handed, the group depended on women for their food supply. "It was woman the gatherer, not man the hunter, who fed the primitive family."[20]

It is said that men are dominant over women because men are stronger than women. But if men are stronger that women today, that has not always been so. The work-roles of males in prehistoric times were not as strenuous as the work-roles of females. When nomads traveled, the men needed to have their arms free to attack or defend. Women, therefore, carried whatever needed to be moved.

Bodies become conditioned to the work required of them. Men needed to be able to run fast and to throw spears a great distance. For that, they developed leg and arm muscles. Women stooped in the search for food and they carried food, water, and the heavy loads of timber needed to build huts, and as a result they developed strong, muscular bodies. Fossil skeletons of female bones are as massive as males and the muscular attachments are almost as large.

Today a man of the Kikuyus tribe in East Africa would consider forty pounds a reasonable burden to carry, whereas women will carry 100 pounds. "A Kikuyu is quite unequal to carrying a load that his women think nothing of."[21] King Bushmen of The Dobe Area, ". . . are conscientious but not particularly successful hunters; although men's and women's work input is roughly equivalent in terms of man-day of effort, the women provide two to three times as much food by weight as the men."[22] As a result of their hard work, women were as strong or stronger than men. "The labor record of primitive women does not warrant the assertion that they were physically weak or helpless."[23]

> The difference which now divides the sexes hardly existed in those days, and are now environmental rather than innate. Woman, apart from her biological disabilities, was almost the equal of man in stature, endurance, resourcefulness and courage; she was not yet an ornament, a thing of beauty, or a sexual toy; she was a robust animal, able to perform arduous work for long hours, and, if necessary, to fight to the death for her children of her clan.[24]

Puberty Rites

There are certain rituals or ceremonies in society which mark a person's passage from one stage of development to the next. These are known as "Rites of Passage." In contemporary society we have, among others, graduation ceremonies, wedding ceremonies, baptismal ceremonies, wedding anniversary ceremonies, retirement, and funeral ceremonies. Margaret Mead, the famous anthropologist, has said that a society with emphasis on rituals, and myths behind the rituals, has a good sense of purpose and integrity.[25] Conversely, societies whose rituals are weakened for whatever reason, either flounder until they can restructure the myth and ritual, or they disintegrate.

The Masai warriors of Africa, though they are exposed to civilization, which has destroyed many tribes, hold strong to their rituals and myths, and consequently they are a prideful tribe.

On the other hand, many tribes too numerous to mention here, have been so affected by civilization that their heretofore sacred rituals are observed only by the elders, while the young people of the tribe go off to the towns to learn the rituals of their "civilizers." Returning, they demean their own tribal customs, many of which have come down through thousands of years from prehistory.

One of the important rites of passage which has descended to today's tribal peoples is the puberty rite. This is the ritual, different from tribe to tribe, and almost non-existent for girls, which marks a boy's passage into manhood. These rituals affect the way boys are conditioned to value "manhood." Also, because the rituals reserve the knowledge of the secret tribal myths for males only, they create a sense of male importance by excluding women. Boys grow up in the "family" with their brothers and sisters. When childhood ends at about eleven to thirteen years of age, the boys are separated from their mothers to be initiated into manhood by the elder men of the clan. The boys are isolated from the rest of the clan and put through ceremonies intentionally meant to scare them and to scar them. Boys, in order to become men, have to prove that they are unafraid, and that they can take pain "like a man." Only then can the boys see the sacred objects, learn the secrets of the clan, and the history of the clan's great achievements.

As a manhood test, the Txukahamei of South America require that the boys hit a wasp nest and "suffer the angry stings and fever."[26] Among the Kavirondo,

> If a victim does show pain his father is so humiliated that he runs away and hides in the bush . . . Another element in the ceremony is the fact that it is so rigidly taboo to women that the boy is supposed to reject his mother . . .[27]

In some clans the boys' teeth are knocked out and these gaping holes are a mark of pride, proving the boys' manhood. In other tribes the boys' bodies are purposefully cut and ashes put on the wounds to raise permanent welts that serve as badges of honor. All of these activities create a bonding and a brotherhood of males, collectively shocked into manhood by pain and fear. The initiates form a bonding which lasts all their lives.

The Herero of Southwest Africa, who have been initiated together ". . . regard themselves as 'coeval,' members of a special kind of brotherhood, who can call upon each other as a right in times of stress and difficulty, and can count on each other's support in all circumstances. A Herero cannot refuse a coeval anything."[28] In prehistoric times and today, it is the uncles of the boys—their mothers' brothers—who guide the initiates.

Women had not always been excluded from these rituals. In the earlier puberty rites women were allowed to watch and to participate, but later their presence was forbidden.[29] In fact, in some clans today a woman can be put to death if she even accidentally comes upon the secret male rituals. For women are not only forbidden to learn the clan secrets, but they also may not learn that the mysterious noises associated with male initiations are not the noise of their god, but the noise from bamboo flutes or bull-roarers. As John Langdon-Davies writes:

> Since women are unclean they were, in the early stage of savage society, rigidly excluded from the religious life of the community; thus in Australia tribal ceremonies may be divided into major and minor, and at the latter only women could participate.

> Both alike centered in the great moment when the boy, having reached the age of puberty, was to be received into full tribal membership, to leave the company of women and children and to become a man, with all the privileges of that state. As the moment, when the central mysteries that were to be revealed

11

was approaching, all the women had to leave the sacred ground and return to their own camp; for the ceremonies about to be held were those which no woman might see and live. At these Tunden, God himself, came down and made the boys into men, and, though the roaring of his voice could be heard far and wide, no woman must see him. So strong was this feeling, Howitt tells us, that fifty years after the country was settled by the white man, a headman said: "If a woman were to see these things or hear what we tell the boys, I would kill her."

The boys who are to be initiated are told that they are going to be "shown their grandfathers." They are placed in a row and covered with blankets so that they are unable to see anything which is going on about them. Shortly an appalling noise is heard, a roar like a ship's foghorn, rising and falling, wailing and groaning in the air about their heads. In spite of the frightening experiences already suffered by the unfortunate novices, sweat pours from them as they listen to the voice of their God. Next they are bidden to stand up and look into the sky. "Look there! Look there!" cries the headman, pointing with his throwing-stick first upwards, then gradually lower till he reaches sixteen men, who have been responsible for the noise. The terrified novices learn then the secret of Tunden's voice; it is made by whirling a "bull-roarer," a flat piece of wood on the end of a string, like a civilized child's "buzzer," which howls loudly as it is whirled about their heads.

Next, two old men run to the novices and in a very earnest manner command them, "You must never tell this. You must not tell your mother, nor your sister, nor anyone who is not initiated." After further explanations the boys take the bull-roarer in their hands and whirl it with some reluctance for the first time.

Later in the day a great ceremony takes place with the name, significant for our history, of "Frightening the Women." Each novice, bull-roarer in hand, advances toward the camp where are the women and children. These have always been taught that the hideous noise heard in the distance is Tunden himself come to "make boys into men," and they have been warned never to leave the camp while he is about, lest he kill them. Concealing themselves behind the trees and bushes, the initiated youths walk around and around the camp, whirling their bull-roarers with gusto, thoroughly entering into the fun of frightening the women, who are terrified at the sound.

Thus in primitive societies women are excluded from the Holy of Holies, unfit for the crowning mysteries of life; they remain children where social maturity is the sharing in just these ceremonies which are forbidden to them. They themselves have the firmest belief in the wickedness of their seeing any of the mysteries. Dr. Codrington tells how a woman in the New Hebrides accidentally saw a newly initiated youth during his purificatory washing, and fled to a neighboring mission school in terror at her sin; when her people came after, she voluntarily gave herself up, and returned to be buried alive without a murmur.[30]

Even though keeping these secrets from women brands women as incomplete, the women participate in the secret-making because keeping myths and rituals is important to the stability of the culture. By protecting their men's secrets, they help to perpetuate tribal pride, even at the expense of maintaining their own inferiority in the culture.

In many tribes the boys experience a mock birth ceremony, being regurgitated, for instance, by a man-made crocodile where they are then declared "twice-born," for it is believed that women make children, but only men can make men. The Arapash male elders in New Guinea cut their arms, draw blood and mix it with coconut milk. The novices drink this and ceremoniously become the elders' children, for the child at birth has only its mother's blood, which is deemed inferior.[31]

No young man in prehistoric times or in today's tribes who has been initiated may return to his mother's hut to live. He will move to the men's house which is the center of ritual activity, taboo to females and uninitiated boys. His life will be forever after different. He will transfer from women's food to men's food, with more meat in it. But the most important change will be that he is now ready for mating. That does not mean that he will now participate for the first time in sexual activity; that has been a part of his growing up. But mating is a different thing. No tribal woman would be mated with a male who did not have the scars to prove that he had successfully passed the test of manhood.

Puberty rites for girls were and are more inclined to mark them in a tabooed condition, that is, with red powder on their bodies to make their "untouchability" or menstruation visible so nobody will come near them. For girls, there is no elaborate ceremony in which they are born again, nor do they learn the clan's secrets or accomplishments. These are reserved for males.

In Brazil the Xingu girl retreats to seclusion at her first menstruation, some remaining secluded for as long as two years. Xingu boys also spend several years in seclusion.

The southern Xingu tribes believe that the transition from adolescence to adulthood is a dangerous period, when you must be protected and cared for.

The entrance of the secluded girls into the village plaza is an exciting moment in the *kuarupe* ritual. Out they come, beautifully adorned with the family's shell belts and beads, from the windowless village houses. Their bodies are white and corpulent from months of seclusion and inactivity; cotton yarn has been tightly wound around their swollen legs. Precious yellow feathers have been woven into their long black hair which covers their eyes as it has not been cut since the first menstruation. They are now marriageable women, and they walk before the chiefs of the visiting

14

tribes placing before each a handful of fruit nuts that symbolize the fertility and sexuality of these girls now returning to tribal life as women.[32]

Among the Xhosa of South Africa, "A feast is held to celebrate a girl's first menstruation to which all including passers-by are invited to celebrate, the information now being broadcast that the daughter of the house has reached marriageable age."[33]

Totems and Taboos

Totems and taboos which governed prehistoric clan customs exist in all of today's tribes. A totem is a symbol for the clan or the tribe, and all the people living under the same symbol are considered of the same "family." People living under the same totem symbols are bound together forever, and they are different from anyone else.

Just as a high school may call itself "The Tiger," and wear tiger insignia on their band uniforms and football jerseys, a clan's totem also could be a tiger. But unlike the high school student who might treat his insignia rather light-heartedly, each member of the tribal totemic family would have a deep, spiritual association with the tiger; it would be considered the spiritual ancestor of each clan member.

Totem is an ancestor, a protector, an aid in hunting, and is full of the vital *mana* which infuses all of the members of the clan. Likewise, the clan members are thought to fuse with the ancestral totem in a sort of incarnation after death.[34]

Some totems are animals the tribe depends on, or ones that are feared. In some clans the totem is a plant, which may not be eaten, or it may be the wind, or the stars. Whatever it is, the totem must be respected more than human life.

15

Within each totem family there were and are strict taboos. Evelyn Reed explains the necessity for these totemic taboos:

> The survival of a species, whether human or animal, depends upon the fulfillment of two basic needs: food and sex. Food takes priority; without regular nourishment the animal dies. But mating is also mandatory if the species is to continue. These twin needs are the dynamic of the behavior and evolution of mammalian species.
>
> Hunger is the organic mechanism worked out in natural evolution to prod species into action to satisfy these needs. It has two forms: hunger for food and hunger for mates. Driven by these imperatives, animals seek out the closest available sources to satisfy both hungers. In one species alone, the human species, survival came to depend upon social controls over these biological needs.
>
> This is the underlying meaning of the primitive institution of totemism and taboo. It represents the earliest form of social control over food and sex hungers, classifying that which is forbidden in both realms. The sex clause is well known; under totemic law a man could not mate with any woman belonging to his totem-kin group. Under the food clause, a man was prohibited from killing or eating totem-kin animals.[35]

The most widespread taboos were and are, the food taboo, the blood taboo, the incest taboo, and the mother-in-law taboo.

The Food Taboo

The food taboo forbid men and women from eating together.[36] As each sex lived separately, they also ate separately, and they ate different kinds of foods. The men were essentially meat eaters and the women were primarily vegetable and fruit eaters. Among the Jale in the New Guinea Highlands,

The women gather insects, lizards, mice and frogs, while the men hunt birds, bats, and a number of small mammals such as the tree kangaroo, cuscus and giant rats . . . An elaborate code, enforced by ritual sanctions against any offender, defines the range of foodstuffs that must not be eaten by males or females respectively.[37]

This food segregation taboo in prehistoric times which persists today, refutes the theory that man has always been the provider for his mate and children. More often the case was that when men returned unsuccessful from the hunt, it was the women who had the more reliable food source to give to the men. The food segregation of the sexes was even more pronounced between mates.

The spouses belonged to different clans. Under the classificatory system the term 'marriage division' was more importantly the 'food division' to which each of the spouses belonged. The wife belonged to her food division in *her* matriclan, the husband to his food division in *his* matriclan. Thus, even though a husband had sexual intercourse with a woman he could have no food intercourse with her.

The taboo against males and females eating together comes down to modern times. When Captain Cook visited Polynesia he wrote that the women never ate with the men and that eating together was more taboo than sex. The Trobriand Islanders never have a meal together unless they are married. "To take her to dinner before he married her (even though they had spent nights together in approved cohabitation) would be to disgrace her."[39]

Today, the engagement-party dinner, with members of both families, often with newspaper publicity, is a carry-over from the food taboo. Eating together publicly signifies that members of each family accept each other.

The Blood Taboo

Women, wanting not to be harassed by men during specific times in their lives, namely during menstruation and after their babies were born, told men that their blood would be bad for men, and that men's spiritual world would be damaged in the presence of women's blood. This taboo that women created to protect themselves was turned against them. Menstruating women, and women after childbirth, were then, and in some major religions today, and in all tribal groups, considered contaminators and polluters.

Briffault sums it up in his book, *The Mothers:*

> The most fundamental of all primitive tabus are those referring to women and sexual intercourse. Tabus on the approach of men to women during and after parturition, and during menstruation, are the most strictly observed of all primitive tabus. All the world over, and not only among primitives, the tabus attaching to menstrual women are similar. And those which refer to women in childbed are practically identical with them. The latter have little reference to the child, but refer to the lochial discharge. Premature births and all issues of blood are treated in the same manner as full-time births as regards tabu.

> It would weary the reader to recapitulate the vast array of evidence from societies in every part of the world which can be brought together to demonstrate the similarity of such tabus. The practices of the Eskimo may be taken as representative of all others. Four weeks before her confinement a woman retires to a separate hut, which no man is allowed to approach. She remains there for a month after she has been delivered, when the father is allowed to see his child for the first time. Should a woman be unexpectedly

18

seized with labor pains, all the men stop work and build a snow-hut as quickly as possible. During her period of seclusion the woman cannot eat or drink in the open air; even the remains of her meals must be disposed of inside her hut. She has her own cups and dishes, which men must be careful not to use, and is subject to dietary regulations. If the few kinds of food which are permitted are unobtainable, she may have to go without eating. Among the Tlinkit, females are driven out of the house at the time of childbirth, and only some time after birth is a mother allowed to enter a rude shelter erected for the purpose.

In the same way, a menstruating woman is regarded as a being with whom all contact, however innocent, would entail dreadful consequences. In most societies a special hut is provided to which women must resort during their menstrual period. Special ceremonies regulate the first menstruation. Thus among the Dene, a girl at her first menstruation remains isolated for two lunar months. She must not touch even her own food with her hands, and is provided with a stick to scratch her head. In some cases the woman's head is wrapped up so that she can see nobody, and she is submitted to purges and fastings. In other cases a girl, at her first menstruation, is placed in a hammock near the smoke-vent of her hut so as to be thoroughly fumigated, and only at night may she rise to cook a little food for herself. The vessels which she has used are immediately broken and buried. Among the Guaranis and other tribes the girls are sewn up in their hammocks in the same way as corpses, only the smallest opening being left to allow them to breathe, and are suspended over the fire for several days. Not infrequently the unfortunate girls die under the process of disinfection. In some cases the women are beaten and all their hair is plucked out.

Some observers have thought that this retiring of the woman was due to an instinctive sentiment of modesty, but since, in some cases the women are allowed to deliver their children upon their knees in the public street in the presence of everyone, this is hardly likely. In Russia, a woman after delivery is regarded as being in a state of impurity, and may not hold any communication with others until she has been purified by a priest. In the province of Smolensk she is confined in a barn or hut some distances from houses.

The Hebrews attached the greatest importance to the primitive tabu. "If a woman have an issue and her issue in her flesh be blood, she shall be put apart seven days; and whosoever toucheth her shall be unclean until evening." Anyone who touched her bed or anything that she sat upon was required "to wash his clothes, and bathe himself in water, and be unclean until the evening." On the eighth day, after, she had to take two pigeons to the tabernacle, one as a sin-offering and the other as a burnt-offering, and the priest has to make atonement for her.

In Ancient Persia the very glance from the eye of a menstruous woman was so polluting that she must not look upon a fire or upon water, nor converse with any man. She was confined during menstruation to an isolated portion of the house, no fire was to be kindled and everyone was to remain at least fifteen paces from any fire or water. When the period was over, the clothes which she had been wearing must be destroyed, and she must be purified by being washed with bull's urine. The tabus attaching to childbirth were exactly similar. The rule mentioned by Herodotus that a man might not see his own child until it was five years old probably refers to a similar length exclusion of a man from the house of his wife. The modern Parsees still observe most of the rules of their ancestors, and it is not long since there were in Parsee communities public menstrual houses to which women resorted at their periods.

Much the same is true among races of the Malay Peninsula. In Africa, Akikuyu women menstruate in a hut, which is at once then destroyed as unfit for human habitation. Among the Menangkabau of Sumatra if a menstruating woman were to go near a rice field the crop would fail. Among the Visayans of the Philippine Islands when a woman is overtaken by childbirth everything is removed from the house, else the weapons would no longer be efficient, nets would catch no more fish, and fighting-cocks, their most valued possession, would no longer be able to fight. Among the Caroline Islanders, women are wrapped up in mats from head to foot during the whole duration of pregnancy, and seclusion continues for five or six months after delivery. They may not paint their faces nor anoint their hair, and are unfit to undertake any cooking. Were a man to touch so much as a drop of water from the pools in which they wash, it would be impossible for him to catch any fish. In Nauru, one of the Gilbert Islands, not only may not food be eaten that has been touched by a tabu woman, but it is considered that the nuts of any trees within a hundred feet of such a woman's dwelling are unfit.

As these instances show, the tabus are not derived from any abstract principle, but from dread of the dire effects of contact with women in these conditions. The Dene believe that a contact with menstrual blood will turn a man into a woman. The Tlinkit are persuaded that a single look from a menstruating woman would completely destroy the luck of a hunter, fisherman, or gambler, and that it might even, like the Medusa's head, believe that contact with a menstruating woman will deprive a man of his manhood . . .[40]

Today, menstruating women are forbidden to enter Buddhist temples in Bali, and ". . . menstruating women may not enter the temple, or women who have just had a child may not go into the inner courtyard of a temple or

21

go too near a priest whose purity must be preserved."[41] In South Africa, the Bacas tribe believes a man's bones will become soft if he touches a menstruating woman. A man could turn into a tree if he were a Bushman and a menstruating woman looked at him. And in Queensland, Australia, it is believed if a man came upon a place where a menstruating woman stayed when she was segregated he would die.[42]

The blood taboo against women is not just a prehistoric or tribal belief. It has come down through history, used as rationale for excluding women in various professions, and is the basis for many religious purification ceremonies.

The Incest Taboo

To protect women and girls from the sexual drive of males in the clans, women originated the incest taboo which forbids members of the same totemic family from having sex together. While other taboos have been weakened or destroyed through the ages, the incest taboo is today one of the strongest social taboos in all societies. Members of the same family are forbidden to have sex together or to marry. But the "family" in prehistoric and in many of today's tribes, as was said before, means the clan. One must go outside the group for sex and for marriage. "The incest taboo, initiated to protect the women of the family group was eventually extended to include all women of the tribe, and the custom of marrying out was adopted."[43] A man who married within his mother's totemic clan would probably be killed along with his mate.[44]

Every society has an incest group which puts its women off limits to its men. But these groups differ in different societies.

No known people regard all women as possible mates. This is not an effort, as is so often supposed, to prevent inbreeding in our sense, for over great parts

22

of the world it is an own cousin . . . who is the pre-destined spouse. The relative to whom the prohibition refers differs utterly among different peoples, but all human societies are alike in placing restrictions.[45]

Children in most tribes take the totem of their mother's clan. If the totem of the clan is a deer, the child could not grow up to marry a person in the deer totem-clan. That would be forbidden by the incest taboo. In some clans a complex marriage system determines that clan totems must be opposites. The Kogi of Colombia cannot marry into a clan unless it is a clan that has a totem very different from a deer, a puma clan being an example.[46]

The Mother-in-Law Taboo

In today's tribal societies the custom of avoidance of certain persons comes down to present times from the prehistoric period. In the days of distrust between clans with different totems, those outside one's totem were to be considered deadly enemies. Yet the incest taboo prescribed that mating must be between members of different totem clans. A young man who was invited into his mate's compound after he had successfully passed his puberty rites in his own clan would naturally have been instructed to avoid people who were dangerous to him. The most dangerous would be the mother of the girl he wanted to mate, also the girl's brother, and her mother's brother. In some tribes the word for mother-in-law and her brother is the same.

As early mating, under the exogamous totemic law, was done on enemy grounds, the young man had been warned by his own clan elders to be wary of enemies, sorcerers, and witches. Witches were among the wise, old females in the group, and wizards were among the wise, old men. Witches could be dangerous, for they were believed to have great magical power, for both good and evil. It behooved a young man, a stranger in his mate's clan, to avoid any contact with his mate's mother for she could be a witch.

23

As all women are mothers to all children, a man in the Kariera clan of Australia, regards all married women of his wife's mother's age as those to be avoided. He must not speak to or look at them. This custom does not break down until the husband himself becomes an elder.[47]

Eventually, as distrust changed to friendship, the avoidance between males decreased, but the mother-in-law avoidance continues to this day. In some societies if a man speaks to or even looks at this mother-in-law this is viewed with as much horror as is a breach of the incest taboo.[48] A tribal man will hide in the bushes to avoid his mother-in-law if she is approaching.[49]

Among today's tribal peoples avoidance does not now symbolize fear. It has grown to symbolize respect. However, in our present-day industrialized cultures we acknowledge the tension in the mother-in-law situation by ridiculing her in the familiar "mother-in-law jokes."

Sexual Morés

Morés, or customs, reflect moral values which are often different from group to group, and from one historical period to another. As times change, values often change. People gradually abandoned their day-to-day existence in small nomadic hordes and settled in larger and larger groups. They accumulated and valued private property, set up stable communities, and eventually over thousands of years established nations. In all of this, their moral values and behavior changed as their conditions changed.

We judge others from our own perspective, and if people have different values than we do, we might be tempted to call them "weird," or even "disgusting." A more appropriate word to describe the various morés this book explores is the word, "different." In earlier times, and today in other places in the world, people are different and they have different moral values.

It is clear that what men are ashamed of depends entirely upon the local taboos and customs of their group. Until recently a Chinese woman was ashamed to show her foot, an Arab woman her face, a Taureg woman her mouth; but the woman of ancient Egypt, or nineteenth century India or twentieth century Bali (before tourists came) never thought of shame at the exposure of their breasts.[50]

In prehistoric societies, as children were considered the children of all the mothers, there was no sense of illegitimacy. Sexual activity before marriage was not, and in many tribes today, is not, frowned on. Consequently no value was placed on virginity. When missionaries stressed the virtue of virginity, tribal peoples could not comprehend how it could have any value for "what the primitive maiden dreaded was not the loss of virginity, but a reputation for sterility."[51] Proven fertility was a young woman's value. If she had children, that proved she was blessed with the supernatural gift of being able to create human beings.

In today's tribal societies, as among the Gonds of Bastar, in non-Hindu Central India, "boys and girls enjoy many years of sexual liberty."

Premarital intercourse is left for the most part free in the simplest societies. Among the North American Indian the young men and women mated freely; and these relations were not held an impediment to marriage. Among the Papuans of New Guinea sex life began an an extremely early age, and premarital promiscuity was the rule. Similar premarital liberty obtain among the Soyots of Sibertia, the Igorots of the Philippines, the natives of Upper Burma, the Kaffirs and Bushmen of Africa, the tribes of the Niger and the Uganda of New George, the Murray Islands, the Andaman Islands, Tahiti, Polynesia, Assam, etc.[52]

It should be repeated here that what was or is acceptable in one culture may be cause for social ostracism in another.

It is possible that once mated, men and women lived monogamously, at least for as long as the marriage lasted. Girls could send their husbands away if the man did not please her or her mother's family As no property was involved and children were believed to be only the wife's, dissolving a relationship did not entail lengthy dispute.

The Great Shift: 15,000—2,500 B.C.
From Hunting and Gathering to the
Age of Cultivation

About 15,000 to 10,000 BC., long after the last ice age had ended, when the earth's surface had warmed sufficiently, the human life-style began to change. This has been called the agricultural revolution which started the Age of Cultivation.

It is not known how it was learned that seeds could be planted and their crop later harvested so that people did not have to move from place to place in search of food. Some suggest that this knowledge was associated with death, where grain was strewn on burial grounds for a departed's after-life. With some rain, or possibly some blood from a sacrifice, the seeds later sprouted. When agriculture was established as a way of life, seeding the soil was often accompanied by human or animal sacrifice, urging the fertility Goddess to bless the people with bountiful crops.

Changed Gender Roles

Women being especially familiar with plants and their productivity are credited with being the first planters.

If anyone deserved credit for one of the few historical developments that can truthfully be described as epoch-making it must have been women, for hers was the knowledge on which agriculture was based.[53]

26

At first, women used the fire-hardened digging stick to cultivate the ground. When men were away on the hunt, women refined their tool-making skills.

The business of learning agriculture, selection, planting, weeding, and so forth was an extended process that took place over many hundreds of thousands of years. To accomplish it, women had to invent many other things besides methods of cultivation and better hoes. They learned enough chemistry to make pottery that would hold water and could be cooked in . . . Women learned enough mechanics to construct looms for spinning textiles, as well as better ways of home building (which is a purely feminine occupation in some neolithic tribes). They also learned—and shaped tools for—grinding wheat, constructing ovens, and using the biochemistry of yeast to make bread.

In mainly agricultural societies of the primitive hoe type, women were the most important food providers. The meat provided by male hunters was much less in quantity and more unstable in supply. As a result, women had a very high status in most of these societies.[54]

Women also established trade between other villages and became priestesses who conducted religious rituals. As McGowan writes, "Women invented work, for primitive man was only an idler."[55]

At first men did the unskilled labor as assistants to women. They cleared away the brush, felled trees, and prepared the ground for cultivation by the women . . . Men eventually began to initiate improvements in a whole series of industrial techniques. With the potter's wheel, for example, men took over potmaking and made it one of their specialized trades. They took over the ovens and kilns invented by women and developed these into forges where they smelted the earth's metals—copper, gold, iron . . .

Social labor is the prime feature distinguishing humans from animals. In the beginning this was largely in the hands of women. They were, so to speak, the first farmers and industrialists; the first scientists, doctors, nurses, architects, and engineers; the first teachers, artists, linguists, and historians. The households they managed were not merely kitchens and nurseries; they were the first factories, laboratories, clinics, schools and social centers. Far from being 'drudgery,' woman's work was supremely creative.[56]

Will Durant writes:

Most economic advances in early society were made by women rather than men. While for centuries he clung to his ancient ways of hunting and herding, she developed agriculture near the camp . . . rolled thread into cotton cloth . . . developed sewing, weaving, basketry, pottery, woodworking, and building.[57]

Later in this new period, somewhere around 6000 BC., women began to domesticate animals. They captured wild sheep, or cattle around their village, or took animal offspring from their lair, raising them for milking or for eating, ". . . during the early agricultural, precivilization era in human history. If woman ever 'ruled,' it was at this time."[58]

. . . new agriculture made livestock farming almost inevitable. The fields that attracted humans also attracted some of the smaller game animals . . . and it must have seemed easier to pen the marauders than protect the fields.[59]

With agriculture and with animal husbandry it was no longer necessary for men to go on the hunt for food. Hunting then became a sport. Men, having experience with animals in the hunt, came to look on domesticated animals as their domain. Freed from the daily hunt, they could spend more time in the community.

When cattle were domesticated somewhere around 6000 BC., man learned to castrate the bull and use it as a draft animal—humanity's first power tool, as revolutionary in its way as the first steam locomotive. It was man, the expert on animals, who was the one to handle it when it was yoked to the hoe or plough.[60]

Gradually men took over the cattle-raising from the women.

Anthropologist Leavitt writes: "The most important clue to woman's status anywhere is her degree of participation in economic life and her control over property and the products she produces . . ."[61] "In most primitive societies the group doing the labor and providing the food has a high status, while the opposite is often true in more advanced societies."[62]

The Advent of Property

Cattle became man's first property. A man's wealth was measured by the number of cattle he owned. Where private property in nomadic life had been virtually unknown, or at least shared with everyone in the group, with the raising of cattle, property became important on an individual basis. Cattle was the standard by which most other things were valued.

Crops, initially women's product, were already usurped by men. When the lands were cultivated by the digging stick and only for the immediate needs of the group, they were women's work. But by the time crops were planted for surplus and for trading, agriculture was moving out of the hands of women. Men, slaves, plows, and work-animals replaced women in the field, or put them under the supervision of men.

The very economy which women developed, destroyed their equality with men. Women domesticated the animals, and men who had previously related to animals in the wilds related to domestic animals. They took to raising them and claimed them as

29

their own. Cattle became the first property of man which elevated him above women. A man could buy a wife or many wives by giving women's family cattle. Pastoral (cattle raising) were the first patrilocal and patriarchal peoples.[63]

In the pastoral society, man was dominant, and woman was as much his chattel as the beasts he herded. It is no coincidence that the male-oriented society of the West today should be in a direct line of moral and philosophical descent from a few tribes of Hebrew nomads . . .[64]

Men also took over the trading that women had established and became the decision-makers for the growing communities.

An important side-effect of the value of property and the desire to accumulate was the change in the social structure. Where groups had been part of an egalitarian, one-class society, wealth produced a stratified society—that is a society of several classes of people. As men gained wealth they bought slaves. Or, where previously the losers in a tribal war had been eaten, when labor was valued the victors took the conquered home as slaves. From then on, physical labor was considered demeaning because it was the work of the lowest social class. Wives of rich men lived in luxury with slaves to wait on them.

One might say that this is a good condition for women, but if a woman's *work* is not valued—her value becomes that of a sex object.[65]

Agriculture, while generating civilization, led not only to private property but to slavery. In purely hunting communities, slavery had been unknown . . .[66]

Generally speaking, it is in those primitive societies where women toil most that their status is most independent and their influence greatest; where they are idle and work is done by slaves, the women are, as a rule, little more than sexual slaves.[67]

30

Why did women let it all go? Boulding suggests that women may have been suffering from work-overload.

Why didn't women reduce their own work loads substantially, giving themselves more time to think about that 'larger picture?' They had the 'power' to allocate their own time differently, and presumably the men's time too. 'Why didn't they . . . ?' is an old question in history. New social perceptions are slow to form, and we can only say that the women did not shift to the necessary new perceptions of their activities and of the total organization of village life soon enough to prevent loss of 'political power.'[68]

History of Knowledge of Paternity

The history of the knowledge of paternity begins most likely with the domestication of animals. Before animal husbandry it was a world-wide belief that infants were souls who had previously inhabited trees, or were spirits that entered a woman's womb when she ate a certain food, or wore a fertility charm.[69]

When men became involved in raising animals for surplus they had only to observe the regular reproductive process of the sheep or the cattle to learn of their own biological importance in human reproduction. However it was still thousands of years before science provided the correct information.

Aristotle, around 400 BC. said that the child was the seed of the father, and the mother was merely the vessel. This theory persisted until after the invention of the microscope, sixteen hundred years later. In 1786 Spallanzani discovered male germ cells, and in 1843, the fusion of male and female cells was understood. In 1879, barely 100 years ago, this fusion was demonstrated by Hermon Fol.[70]

Little wonder that prehistoric primitives had no knowledge of paternity when our own scientific civilization has only so recently learned the actual human procreative process.

When men learned that their mate's children were not hers alone, men laid claim to their children. Unlike children in nomadic hordes who were often left behind when food was scarce, children in the Age of Cultivation were assets. They could work the field or herd the animals. Men began to reckon lineage through themselves and bequeathed their property to their sons. They placed a property value on their daughters, determining their daughters' worth by how many cattle they could get in exchange for their daughters in marriage.

The planting of crops, domestication of animals, knowledge of paternity, together with the value of property and slavery all combined to change society. Matriliny which reckons descent through the mother, and in which children inherit from the mother, does not fit in the male's desire to leave his possession to his kin only. Matriliny branches out to woman's children, brothers, and sisters. "Patriliny reserves all for a man's nuclear family, excluding all else."[71]

Men needed to ensure that their property would go to their own children and not to some other man's children. To do this, men restricted the sexual freedom which females had exercised in pre-propertied society. After men discovered their role in procreation

> . . . it was now possible for a man to look at a child and call him 'my son'; to fill the need to call a woman 'my wife.' Whatever the marital custom before that time . . . after it, woman's sexual freedom began to be seriously curtailed. A man might have a harem if he could defend it, but the concept of "my" son required the woman to be monogamous.[72]

Changed Sexual Morés

In cattle-raising property-conscious groups, no longer were boys and girls permitted to play at sexual intercourse. If a man was to be assured that the bride he purchased with cattle would have no children except his, he must be guaranteed of her virginity. Female virginity therefore developed a marketable quality. A male suitor's virginity, however, was not an issue as his sexual freedom was not restricted. Thus property gave birth to the double-standard, one standard for the sexual morés of females and another for the males, though in hunting and gathering societies there had been no difference in the sexual morés between the sexes.

If girls must be virgins at marriage, but males need not be, where would unmarried males find their sexual partners? Property, thus, also gave birth to prostitution.

Once a girl was married there were strict rules of chastity and fidelity. But no society in the world has concerned itself with male chastity.[73] Severe punishment for adultery and rape developed. These crimes were considered theft of a man's property. The punishment was especially severe if a woman was raped who came from the upper class.

> The Incas burned alive any man suspected of adultery with any of the Inca's wives or concubines, together with the woman. Also, 'his parents, sons, brothers, and all other near relatives were to be killed and even his flocks slaughtered, his native town or village was to be depopulated and sown with salt.'

> Among the Niam, seduction of the wife of a chief is punished with horrible mutilation, but among the ordinary people a present of cloth or beads salves the feelings of the husband.[73A]

> Among the Cayupa of Ecuador, where land is valued, they 'tend to lay the blame for adultery on the woman.' It is woman, they say, who incite the men. Indeed, the punishment—with cat-o'-nine-tails—falls more often to the women. It is common for a man to plead innocence, claiming he was coerced by the woman.[74]

Where there had been no such thing as illegitimacy in hunting-gathering societies, with the advent of property, children born to an unmarried woman were often near outcasts of society. Thousands of years later, Dr. Samuel Johnson wrote that illegitimate children should be penalized from birth, "because the chastity of women being of the utmost importance as all property depends on it."[75]

"In primitive societies there was no difference between children born of paired peoples or not."[76]

Regardless of why the social life of humankind changed with the coming of the Age of Cultivation and its attendant knowledge of paternity and the value of property, the fact is, agricultural and herding societies, compared with hunting and gathering societies, became patriarchal when they had been previously, at least mildly matriarchal, and certainly matrilocal and matrilineal. In hunting and gathering societies today, remnants of prehistoric matriliny still exist though marriages are often now patrilocal and based on property. The family as we know it, makes its appearance with the arrival of the value of property.

The Development of Pair-Bonding and Marriage

In order to find out how the earliest modern man, say 30,000 years ago, managed their breeding we have to look at the most primitive kinds of men who survive today. Anthropologists have searched out these people. They have described their habits with great accuracy and their evidence has given us a picture which shows most significant agreement; significant, that is, of the behavior of our common ancestors.[77]

From anthropological and archeological study, it has been surmised that in hunting-gathering societies, when the men were away from the camp hunting, and the women and children were gathering food, if a woman saw a man from another clan, and if she were attracted to him, she could make arrangements for him to visit her in her mother's hut that night and for as many nights as she wished. This would be very dangerous for the man because he would be going into enemy territory where he might be killed unless he could be given some protection. All this being known, the woman would arrange with her brother to give the stranger "safe passage" to and from her mother's hut. If any children resulted from this mating they were the woman's, fatherhood being unknown. This type of mating required no new family grouping because the man did not live with the woman.[78]

> Far from being eternal, pair-unions developed slowly and precariously over a long period of time. The right of safe passage . . . was a signal advance over earlier fleeting encounters between the sexes in the forest . . . This precarious situation can be seen more clearly in what is sometimes called 'institution of the visiting husband.' In the earliest stage of matrimony the husband was little more than a visitor to his wife's community. He did not start out by occupying a separate house or hut with his wife; he was given accommodations in the male clubhouse reserved for strangers and visiting husbands. There under the surveillance of his wife's male kin he slept and took his meals.[79]

"In primitive states women enjoyed independence and influence not achieved under patriarchy. There is no evidence to suggest that patrilocal marriage existed before matrilocal."[80]

Protection by the brother in a clan to a member of an enemy clan, related the two men. The stranger became an extended family member—a cross cousin.

An interesting matrilocal primitive marriage custom practiced by the Dobu Islanders in the Western Pacific is the "sleeping over" betrothal. When a man and woman decide to make a marriage of their previous sexual arrangement, the man who has visited his wife's hut, purposefully "sleeps over." He does not leave her hut in the middle of the night as he had previously done. The girl's mother, recognizing the man's action as an application for marriage, has to make a decision. If she lets him go, she is indicating that he has not met with his future mother-in-law's approval. If, however, she sits in the doorway, blocking his exit, she is publicly demonstrating that she has accepted him. The neighbors are then curious. What young man from what clan will emerge? They send for their friends and relatives from far and wide. The young man and woman emerge and sit on the ground in front of the hut. The whole tribe stares at them for as long as a half hour. The staring is a public announcement of the marriage. That is all it takes. There is no further ceremony.

When the crowd leaves, the mother-in-law gives the young man a gardening tool, a digging stick, and tells him to go to work. His work buys him the right to the marriage he has just begun. Now he will live in the men's house, but he will work for his mother-in-law, returning to his own clan for his totemic ritual celebrations.[82] "Thus the husband makes his appearance in history as a gardener working for his wife's kin."[83] The Kung Bushman "groom usually joins the girl's band and works for her parents for a number of years."[84] These bondings or marriages would be called "marriage by service."

Early pairing and early marriages were matrilocal. The men came and visited, and eventually came and lived in the women's mother's house. Matrilocal marriages were difficult for men. Only a visitor in his wife's house, the man, for all important occasions returned home to his own clan. It was at his mother's house that the grain and the sacred objects were kept. When his mother died, a man's first allegiance then went to his sister. A sister-brother relationship was stronger than a husband-wife relationship because a sister would always be a sister, but a wife could later be someone else's. If a wife died before him, a husband was pushed out of the hut to return to his own clan.[85]

Marriage in an early primitive pattern exists among the Xikrin of Brazil:

> . . . often a youth slips silently into a girl's family hut every night. He does not eat while there and tactfully slips away before dawn. However, when his first child is born, he moves in with his in-laws. He hunts food for them, cuts down a forest plot for his wife's garden, and fully supports her and the children. Nevertheless he has little prestige among her relatives and almost no say in family matters. He is accepted into his wife's family slowly as his children grow older and as his children have children. A grandfather is highly respected.[86]

A form of migratory marriage evolved with a husband making a garden at this wife's home, and a garden also at his mother's where his wife came to live from time to time. But women returned home to their mother's for long periods of time, especially at childbirth, before marriage became more firmly patrilocal.

Marriage evolved from matrilocal, to migratory, to patrilocal. Instead of working for his mother-in-law, as a price he paid to be married to his wife, a man would pay his mother-in-law goods valued at what his work was worth for a period of time. As soon as a man pays a "bride-price" for his wife, this is the beginning of removing her from her mother's home to *his* mother's home. If he married without a bride-price, she stays in her own home. But if he pays, he can take her and sell her, even at a profit.[87]

The first marriages that were related to property developed in the cattle-raising countries of Africa, Asia and Europe.[88] Marriage developed alongside the development of animal husbandry and is distinctly aligned with property. The man buys his wife with a "bride-price," or, in other instances the girl brings into her marriage a dowry, her wealth, which in a sense buys a husband for her.

37

Among the African Masai, "The number of a man's wives depends on his wealth in cattle. Bride-wealth is usually about three cows, two sheep, and an ox."[89]

Will Durant explains the development of the dowry system of marriage:

Marriage by purchase prevails throughout primitive Africa . . . it flourished, in ancient India and Judea, and in pre-Colombian Central American and Peru; . . . It is a natural development of patriarchal institutions; the father owns the daughter, and may dispose of her, within broad limits, as he sees fit. The Orinoco Indians expressed the matter by saying that the suitor should pay the father for rearing the girl for his use. Sometimes the girl was exhibited to potential suitors in a bride-show, so among the Somalis the bride, richly caparisoned, was led about on horseback or on foot, in an atmosphere heavily perfumed to stir the suitors to a handsome price. There is no record of women objecting to marriage by purchase; on the contrary, they took keen pride in the sums paid for them, and scorned the woman who gave herself in marriage without a price; they believed that in a 'love match' the villainous male was getting too much for nothing. On the other hand, it was usual for the father to acknowledge the bridegrooms' payment with a return gift which, as time went on, approximated more and more in value to the sum offered for the bride. Rich fathers, anxious to smooth the way for their daughters, gradually enlarged these gifts until the institution of the dowry took form: and the purchase of the husband by the father replaced, or accomplished, the purchase of the wife by the suitor.[90]

Among the Jalé in New Guinea Highlands, a married girl goes to live with her husband's family. Her children belong to her husband's lineage and therefore her procreative ability is "lost" to her group. The man gives his wife's kin a pig to validate their marriage, and pay for what her group lost.[91]

The marriage relationship among Pygmies is complicated. In some groups the task of locating a potential wife is a problem for young men, because of the economic value of women. Females may be valued for their individual qualities, but in the main they are looked upon as essential workers and as the producers of more pygmies. A family group, as tenacious of its collective life as the individual of his own life, will not let a girl go without acquiring another in return. Thus there has arisen the "head-for-a-head" system, called in Kingwana kichwa-kichwa.

A young man of sixteen or seventeen may find in a neighboring group a girl of thirteen or fourteen he would like to marry. The basis for his choice may depend in part on her beauty and figure, but her aptitude for hard work carries more weight. The young man must not only win the consent of the girl's father and pay him a purchase price—which might be six arrows and a spear, or eight arrows and so much bark cloth, or four arrows and a good piece of iron—but he must also become matchmaker and persuade a girl in his own family group to marry a young man in his girl's neighboring group. When all this is accomplished, the girl goes home with her husband, without any ceremony. But this is not the end. When the wife bears a child, the husband makes an additional payment to her father. Even if she has no child, he makes a further payment at the end of six months or a year, when both parties to the marriage decide it will probably work out. If the girl should prove sterile, or if the young couple should decide the marriage is not good, the man can return the girl to her father and get his payment back. But this is complicated by the other couple involved, who may want to continue their marriage.

Even after many years of happy, successful marriage, a girl's strongest ties remain with her original family group and never with her husband's. She knows that her family will welcome her back happily—and her husband knows it, too, which puts a brake on his dictatorial power over her. A wife is his property; she is there to work and everyone knows it. It is all right for her husband to beat her once in a while, if only to remind her who is boss. But there are limits beyond which he cannot go. If he beats his wife too hard or too often, if he philanders regularly, if he fails to provide the necessities of life, if he is constantly mean to his children—then the wife will just walk back to her family. The family will welcome her and protect her, unless she is being too sensitive about an occasional smack on the head, in which case her family tells her to go back to her husband. Usually a wife leaves her husband only for very good cause.[92]

As has been said before, with the advent of the value of property, a girl's value depended on how many cattle her father could get for her at marriage. But the cattle were paid not only for her, but also for the children she would produce for her new husband. As children became valuable, infanticide decreased. If a wife had no children, the husband could demand another wife for the cattle he had given the girl's father.

Under these circumstances it was difficult for a woman to leave an unhappy marriage because she either had to give her husband a certain number of children, or the family had to return to him the cattle he had paid. In some cases she could leave after she gave him five children, but in other cases this could be only three children. If she had no children in her first marriage, but did in her second marriage, she had to give the children to her first husband.[93] A man therefore buys the woman and her offspring with the same rights as a man buys a cow and its calves. When the right to purchase women became a regular practice, women's freedom in some tribes was curtailed. Of course practices vary widely. In many tribes women keep the property they bring into the marriage and take it with them if they leave. But with the advent of property, men make marriage deals for their daughters with other men, based on property.[94]

The *lobola* among the Bantu today is the price a man pays to his wife's father for the children she will have which will be his if she leaves him.

> Once girls begin to leave the villages of their mothers to marry, and had to enter the villages of their husbands' fathers, patrilocality, the fluidity of earlier relationships disappeared and the practice of male dominance began.

> There are few dominance patterns in hunting-gathering type families.[95]

Women in most primitive cultures are ". . . freer, more powerful, and above all, economically more secure . . . than they are in civilized cultures."[96]

To summarize this section on pair-bonding and marriage, when wealth arises it is acquired by males, and the habit of buying a bride develops. The first commodity to be exchanged for a bride is cattle, from which the word "chattel" is derived, meaning exchangeable, movable property. When the bride goes to live in the male's domain she generally reckons the descent of her children through the father's lineage, especially after fatherhood is known. Fathers then assume the right to bequeath the family property to their sons.

Goddesses to Gods

"Among our ancestors in Western and Northern Europe, as elsewhere, it would appear that formerly religious and priestly functions belonged originally to women."[97]

Until paternity was known, women were considered sacred because it was believed that they were endowed with a supernatural gift given only to females to create other human beings. Johann Bachhofen, a Swiss historian, substantiated his intuition that pre-Hellenic (pre-

41

Greek) cultures were more female oriented than male, in his discoveries of thee agriculture-based mother-right cultures of Asia Minor which transferred later to Greece and Rome.

Small stone statuettes of Mother Goddesses found from Russia to Spain, sculptored as early as 25,000 BC., attest to the Great-Mother Goddess worship. Some have demeaned this worship as cult worship, but as this was a world-wide concept at the time, that would not fit the idea of a "cult."

> The appearance of these figures in a territory extending from Siberia to the Pyrenees seems to presuppose the presence of a unitary "World View" centering around the Great Goddess . . . They exemplify the dominance of the matriarchal, regardless of whether and to what extent the male, e.g. the hunter group, seized power over the woman in this epoch.[98]

> "Dating back to the 7th millenium BC. large settlements as large as small cities . . . display wall paintings and plaster relief of goddesses . . ."[99] "The All-Mother is older than the All-Father. Ishtar and Isis were the Universal Mother long before any sky god or tribal male deity had evolved from universal fatherhood."[100]

> The female theme of conservation and propagation of life . . . all the mysteries of life and death were hers, not his. All over the world this metaphysical supremacy of the female principle has asserted itself whenever horticultural production and human reproduction were linked.[101]

Learning about the religion of the historical period is an aid in understanding the relationship between females and males at that time. In history there are females among the deities and human females participated equally with men in the religious ceremonies. Elizabeth Dobell's recent article traces the historical process from a belief in goddesses and gods to a belief in one male god.

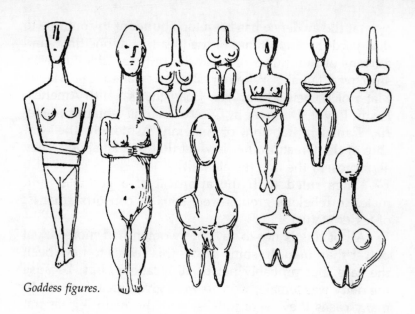

Goddess figures.

The great mystery of the creation of life was attributed to some divine power in women. Because women could bring forth life, it was believed that the female spirit was responsible for the creation of all life—plants and animals—even for night and day.

Whenever in history a mythology develops, it is most often accompanied by the need for a place to practice the rituals associated with the ideas. The earliest places of worship have been found in the Ukraine in Russia. Evidence tells us that as far back as 30,000 BC., worshipers gathered there to honor the Goddess. All over the world other ancient places of worship of the female deity have been found. In the goddess temples the mythology was reinforced in the same way it is reinforced in today's temples, churches and synagogues.

Because over the past 3000 years the idea of a single male god has dominated the thoughts of men and women, the concept of a female deity has been disregarded. The evidence of numerous goddess temples all over the world unearthed by scholars and archeologists was written off—referred to as places of mere cult worship.

Yet the evidence has been too abundant to continue to disregard the importance of the idea that at one time, and for tens of thousands of years the principal deity of worship was female. Whether she was called the Magna Mater of Rome and Phrygia, Coatlicus of South America, Isis in Egypt, Demeter in Greece, Inanna Ishtar in Sumeria, Tiamat in Babylon, of Asherah, Ashtoreth, the worship of the Great Mother is what that was all about. They all represent the one female deity.

Kings ruled with the approval of a goddess, and males in religious groups were sons or consorts—that is, of lesser status.

All of this is not to say that women had more actual power than men. In some places this seems to have been the case, but probably not in all locations. But, because the deity was female, women were given great respect. In many cases they were judges, and the main legislators, and there are records of women generals.

With the knowledge that men had a part in human reproduction, the women's role and importance in society was diminished. She was not divinely gifted, after all. She was relegated to the role of being simply the carrier of the male's seed. This was the beginning of male domination. In order for men to know that the child who inherits his name and property is his, it became necessary to restrict women, to put women out-of-bounds to any other male. Rules about virginity and adultery were eventually written into the male-dominated religious dogma.

The mysterious, spiritual side of life for which women had been responsible began to be seen as weak. And this consciousness was transferred to mythology. Female deities were gradually replaced by male deities. Sons and consorts of goddesses began to dominate goddesses and even to murder them if necessary in order to rule in the religious sense. In this way Tiamat was murdered by her great-great-grandson, Marduk, so he could replace her and be the King of the Universe.[102]

With the advent of male gods, ". . . what had been good became bad. Former heroes became demons."[103]

"Woman's magic powers became witchcraft."[104]

"The downfall of the Great Mother some three or four thousand years ago was a psychological event of the first magnitude."[105] The ascendency of male gods, ". . . shaped the relationship of the sexes . . . in such a way as to assure the complete predominance not always or necessarily of men, but of the masculine principle . . ."[106]

Whereas goddesses had represented abundance from the Earth, the gods functioned from above—the sky. Early gods were rain-makers.[107] "The Great Goddesses had to be overcome for men to become dominant."[108]

As time goes on it is predicted that archeologists will unearth more evidence of goddess worship. Since 1977, when the Goddess of Wisdom Temple was unearthed in Rome, two more relics have been discovered, the statue of Sekhmet, the ancient Egyptian Goddess, and the stone carving of the Aztec Moon Goddess, Coyolxahuqui, excavated in Mexico City, May, 1979.

Matriarchy vs. Patriarchy

Any book on the history of women must look at the controversy of whether or not there was a matriarchy before the existing patriarchy. Prejudice in favor of one theory or the other is apt to cloud the issue. Though there is not definite proof of the matriarchy, literature and archeological evidence supporting the matriarchy theory are abundant.

The accumulating archeological evidence of a matriarchal origin of human society calls for a drastic rewriting of the history of mankind on earth. 'The original matriarchy is obvious,' writes Graves, 'despite the patriarchal interpretation of the Old and New Testaments.' And James Hastings' *Encyclopedia of Religion and Ethics* states that 'it is certain that by far the more frequent process throughout the world has been the transition from mother-right (matriarchy), to father-right (patriarchy).[109]

45

'The violence of the antagonism against the theory of matriarchy arouses the suspicion that it is . . . based on an emotional prejudice against an assumption so foreign to the thinking and feeling of our patriarchal culture.' writes Erich Fromm.[110]

Yet the theory 'has been irrefutably confirmed,' says Campbell, by such archeological breakthroughs as the decipherment of the Cretan Linear B tablets—'a pre-Hellenic treasure trove.'[111]

In 1861 Bachofen proved the existence of matriarchies in Lycia, Athens, Crete, Lemnos, Egypt, Tibet, Central Asia, India, Orchomenos, Locris, Elis, Mantinea, Lesbos, and Cantabria. "He also predicted proof for similar conditions for a majority of the greater part of the earth and he was borne out."[112]

The institution of matriarchy

. . . ignored the male's role in the child's procreation and traced descent solely from the maternal line. "Descent," is here used in the literal sense, 'to come from.' Genealogy, therefore, was strictly feminine. There was no difference between children born inside or outside of wedlock, for all children inherited their mother's class and bore her name or that of her clan. Property was also inherited solely in the feminine line: it passed from the mother to her daughters, and so on. The sons received nothing, though occasionally their sisters gave them a dowry when they got married. They could not inherit anything from their bodily father, because he was not considered related to them. Whatever he captured or earned in his lifetime was logically bequeathed to his uterine clan through the common mother, or through her to the children of his sisters. These nephews and nieces were considered much more closely related to him than to their own fathers. During the transition between matriarchal and patriarchal law, the mother's brother was the only man who was accorded any influence upon the feminine clan.[113]

Recently three towns were unearthed in Anatolia, a region now called Turkey: Mersin, Hacilar, and Catal Huyuk. These three cities, dating back to at least 6000 BC., all worshipped goddesses.

James Mellaart, the archeologist in charge of the first digs at Catal Huyuk, was overwhelmed by the implications of the earliest revelations there. That the civilization expressed at Catal Huyuk was woman-dominated, he writes 'is . . . obvious.' Mellaart commenced his excavations at Catal Huyuk late in 1961, and the work still goes on. For the ancient city covers more than thirty-two acres of land and consists of at least twelve levels—city piled upon city dating back perhaps to the year 10,000 BC. The earliest radio-carbon dating available gives a reading of 7000 BC.—nine thousand years ago—but internal evidence suggests that the city may have been over a thousand years old even then; and the lowest levels had not then been reached.

Mellaart's report, written in 1966 before the completion of the excavations, shows that Catal Huyuk, whatever its name may have been ten thousand years ago, was not only a matriarchy but a utopian society. There had been no wars for a thousand years. There was an ordered pattern of society. There were no human or animal sacrifices; pets were kept and cherished. Vegetarianism prevailed, for domestic animals were kept for milk and wool—not for meat. There is no evidence of violent deaths. Women were the heads of households, and they were reverently buried, while men's bones were thrown into a charnel house. Above all, the supreme deity in all the temples was a goddess.[114]

Boulding writes of Catal Huyuk that "the preponderance of the evidence points to an all-female priestly class." Priestesses conducted funeral rites and women even had larger beds than men. "In Catal Huyuk . . . we are shown a society in which women are masters."[115]

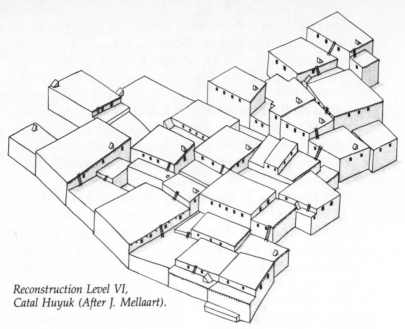

Reconstruction Level VI,
Catal Huyuk (After J. Mellaart).

Catal Huyuk is one of many examples. Yet as the idea of a matriarchy before patriarchy gathers strength and evidence, so does the opposition to the idea. As Reed says:

The most formidable barrier to recognizing the priority of the matriarchy is the reluctance to accept the maternal class as a unit of society that preceded the father-family. Such an acknowledgment would invalidate the claims that male supremacy has always existed because men are physically stronger and thereby socially superior to women, and that women as child-bearers are the weak and helpless sex and have always been dependent on men for the support of themselves and their children.

These assumptions are not borne out by the anthropological record. Women have always borne children, but there was a time when this did not interfere with their economic independence, as their productive record shows. Communal production was accompanied by collective child care. Women were not always beholden to husbands and fathers; before marriage and the family existed, their co-workers were the brothers and mothers' brothers of the clan.

Moreover, even after the husbands and fathers made their appearance in the clan system, it took a long time before marriage and the father-family were solidly instituted. Evidence for this can be seen in the segregation of wife from husband and of father from child.[116]

Opponents of the matriarchy theory point out, in spite of Mellaart's conclusions, that there is little if any scientific proof that matriarchy existed in prehistory. They reason that the lack of written evidence makes proof impossible. In answer to that charge, Pomeroy suggests that in all fairness, if prehistoric matriarchy cannot be proved, then by the same reasoning, prehistoric patriarchy should not be assumed.[117]

The author of this book believes that matriarchies probably did exist in some places in prehistoric societies. But though there is no conclusive evidence that women actually ruled "world-wide," there is evidence left from archeological sites, wastes, and artifacts that women in hunting-gathering societies were the major food providers for the group which indicates a reliance on their decisions for, among other things, movement from one place to another. In hunting-gathering cultures there is no dominance of one sex over the other. What can be said about the relative status of males and females is that in these tribal cultures females had and do have a higher status in their societies than women in other societies.

The Great Shift in Summary

Matriarchy or not, social groups had evolved from nomadic hunting-gathering clans to tribes. Over thousands of years people in the tribes settled, established villages, and learned to plan for the future.

In hunting-gathering cultures people did not generally store up supplies for the future. Frequently on the

49

move, searching for new food to eat, they considered possessions burdens. They ate what they found on the spot and moved on. Once they began to settle in one place, people could store food for the future. Also, once cattle had been domesticated and men took over animal husbandry, those who remained nomadic, bred cattle to increase their herds beyond the immediate needs of the group in order to gain wives, wealth, and prestige. Cattle-raising groups are most often male dominated. "Yet even where the man is dominant, there is not the demeaning subordination of women found in later class-divided, exploitive societies."[118]

The desire to accumulate possessions, property, wealth, and slaves created a new class structure, dividing those who had possessions and those who did not. Usually this was an upper class who lived in relative idleness and a lower class, or slave class, who worked. As work was relegated to the lower classes, work was demeaned.

> Agriculture was totally changed by the use of the plough from a female to a male occupation. This ended some of the hardest labor for women, but it also ended their control of the main food supply and reduced their socioeconomic status.[119]

> Where women's shoulders were the oldest means of transport, they were replaced by animals pulling wheeled vehicles. Along with the animals came male drivers. Besides the wheel for vehicles, men also invented the potter's wheel; and henceforth pottery was done by men. These male inventions helped women live better but reduced their status. When women no longer carried the heaviest burdens, did most of the agriculture, and made the pottery, the new situation removed the economic bases of women's equal or superior status. After men took over agriculture, transport, and pottery, as well as cattle raising, most societies became patriarchal. The male dominated the family or household, which included married sons and their families.

Yet even male economic dominance did not automatically mean the total subordination of women—any more than it did in the predominantly herding societies. What sealed the doom of women was the coming of slavery and/or serfdom, which ended both collective ownership and the matrilineal clan system. The clan system slowly gave way to individual families based on private property, beginning with the cattle owned by the male.[120]

. . . private property became the rule and . . . armed forces were formed to support the rule of the wealthy owners over the slaves and serfs . . . the male chief found ways to give his sons, not only his wealth, but also his authority and this ruling line of wealth and power finally became hereditary.[121]

In such societies, even ruling-class women came to be treated as property, the same as slaves and serfs, sometimes more valuable, sometimes less so. Woman's value declined both because slaves could do the productive work and because slave women could be used for sexual pleasure. The double standard was instituted whereby a husband could have sex with any woman but the wife was to be strictly monogamous. The reason for the strict control and seclusion of wives was to ensure that only legitimate sons inherited all of the private wealth.[122]

Recognition of fatherhood and the advent of property subordinated women, as women relinquished the work they had created when they domesticated animals and initiated the Age of Cultivation. . . . for the male now demanded from her that fidelity which he thought would enable him to pass on his accumulations to children presumably his own. Gradually man had his way: fatherhood was recognized and property began to descend through the male; mother-right yielded to father-right; and the patriarchal family, with the oldest male at its head, became the economic, legal, political and moral unit of society. The gods, who had been mostly feminine, became great bearded patriarchs with such harems as ambitious men dreamed of in their solitude. The passage was complete to the patriarchal-father-ruled family.[123]

Chapter 2

ANTIQUITY:
2500 BC. to 400 AD.

History is said to begin with Antiquity, and everything that occurred before about 2500 BC. is *pre*history. Because people consciously began to leave a record of their existence around 2500 BC., history is therefore about 5000 years old. That would include the 2500 years before the birth of Christ and the nearly 2000 years since Christ's death.

History begins in Mesopotamia with civilizations there rising and falling and shifting. The approximate dates of the various civilizations and of early Christianity included in Antiquity follow:

Mesopotamia:

Sumeria......................2500 BC.—1750 BC.

Babylonia ....1900 BC.—1600 BC.

Assyria ....900 BC.—600 BC.

Judea...........................1300 BC.—60BC.

Egypt...........................3000 BC.—332 BC.

Greece..........................800 BC.—146 BC.

Rome............................800 BC.—400 AD.

Early Christianity ....30 AD.—400 AD.

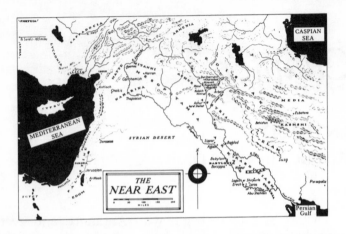

Sumeria

Historical Background

People settled in the warm Mesopotamian climate by the Tigris-Euphrates Rivers that empty into the Persian Gulf which is now a part of Iraq. There, with a dependable water supply, food grew abundantly and gradually the settlers replaced their hunting-gathering style of life with a more complicated society. ". . . the rich delta of Mesopotamia's rivers saw the earliest known scenes in the historic drama of civilization" (Durant I, 109).

The history of Sumer lay buried under the earth until 1834 when archeologists first began to dig into the Mesopotamanian soil. A new surge of archeological interest in Sumer, initiated in 1958, produced the history of the beginnings of western civilization.

Archeologists unearthed cities and irrigation systems dating back to 4000 BC. (Durant, I, 124). They also found the earliest written records—voices from that early civilization. The Sumerians, who are credited with inventing writing, chiseled symbols into clay tablets to record their business transactions and their laws. Ancient librarians in Sumer accumulated and organized 30,000 tablets found some 5000 years later at Tello. Frum these and other sources historians have learned that Sumer became an area of separate city-states; Nipper, Ur, Lagash, Uruk, Khafajah, Larsa, Erich, and Kish, all with their own temples.

The city-states began warring with each other over territorial and water rights. Victorious soldiers brought captives home to their city-states and expanded the system of slavery that goes hand-in-hand with war and civilization.

Sargon from Akkad in about 2300 BC. conquered and united the cities of Sumer, and with other lands he had vanquished, established the first empire in history. That empire collapsed about a hundred years later and was followed by numerous other short-lived conquerors until Hammurabi of Babylon, about 1750 BC. conquered Sumeria which was henceforth known as Babylonia.

Religion

As was true in some earlier religions, the deities of Sumeria lived in human forms. The government officials were the earthly "deputies," or priests of the universal deities whose statues were believed to have human qualities and desires and were ritually offered food and other comforts.

Each city-state worshipped its own god and goddess. In Nippur, the god Enil and his consort, Ninlil reigned; in Urak, the virgin earth-goddess, Innini; in Kish and Lagash, the mother-goddess, Ninkarsag; and in Lagash, the goddess, Bau.[1] In Nippur, the temple of the goddess

Inanna was unearthed as recently as 1958. Under Babylonian rule Inanna had become known as Ishtar.

Girls worked in the temples as housekeepers or as concubines to the earthly representatives of the gods. Fathers were proud to have their daughters serving religion in this way. They would mark their daughters' entry into temple life with a ceremonial sacrifice and bestow the girls' marriage dowries to the temple.[2]

Male/Female Relationships

The cunieform tablets record that marriage was regulated by many laws. A father gave his daughter and her husband a dowry which they owned together, but which she controlled and could bequest. Equally, she and her husband exercised rights over their children.

An upper-class wife could conduct business on her own, could keep personal slaves or sell them.[3] In Sumeria, society was highly stratified. There were many levels of rich people and many levels of the poor and the slaves.[4] As a result of the double standard, born of the desire to own and bequeath property, adultery was forgivable for a man, but because a wife must bear only her husband's children, the punishment for a woman was death.

A woman was valued for the number of children she had and if she produced no children, she could be divorced. If she did not want to give birth to children continuously, her husband had the legal right to drown her.[5]

"Women's strongest position was in relation to the temples. In general, a female priesthood served the male gods, and a male priesthood served the female gods . . . The fact that the king of Sumer ritually married a representative of the goddess Inanna once every year helped sustain the power of the priestesses for a time at least."[6]

As male power and wealth grew and shifted from city-state to city-state, women's status was reduced. At least one historian suggests that women enjoyed a higher status in the earlier Sumerian years than in the civilization's later years.

The status of women was certainly much higher in the early Sumeria city-state than it subsequently became . . . There are hints that in the very beginning of Sumerian society, women had a much higher status than in the hey-dey of Sumerian culture: this chiefly rests on the fact that in early Sumerian religion a prominent position is occupied by goddesses who afterwards virtually disappeared, save—with the one exception of Ishtar—as consorts to the gods.[7]

Women in Sumerian History

In these early histories it is difficult to find names of women. "Other than a few exceptional royal wives, only a handful of women managed to break through into the pages of history."[8] Even so, one of the first poets of Western civilization is Enheduanna, the daughter of Sargon. She was a "high priestess of the moon god . . . and her influence was so great that she later seems to have been regarded as a god herself."[9] The poetic style in her poem, "The Exaltation of Ianna," served as a model for subsequent poetry. It may be that she is the author of many other poems which are not so well preserved.[10]

Babylonia

Historical Background

The Sumerians, who had been the creative force in developing Western civilization, were overcome in about 1750 BC. by neighboring Semitic people, the Babylonians, whose greatest king gave his famous Code of Hammurabi to history. Babylonia developed a highly commercial civilization, ruling the many diverse city-states in Mesopotamia.

After Hammurabi's dynasty collapsed, Babylonia declined and was conquered by the northern Semites, and in turn by the non-Semitic Hittites, the Kassites, Aramaeans, and the Chaldeans. Then for several hundred years Assyria controlled Babylonia, ousting the Chaldeans and incorporating Babylonian culture into their own. In 689 BC. Assyria destroyed the city of Babylon and carried the statue of the god, Marduk, back to Assyria.

Babylon was rebuilt and prospered again under Nebu-chadnezzar (604-562 BC.), who is probably best known for his "Hanging Gardens of Babylon," which he built for his wife who longed for the greenery of her homeland. Nebu-chadnezzar is also known for destroying Judah and Jeru-salem in 587 BC., and for the Babylonian Captivity of the Jews for the following seventy years.

In 539 BC. Babylon fell to Cyrus the Great, a Persian, and later to the Greek, Alexander the Great, who had wanted to make Babylon his Eastern capitol, but who died before this dream was achieved.

Babylon, strong and powerful as it had been, was abandoned before the time of Christ.

Religion

The principal deities of Babylonia were the god Mar-duk and the goddess Ishtar known previously as Inanna and later as Astarte to the Greeks and Ashtoreth to the Jews. Among other Babylonian gods were Anu, Shamash, Nannar, and Baal. Marduk, however, assumed his supremacy.

In the later Babylonian epic of Marduk, the young male god overcomes and kills his great, great, great grandmother Tiamet the Creator to become King of the Universe. The theme of Marduk's conquest was repeated in many other late myths, until at long last the tales of creation boldly declared that one or another male god alone was the Creator.[11]

Priests and priestesses served the gods and god-desses. The Hammurabic Code details how priestesses might inherit and what they may bequeath, suggesting that they owned property and possibly engaged in business.

Life revolved around religion. Everything belonged to the gods including the workers, the earth, and all it produced. The harvest was stored in the temples where the priests distributed some of the crops to the citizens "according to their social standing."[12] The remainder was used to finance a growing commercial trade.

Temples grew rich from taxation and the spoils of war. The priests, who were also the first judges, were "the greatest merchants and financiers of Babylonia," and even the Kings of Babylon needed to keep the priests happy, which they did by building huge temples. There was no town without at least one temple. The gods were not aloof from men; most of them lived on earth in the temples, ate with a hearty appetite, and through nocturnal visits to pious women gave unexpected children to the busy citizens of Babylon.[13]

In the Mesopotamian temple system there apparently were a high priestess and associated priestesses of elevated rank who only married under certain conditions; there was a second rank of virgin priestesses, the Naditu, and several ranks of women performing special services. One of these services was "temple prostitution." In Babylonia, as in Egypt and Phoenicia, the concept of rendering sexual services on a public basis evidently first developed in connection with temples, and intercourse with temple women was considered an act of worship. All fees for such services took the form of offerings to the temples. The women who provided the services were often of the middle and upper classes. Prostitution as a secular service came later.[14]

The most striking feature of Babylonian life, to an alien observer, was the custom known to us chiefly from a famous page in Herodotus:

'Every native woman is obliged, once in her life, to sit in the temple of Venus, and have intercourse with some stranger. And many disdaining to mix with the rest, being proud on account of their wealth, come in covered carriages, and take up their station at the temple with a numerous train of servants attending them. But the far greater part do thus: many sit down in the temple of Venus, wearing a crown of cord round their heads; some are continually coming in, and others are going out. Passages marked out in a straight line lead in every direction through the women, along which strangers pass and make their choice. When a woman has once seated herself she must not return home till some stranger has thrown a piece of silver into her lap, and lain with her outside the temple. He who throws the silver must say thus: "I beseech the goddess Mylitta to favor thee,: for the Assyrians call Venus Mylitta.* The silver may be ever so small, for she will not reject it, inasmuch as it is not lawful for her to do so, for such silver is accounted sacred. The woman follows the first man that throws, and refuses no one. But when she has had intercourse and has absolved herself from her obligation to the goddess, she returns home; and after that time, however great a sum you may give her after that time, you will not gain possession of her. Those that are endowed with beauty and symmetry of shape are soon set free; but the deformed are detained a long time, from inability to satisfy the law, for some wait for a space of three or four years.'[15]

Male/Female Relationships

Historians have learned about the Babylonian male/female relationship, and the status of women, from the Code of Hammurabi. Said to be the first written law, the Code carved in stone about 1750 BC., was stolen from the Babylonians by the Elamite king in 1200 BC. and subsequently lost. It was unearthed in 1902, after having been buried for 3000 years. The Code embodies the "les taliones," or equivalent retaliation system of justice, known often as "an eye for an eye."

In earlier times the taboos were the law; after that, in Sumeria, justice was through trial by ordeal. For instance, a girl accused of adultery was required to jump in the Euphrates River. If she survived she was innocent. Later, in Christian times, if she survived she was guilty, the theory being that the water would reject the wrongdoer.

Justice was also based on payment of damages. The Hammurabi Code gradually replaced payment of damage by substituting equal punishment on the wrongdoer. Some parts of the 282 regulations in the Code which deals with every-day problems of marriage, divorce, real estate, debts, and slaves, follow:

Selections from The Laws of King Hammurabi, King of Babylon:

1. If a man break another man's bone, they shall break his bone.

2. If a man brings an accusation against another man and charge him with capital crime, but cannot prove it, he, the accuser, shall be put to death.

3. If a man hire a field laborer, he shall pay him eight gur of grain a year.

4. If a man destroy the eye of another man, they shall destroy his eye.

5. If a man be in debt and sell his wife son or daughter or bind them over to service, for three years they shall work; in the fourth year they shall be given their freedom.

6. If a man practices robbery and is captured, he shall be put to death.

7. If a man aids a slave to escape from the city, he shall be put to death.

8. If a man steal the property of a god or palace that man shall be put to death; and he who receives the stolen goods shall also be put to death.

9. If a man destroy the eye of another man's slave, he shall pay the owner one-half his price.

10. If a doctor operates on a man for a severe wound with a bronze knife and saves the man's life, he shall receive ten shakels as his fee.

11. If a doctor operates on a man for a severe wound with a bronze knife and causes the man's death, they shall cut off the doctor's fingers.

12. If a son strike his father, they shall cut off his fingers.

13. If a man slave says to his master: "Thou are not my master" his master shall prove him to be his slave by cutting off his ear.

14. If a robber is not caught, the man who has been robbed shall in the presence of god make an itemized list of his losses, and the city and the governor in whose jurisdiction the robbery was committed shall compensate the robbed man for whatever was stolen.

15. If a woman hate her husband and say: "Thou shalt not have me," they shall inquire into her antecedents for her defects; and if she have been a careful mistress and be without reproach and her husband have been going about belittling her, that woman has no blame. She shall receive her dowry and shall go to her father's house.

16. If she have not been a careful mistress, have gadded about and have belittled her husband, they shall throw her into the water.

17. A woman, merchant, or other property holder may sell field, garden or house.

This very ancient code differs from most other ancient bodies of law in that it gives women a good and independent legal position.

Marriage, while being as usual a form of purchase, was also a contract to be man and wife together, . . . if a wife became ill, her husband was bound to support her unless she preferred to go back to her father's house, in which case she took her dowry . . . The dowry remained the property of the bride and descended from her to her children. The man was responsible for his wife's debts, including those contracted before marriage . . . Divorce was optional with the man, but he must return the dowry, and women kept custody of the children and were given sufficient means from real estate to pay for their upbringing. If she had been a bad wife, the husband might send her away without dowry or degrade her to the position of slave, but she could bring action in such a case against him and seek judicial separation on the ground of cruelty. If she failed to prove her case she was drowned . . . Moreover, women could be judges, elders, witnesses, and scribes; so that in every way their position was high and in many ways higher than in nineteenth century England or America; and yet the Code of Hammurabi is more than four thousand years old.[16]

Though the Code clearly acknowledges the value of property, and women as property, punishment was much more severe if a poor man damaged a rich man, or his property, or a rich man's wife, than vice versa.

According to the Code, a man could divorce his wife simply by saying, "Thou are not my wife." However, a wife who used those words against her husband would be drowned.[17]

Babylonian females were basically property. Their fathers determined whom they should marry and they could sell them to the prospective husbands for an agreed-upon price. Marriage was monogamous for women, but men were free to visit prostitutes, or to take concubines.

Unmarried free women were punished differently than married women. If a married man committed adultery with an unmarried free woman, the man's wife was given back to her father for prostitution and the man had to marry the victim.[20]

Though the Code was severe, a woman could leave her husband, (though she could not divorce him) if she could prove that her husband had been cruel and that she had been faithful. She could take her own property with her and return to her parents. Under certain limitations women could own, inherit, and bequeath property.[20] Women could be witnesses to documents, and they could conduct business.[21]

Because upper class women were considered valuable property, they were confined to quarters and if they went out, they were accompanied by eunechs—male slaves who had been castrated and were considered no threat to another man's property.[22] Lower class women had freedom, but if they had no dowry their status was only slightly above that of a slave.[23]

> In general, it appears that women had less personal and sexual freedom than men did . . . Both law and practice confirm a growing double standard from this point on through history, again applied chiefly in the strata above the semiskilled working class.[24]

And as Stone writes:

> Despite a loss of status in position of women in Babylon compared with their predecessors of Sumer—a loss that was accompanied by the gaining ascendency of male deities such as Marduk, who mythically murdered the Creator Goddess Tiamut to gain and secure his position—the women of Babylon still continued to hold certain rights of independence.[25]

Women in Babylonian History

Though they are not recorded in history by name, women as priestesses, business managers, midwives, musicians, scribes, and textile workers actively contributed to the rich commercial civilization of Babylonia.

Assyria

Historical Background

In contrast to Babylonia with its warm climate and rolling desert terrain, Assyria is colder and mountainous. Also, the Babylonian civilization was based on commerce; Assyria's civilization was militaristic, dedicated to war. ". . . from beginning to end they were a race of warriors, . . . kings and slaves, wars and conquests, bloody victories and sudden defeat."[26]

Assyria's most famous ruler was Sennacherib (705-681 BC.). When he was "irritated by the prejudice of Babylon in favor of freedom, besieged it, took it, and burned it to the ground, nearly all the inhabitants, young and old, male and female, were put to death, so that mountains of corpses blocked the streets."[27] Sennacherib's brutality was matched by his sons' who murdered him, and by other Assyrian kings who came after him, conquering more and more territory and establishing Assyria as a world-wide empire from about 600-500 BC., until it, in turn, fell to Cyrus of Persia to the great delight of the people it had cruelly subjugated.

Religion

Religion apparently did nothing to mollify this tendency to brutality and violence. It had less influence with the government than in Babylonia . . . Ashue, the national deity, was a solar god, warlike and merciless to his enemies; his people believed that he took a divine satisfaction in the execution of prisoners before his shrine. The essential function of Assyrian religion was to train the future citizens to a patriotic docility, and . . . the only religious texts that survived from Assyria are exorcisms and omens.[28]

Male/Female Relationships

As a war-like empire it encouraged a high birth rate because it needed soldiers. Women who bore sons were honored; women who "secured a miscarriage, even a woman who died of attempting it, was impaled on a stake."[29]

Laws governing the rights of women were written into the Middle Assyrian laws (c. 1300 BC.) thought to be amendments to the Hammurabic Code. Nearly all the laws relate to women and appear to be "a further limitation on the rights of women."[30] Also in Assyria wives could not go out unveiled, and strict fidelity was expected of them though their husbands had no restrictions. A husband was legally justified in killing another man making love to the husband's wife, a custom that has come down through history.

Women in Assyrian History

Queen Sammuramet who ruled as queen-mother for three years, 811-808 BC., built temples, participated in the military and is said to have "led troops into battle."[31]

Queen Naqi'a, also called Nitrocris, wife of Sennacherib, (705-681 BC.) with her son, helped to rebuild the Babylon her husband had ruined.

Summuramet and Naqi'a are notable exemplars of the capacity of women to take leadership in one of the most intensely militaristic societies known to date.[32]

Judea

Historical Background

Civilization, like life, is a perpetual struggle with death. And as life maintains itself only by abandoning old, and recasting itself in younger and fresher forms, so civilization achieves a precarious survival by changing its habitat, or its blood. It moved from Ur to Babylon and Judea . . .[33]

On the grade route between Mesopotamia and Egypt lay a tiny territory of Palestine, known in Antiquity as Judea, that was to play a major role in the development of moral standards of Western civilization and "leave behind it an influence greater than that of Babylonia, Assyria or Persia, perhaps greater even than that of Egypt and Greece."[34]

"The Jews, (also known as Semites and Hebrews) believed that the people of Abraham had come from Ur in Sumeria and had settled in Palestine about 2200 BC., a thousand years or more before Moses . . ."[35] According to the Old Testament of the Bible, Moses led the Jews out of their slavery in Egypt into the desert where, at Mt. Sinai he is believed to have received the word of God, the Ten Commandments. After forty years of wandering in the desert, the Jews returned to their Promised Land, conquering the Canaanites possibly around 1280 BC. Instead of unifying as a nation they remained as twelve or more independent tribes with Judges as their leaders and lawgivers. "The authority of the Judges . . . recalls that of the tribal chiefs in the nomadic organization typical of the more ancient phase of Semitic life."[36]

The Twelve Tribes unified under King Saul, about 1150 BC., but he ". . . soon came into conflict with the priesthood." His successors, David and Solomon took the priesthood ". . . under their own protection, . . . and strove to make the religious organization a department of the state." After that, if people were dissatisfied, they directed their protest against *both* the government and religion. The prophets voiced this general dissatisfaction of kingly rule imposing itself on religion.[37]

The city of Jerusalem was not captured by the Jews until the time of King David, who came to the throne about 1000 BC., and whose reign was marked by prosperity. "Political and commercial life reached a high degree of development, while religion retained to a great extent its primitive simplicity and purity."[38] David's son, Solomon (961-922 BC.), spent lavishly, taxed heavily, yet at the same time extended the rich commercial life of Judea. However, with the death of Solomon, the Hebrew political ascendency came to an end, and Judea was divided into two Hebrew nations, Judah to the south and Israel to the north.

After a succession of kings, and small wars, the Babylonian king, Nebuchadnezzar, 586 BC., captured Judah, destroyed Solomon's temple, and "carried 10,000 Jews into bondage,"[39] where they remained until Cyrus of Persia gave them their freedom when he captured Babylon and allowed them to return to Jerusalem. There, for about 200 years they enjoyed relative political and religious freedom though the country was occupied by the Persians.

The Persian Empire of Cyrus the Great was conquered by Alexander the Great, and after his death in 323 BC., the land was ruled by Ptolemy of Egypt, and then it later became a Roman protectorate in 63 BC. During the rule of Herod (37-4 BC.) Jesus of Nazareth was born in Bethlehem.

The Jews revolted against the Romans in 70 BC., again in 115 AD., and in 132 AD., when Jerusalem was set up as a Roman capital, barred to the Jews except for annual pilgrimages. From 135 AD. until the United Nations in

1945 established Israel, a homeland for Jews, they have lived as nationals, elsewhere in the world.

Religion

Unlike other people in the world at that time, the Jews worshipped only one god. Whereas, before, tribal gods and Mesopotamian gods, Egyptian, and Greek gods had wives or consorts, the God of Israel, Yahweh, or Jehovah, was exclusively male with no female consort.

With the knowledge about 3000 BC., that men, too, had some part in human reproduction, combined with the male domination of agriculture and animal husbandry, the western world was ready to accept a male-only divinity, a god who had no wife or female consort. From then on, western religion is patriarchal. The roots of western culture and morality began in Mesopotamia, were incorporated into the Jewish Old Testament, and eventually into the Christian New Testament.

Previous deities had sometimes appeared in animal or human form, but

> The Hebrew God is invisible to men, except in particular conditions and under especial form; as the God of a nomad people, he has no fixed abode, but can be everywhere; he has neither family, nor sex; he is holy and just; he has made a special covenant with Israel, and made it his chosen people.[40]

Early Judaism put an end to goddesses, established a single, male divinity, established the Ten Commandments which are the basis of moral, social life in the Western Hemisphere, and through the Adam and Eve myth explained sin as the primal transgression of man against God, instigated by women.

Male/Female Relationships

Ancient Judaism followed the attitudes of Mesopotamia, rather than Egypt, as far as women were concerned.

It was "a male-oriented religion with women clearly sub-ordinate."[41]

Women of the earlier Semites had a higher status than they did after they entered the Promised Land. "Perhaps the shift toward patriarchy started when the tribes were fighting their way into Canaan; a militaristic orientation works against a high status for women."[42]

When the Jews were in Egypt, they did not subjugate women, and in their first years in Israel, "Rachel and Leah . . . are called 'builders of Israel . . . Deborah was a judge of Israel . . . a continued status for wise women prophetesses, and judges, carried on for a long time after settlement in Canaan."[43] Yet, after a time, as Roland de Vaux, an archeologist and a priest writes in his book, *Ancient Israel*,

> The social and legal position of an Israelite wife was inferior to the position of wife occupied in the great countries round about . . . all the texts show that Israelites wanted mainly sons, to perpetuate the family line and fortune, and to preserve the ancestral inheritance . . . A husband could divorce his wife . . . women on the other hand could not ask for divorce . . . the wife called her husband Ba'al or master; she also called him adon or lord; she addressed him in fact as a slave addresses his master or a subject, his king. The Decalogue includes a man's wife among his possessions . . . all her life she remains a minor. The wife does not inherit from her husband, nor daughters from their fathers, except when there is no male heir. A vow made by a girl or married woman needs, to be valid, the consent of the father or husband and if this consent is withheld, the vow is null and void. A man had the right to sell his daughter. Women were excluded from the succession.[44]

The thrust of the Adam and Eve myth that came from the Hebrew Old Testament, put new burdens on women. True, women had been considered contaminators and polluters in primitive times, but Judaism emphasized the need to avoid sin and for man to protect himself from his "inborn evil tendencies inherited from Adam."[45]

Man's greatest weakness was the lure of sexual pleasures. The urge for sexual satisfaction made man almost a helpless victim in the eyes of Satan. Woman after all to the male mind is often equated with sex. She keeps reminding him of his sexual nature and therefore she must be evil.[46]

Religion, instead of government, was the law, and Jewish family life reflected the patriarchal structure of the religion. The oldest male in the family had unlimited authority. He owned his wife, or wives, slaves, concubines, children, and the land. The children would live only if they were obedient to him. A father could sell his daughters into marriage, or give them away as he wished.[47]

In biblical times a Jewish wife, who was sometimes one of many, could be put away at the wish of her husband. Virginity upon marriage was strictly required, and she might be stoned if found to be adulterous. Confined to domestic chores, which afforded her little rest, she was expected to work hard. At the same time woman was associated with religious taboos, was considered ceremonially unclean, and had no standing before the law. By virtue of her secondary creation, that is, of the merely derivative character of her existence described in the earlier Genesis account, woman could justifiably be considered naturally inferior and subordinate to man. Created out of man and for man, to relieve his loneliness and to help him, woman is shown to be responsible also for man's troubles, not the least of which is his loss of immortality. In the male-oriented religion of the Jews and later of the Christians, these concepts of woman's inferiority and troublesomeness became entrenched in Western tradition remaining virtually impregnable into the twentieth century.[48]

Because it was important for the population to increase, both for militaristic reasons and to fill the conquered land with their own people, there was no room in society for unmarried men or women. Levirate marriages, whereby a man was obliged to marry his brother's widow, even if he already had a wife or wives, assured a woman protection and also continued male ownership.

Marriage was for legal heirs, and to help ensure that a man's child was his, a woman had to prove her virginity at marriage, upon pain of death.[49] Because the woman had been bought by her husband, adultery was a violation of the law of property and usually resulted in death to both parties.[50]

A woman's greatest value was as a mother and fruitlessness was a disgrace. If a wife had no children she could provide a slave girl as a wife.[51] For women, marriage was monogamous, though polygamous for men. Hebrew law assumed polygamy. The first pronouncement against it wasn't until the eleventh century AD., at the Council of Worms.[52] Gidean, the Israelite judge had enough wives to bear him 70 sons. Abraham, Jacob, Saul, Gidean, David, Solomon all had concubines who were either bought or taken as captives.

Women of Early Judaism

Without a goddess-protector, as women had in adjoining lands, the women of the Israelites had to achieve their goals in spite of the society run by men and dominated by a male god. Several women, however, come through the pages of the Old Testament in the Bible as wise, patient, and brave women.

Jochebed, a Jewish slave, and mother of Moses, defied the Pharroah's orders to destroy male infants and after hiding him for three months, saved Moses by putting him in a raft of bulrushes at the river's edge.

72

Miriam, a Jewish slave and sister of Moses, witnessed the rescue of Moses by the Pharoah's daughter.

Shiprah and *Puah*, Jewish slave midwives who, fearing God, cleverly outwitted the Pharoah and his order to kill all males at birth by telling him the Jewish women were delivered of their children before the midwives arrived.

Ruth, the daughter-in-law of Naomi, and the wife of Boaz. She advised Naomi in the art of finding food even in the midst of famine. Ruth is the symbol of love and devotion to a mother-in-law. She gave birth to Obe, the grandfather of David.

Hannah, a barren Jewish wife who prays for a man-child, offering devotion if her prayer is granted. She becomes the mother of Samuel. She gives her prayer of thanksgiving and her son to be a minister.

Rachel and *Leah*, Jewish women referred to as builders of Israel.

Esther, the Jewish Queen of King Ahasueras, who saved the Jews when the king ordered them killed. At the risk of her own life she revealed that she was a Jew.

Deborah, a Jewish prophetess and a judge in Israel to whom the people came for judgment. With Barak, she led 10,000 men to defeat the Canaanite King Jabin, though Barak told her he would not go unless she did.

Jael, a Jewish wife who tricked the Canaanite, Sisera, into trusting her and when he fell asleep she killed him and proudly showed his dead body to the victorious Barak.

Relationship of Religion to the Status of Women

Goddess worship and the practice of matriliny appear to go together in prehistoric societies. During the years

2000 to 1000 BC., Indo-European Hittites, Hurrians, and Kassites moved into Mesopotamia and Canaan about the same time the myth of the god Marduk is said to have killed the goddess Tiamat to become the ruling Babylonian god. Before this time, in Sumeria,

> . . . if a man raped a woman he was put to death. In the Old Babylonian period of Hammurabi, before the major incursions of the Indo-Europeans, though many of the northerners were in Babylonia even at that time, the same punishment was given . . . The reforms of Urukagina (Sumerian king about 2300 BC.) refer to the fact that women used to take two husbands, though at the time of his reign this was no longer allowed. In the laws of Eshnunna (a Sumerian State) a man who took a second wife, after his first had given birth to a child, was to be expelled from the house without any possessions. In Eshnunna, if a woman had a child by another man while her husband was away at war, her husband was expected to take her back as his wife. No punishment for adultery was mentioned. In Hammurabi's laws, if a woman related to another man sexually she was expected to take an oath at the temple and return home to her husband.[53]

Then, with rising dominance of male gods over goddesses,

> In the laws of Assyria, which are dated between 1450 and 1250 BC. (when Assyria was under Indo-European control), we read that if a man rapes a woman the husband or father of that woman should then rape the rapist's wife or daughter and/or marry his own daughter to the rapist. The last part of the law was also the law of the Hebrews, who added that a raped woman must be put to death if she was already married or betrothed. Assyrian laws appear to be the first to mention abortion, assigning the penalty as death . . . The Assyrian and Hebrew laws give the

74

husband the right to murder both the wife and lover . . .[54]

Male dominance was becoming firmly established at the time that male deities became powerful.

. . . The major changes in the laws concerning women affected their right to engage in economic activities, what they might or might not inherit, what they in turn were allowed to pass on to their children, the attitude toward rape, abortion, infidelity on the part of the husband or wife, and, among the Hebrews only, the penalty of death—for women—for the loss of virginity before marriage. These laws since they primarily affected the economic and sexual activities of women, point to the likelihood that they were aimed at the matrilineal descent customs. The very fact that so many of the laws concerned women suggests that both the economic and sexual position of women was continually changing from the time of the first attested northern invasions (about 2300 BC.) until the laws of the Hebrews, probably written down.[55]

Egypt

On the following page a map of Egypt outlines the extent of the Egyptian Empire around 1450 BC.[56]

Though this book does point out women's great contribution to the development of civilization, it barely mentions any specific historically famous women so far. The omission of names is not because there weren't any valiant women, but because Mesopotamian societies were patriarchal, and what women achieved was not considered as important as men's achievement. In Ancient Egypt, however, there are several women whose lives, at least for the time, affected the history of their country. Women's ascendence onto the rolls of history in Ancient Egypt is probably the result of the Egyptian culture being somewhat matriarchal.

Most of the famous women in any country, and in any time up to the modern period, are from either the ruling class or the upper class. Early tribes were not stratified into upper and lower classes—they were all of the same social class. But large-scale war and the accumulation of private property divided people generally into groups: captives brought home from conquered territories became slaves and did the menial work; people who tilled the land and owned little or no property were lower class; and those who owned slaves and property and made the decisions for society were upper or ruling class. The middle class society did not develop until the Industrial Revolution, about 1600 AD.

Men and women whose deeds are recorded were almost exclusively from the ruling, or upper class. Little is known about the lower or slave classes in Antiquity, for men *or* women, except as is surmised from pictures on walls or vases. Who would write of their lives? Very few people in the upper classes could read or write, so it is a reasonable assumption that almost no one in the lower or slave classes could record their own existence.

Even so, writings in Egypt went unread for almost 2000 years because their hieroglyphics and cursive writing could not be deciphered. In 1798 AD., when soldiers in Napoleon's army were digging trenches in Rashid, or Rossetta, in Northern Africa, they unearthed a basalt stone inscribed in three languages. Egyptian hieroglyphics, cursive Egyptian script, and Greek. Even knowing Greek, it took men twenty years to decipher Ancient Egyptian.

But once deciphered, the Rossetta Stone unlocked Egyptian history and began the modern study of Egyptology. Historians, archeologists, anthropologists, and others reconstructed Ancient Egyptian history. The Rossetta Stone, together with pictures on temples and pyramid walls, and the writings of Herodotus, the Greek historian who traveled in Egypt around 500 BC., have provided the modern world with a view of the ancient Egyptian.

Historical Background

History in Egypt is divided into Kingdoms and Kingdoms are divided into dynasties. A dynasty is a time-period when descendents of one family ruled. The ruler was known as a pharoah, a man who was both a king and a god. He had absolute power because he was considered divine. Only men could be pharoahs, though a pharoah had to be a son from a royal queen. descent for all people, not just royalty, was matrilineal.

The Time-period of the Dynasties

Dynasties I—VI . . . . Old Kingdom 3200—2200 BC.

Dynasties VII—XVII
. . . . Middle Kingdom 2200—1600 BC.

Dynasties XVII—XXX
. . . . New Kingdom 1600—300 BC.

In 330 BC. Alexander the Great, a Greek conquered Egypt. "In 30 BC., Egypt became a province of Rome and disappeared from history." (Durant I, 216)

The Egyptians settled along the Nile River for the same reasons their Mesopotamian, distant neighbors, had settled along the Tigris-Euphrates Rivers. The climate was comfortable for year-round living, the regular flooding of the river enriched the soil for agricultural production, and the river was a natural highway for trading. The Egyptian desert, more vast than the Mesopotamian desert, provided more security from invaders. That is probably one of the reasons that the Egyptian civilization lasted over twenty-five hundred years.

Originally divided into Upper and Lower Egypt, the country was united under one pharoah in 3100 BC., the first of thirty dynasties.

Religion

Religion was the main thrust of Egyptian life, and immortality, or life after death, was the religion's main emphasis. It was believed that everyone had a double, or a *ka*, and the *ka* could be kept alive and fed and clothed. In the early days of pyramid or tomb-building, these graves for the pharoahs, included their wives, slaves, and horses, who were buried with the pharoahs. Later, pictures were painted on tomb walls of wives, slaves, and horses, and things that were assumed to be necessary for the deceased's after-life, rather than burying the people. These pictures of wives and slaves told more history of how people lived than the bones of actual wives and slaves ever could.

"Worship of animals and nature commonly occurs in very early societies, which are dominated by the world roundabout . . ."[57] The cults of the numerous gods and goddesses who also had animal counterparts, were brought into the culture of Ancient Egypt from its beginnings. Belief in the supernatural was intricately woven into the Egyptian's daily life. And the numerous goddesses attest to the high position of women in Egyptian society.

In addition to Isis, who became so popular she supplanted all other goddesses, there was Nyphthys, Isis's sister; Hathor, goddess of creation, Hekhebet, goddess of childbirth; Buto; Mut, the divine mother, consort of the great god Amon; and the goddess Bast, worshipped as long ago as 3200 BC. Taueret, from prehistoric times a mother goddess, protective of pregnant women or women in childbirth; Selket, the protective goddess of four sources of the Nile, of burials, and fertility (the most famous sculpture of Selket was found in the tomb of Tutankhamun); and Mayet, goddess of justice and truth.[58]

Tutankhamun, in his famous headdress, wears the "protective goddess Nekhebet of Upper Egypt and Buto of Lower Egypt."[59] The famous Rameses II statue wears the emblem of the goddess Buto.

But Isis overshadows all the other goddesses. She was the sister and wife of Osiris. She represented creativity and rejuvenation, and the originative leadership of women in tilling the earth.

Among all these mother-gods alike, save only in name, none other gained so wide an influence as Egyptian Isis. She passed from country to country absorbing all the local deities, until Greece and Rome identified her with Selen, with Demeter or Ceres, with Aphrodite, Juno, Nemesis, Fortuna, and Panthea.

'I am Isis,' reads an old Greek inscription, 'the mistress of every land; I laid down laws for mankind, and ordained things that no one may change; I am she who governs Sirius the Dog Star; I am she who is called divine among women; I divided the earth from the heaven; I made manifest the paths of the stars; I prescribed the course of the sun and the moon; I found out the labours of the sea; I made justice mighty; I brought together man and woman; I burdened woman with the newborn babe in the tenth month; I ordained that parents should be beloved by their children; I put an end to cannibalism; I overthrew the sovereignty of tyrants; I compelled women to be beloved by men; I made justice, more mighty than gold and silver; I made virtue and vice to be distinguished by instinct.'

In short, Isis, the fertile mother, the feminine principle, had taken to her the attributes of most minor deities and triumphed over the civilized world. It is well to remember that this signifies the full worship of women as givers of fertility and their exaltation over all mankind; it is, . . . the logical outcome of women's chief claim to power, of her one gift which no man can share with her . . . Such as Isis: 'when her cult finally broke down through the development and mighty spreading of Christianity in Egypt, Isis was to her votaries the type and symbol of all that is greatest and best in woman in her character of all that is unselfish, true, tender, and loving and eternal World Mother and Earth Mother, the exaltation of the soil because of its fertility, and of women in general because they by their mysterious *mana* made this earth fertility possible.[60]

Isis, as the sister and the wife of the god Osiris, is seen not to embody the sister-brother marriage, but as the religious reflection of the shifting from brother-sister clan partnership of prehistoric times to the husband-wife relationship emerging with civilization. ". . . Isis personified the full transition from maternal clan to father family . . ."[61]

Women's religious activities and participation in religious ceremonies were greatest in the earlier years of Ancient Egypt. "During the first several dynasties there often were female names listed among the list of priests; they disappeared after about 1785."[62] From 3000 BC. to 1300 BC., the goddess, Hathor was served by 61 priestesses and 18 priests. By 1300 BC., women were not even a part of temple life. They served only as musicians.[63]

One of the first steps in limiting women is to take away their religious or magic functions, as also happened among the primitives. Even so, as the Pharoah was a god, his wife then was a consort to a god. And if she bore a son, she was a mother of a god. A woman's power in Ancient Egypt lay in her ability to influence her husband, or, later, her son.

Male/Female Relationships

Perhaps the oldest book in the world, *The Maxims* of Ptah-hotep, governor of Memphis and Prime Minister to the King, who lived around 3000BC., reveals the nature of the Ancient Egyptian marriage relationship. The husband states,

I acknowledge thy rights as wife. From this day forward I shall never by any word oppose thy claims. I shall acknowledge thee before anyone as my wife, but I have no power to say to thee: 'Thou art my wife. It is I who am the man who is thy husband. From the day that I become thy husband I cannot oppose thee, in whatsoever place thou mayest please to go. I cede thee (here follows a list of possessions) that are in thy dwelling. I have no power to interfere in any transaction made by thee, from this day. Every document made in my favour by any person is now placed among thy deeds, and is also at the disposal of thy father or of any relatives acting for thee. Thou shalt hold me bound to honor any such deed.'[64]

"For centuries women owned property in Egypt to such an extent that in some households the husband was practically nothing but a boarder."[65] At marriage, by contract, a husband deeded all his property to his wife. In this way his children, through her, could inherit his property. Otherwise his sister's children would inherit.[66]

Ptah-hotep advised his son,

If thou art wise, keep thy home, love thy wife, and do not dispute with her. Feed her, massage her. Caress her and fulfill all her wishes as long as thou livest, for she is thy property that brings great gain. Attend to that which is her desire and to that which occupies her mind. For in such manner thou persuadest her to remain with thee. If thou opposest her, it will be thy ruin.

"The mother's name is always given, the father's name may be omitted; the ancestors are always traced back in the female, rather than in the male line."[67] Descent was traced from the mother's ancestry. All children belonged to their mothers, therefore there were no illegitimate children.[68] Illegitimacy arises in societies where a father's claim to his children must be definitely established. Children took on the mother's social "class," in the same way that children of earlier tribal peoples were members of their mother's matriclan.[69]

For a woman,

> Possibly because of the mastery over her own affairs, infanticide was rare; Diodorus thought it a peculiarity of the Egyptians that every child born to them was reared, and tells us that parents guilty of infanticide were required by law to hold the dead child in their arms for three days and nights."[70]

The paintings on temples and pyramid walls show women working right alongside men. In some matters, however, women were subordinate to men. Adultery for a women meant she forfeited her dowry to her husband. For men, adultery was not a sin.[71] A woman could not divorce her husband, but a man could divorce his wife. If it were for other than adultery, he had to give her a large share of the property.[72]

Marriage for women was monogamous, though most men had several wives or concubines and every Pharoah had a harem. Yet women could hold and bequeath property, pay taxes, regain their dowry if the marriage broke up, testify in court and bring actions against men, receive equally from their father's estate, remain free of guardianship in legal rights, that is, they did not need to be represented by their father or brother, they could eat in public and eat with their husband in public, go about town unattended, and unveiled, and engage freely in business.[73]

Ramses II said, "The foot of an Egyptian woman may walk where it pleases her and no one may deny her."[74]

> In sum, the Egyptian woman had a relatively pleasant life and we do not need to resort to questionable generalizations like that of primitive matriarchy in order to explain it. Her somewhat higher status than the Mesopotamian woman still did not mean that she was

considered equal to men. Women were clearly subordinate, and compared to men their lives were circumscribed. It might well be that the very passivity of living in Egypt due to the great fertility of the soil and to the regularity of life lent less emphasis to war and to the making of war. Women worked in the fields along with the men in ancient times, as they do now, although their assigned functions differed. Even the fact that women appeared as rulers does not mean that they had equality, since all apparently exercised their power in the name of their son or took a male name. It is also worthy of comment that most of the women rulers appeared at the end of a dynasty, apparently striving to keep the family in power either because their sons were young or their husbands enfeebled. Hatshepsut, of course, was an exception. Some Egyptian women worked outside of their homes, but the professions were not open to them nor were any of the crafts, except the traditionally female ones. They were not priests, nor were they carpenters, sculptors, or scribes. Woman's place was in the home, and it was as mothers that they had their greatest influence. If Egypt is the example of the power that women had under what some have called a matriarchy, their status in times past must never have been very high.[75]

The position of Egyptian woman presents an anomaly. On the one hand, Egypt's society was typically male dominated; the word of the man of the house was law, and a wife was in many ways her husband's chattel. On the other hand, Egyptian women enjoyed far more rights and privileges than in other lands, modern as well as ancient.[76]

"No people, ancient or modern, has given women so high a legal status as did the inhabitants of the Nile Valley."[77]
It appears that after tribes settle into one area and develop trade, build permanent buildings, and set up govern-

ments, at first women have many rights, almost an equality with men. Then as society develops further and becomes more complex, men dominate the society and women's status seems to suffer. But as Boulding says, ". . . Egypt never became as militarized as other societies, just as it never became urbanized, so the loss of status of women was more gradual and never went as far as it did elsewhere."[78]

Notable Egyptian Women
Queen Hatshepsut

Though only a man could be a pharoah, one woman, Queen Hatshepsut, actually ruled as a pharoah by declaring herself aman, wearing the traditional false beards of the pharoah, and declaring also that she was a god; all requisites for ruling.

A matriarchal system of inheritance persisted in Egypt from the earliest times, and the throne could be gained by marriage to a royal heiress. Hatshepsut was daughter of Tuthmosis I, and while she acknowledged that her brother (and husband) had a right to the throne and saw him reign as Tuthmosis II, she believed her own claim to follow him to be stronger than that of her half-brother who eventually reigned as Tuthmosis III. She had no compunction about declaring herself the daughter of the god Amon . . ."[79]

It should be said here that in Ancient Egypt there was the unusual practice of brother-sister marriages, following the examples of the god and goddesses, Osiris and Isis. This does not say that these alliances occurred often, or that "marriage" meant sexual relationship. Nevertheless among royalty, brother-sister marriages and father-daughter marriages (as with Rameses II and Nefertari who has a tomb of her own) kept the family fortune in the family.[80]

Hatshepsut ruled for twenty years, from 1489-1469 BC. She was one of Egypt's most successful rulers. She restored the ancient ruins and established peace in her kingdom. She built the magnificent temple at Deier el-Bahri on the west side of the Nile near Thebes, and two obelisks at Karnak. Rulers before and after her are noted for building up Egypt's military strength. Queen Hatshepsut's reign is noted for peace.[81] She opened up trade routes to sell Egyptian goods in other lands and to buy the things Egypt could not make or raise.[82]

When her son-in-law Tuthmosis III took over the throne he discontinued all the reconstruction work Hatshepsut had started and set Egypt's course once more on military conquest[83] erasing Hatshepsut's name wherever it could be found.[84]

Mortuary Temple of Queen Hatshepsut, Deir el-Bahari, c. 1500 B.C.

Queen Nefertiti

Known for her great beauty, the wife of Ikhnaton supported her husband's belief in the monotheistic, revolutionary idea of one god in a land that worshipped a pantheon of gods and goddesses. Ikhnaton protested the corruption he saw in the temples and proclaimed that there was only one god—Aton—a divinity in the sun. Though Ikhnaton banished Nefertiti from the main palace, as opposition for his religious idea grew, Nefertiti remained steadfast and loyal to her husband and his belief. Together they had six daughters and there are many pictures showing an idyllic family life.[85] After his death, the god Aton was overpowered by the god, Amon, and polytheism once again was Egypt's religion.

Nefertiti

Queen Cleopatra

Cleopatra, who was actually of Greek origin, and an astute politician, was the oldest daughter of Ptolemy XI. She shared the throne of Egypt with her elder brother, Ptolemy XII. When their father died in 51 BC., both Cleopatra and her brother were minors. In 59 BC., her brother was persuaded by advisers to depose Cleopatra of her share in the government and to exile her. She began plans to regain her rights when Julius Caesar arrived in Alexandria and supported her fight in which her brother was killed. Cleopatra was proclaimed Queen by Julius Caesar.

According to custom she took her younger brother Ptolemy XIII, eleven years old, as her husband in name, as a colleague on the throne. When he was fourteen years old he demanded his share in governing. It was rumored that she had him poisoned, and made her son Caesar her associate in ruling Egypt.

After Caesar's death, and after a romance with Mark Antony, Cleopatra killed herself as the victorious Octavius defeated Antony. It is claimed that she preferred death to sharing her throne with a conqueror or being taken captive back to Rome. With her death, ended what little there was of Egyptian queens who actually ruled.

Greece

Origin of the Name

Greece, or Hellas, means all lands occupied by people speaking Greek. The Greeks, known in previous times as Hellenes, derived that name from the myth that ". . . the inequity of the human race provoked Zeus to overwhelm it with a flood, from which one man, Deucalion, and his wife Phrrha, alone were saved, in an ark or chest that came to rest on Mt. Parnassus. From Deucalion's son, Hellen, had come all the Greek tribes and their united name, Hellens."[86]

*Approximate Dates and Periods
in Greek History*[87]

Late Minoan Period ....1600—1400 B.C.
   (Island of Crete)

Mycenaen Period ....1400—1300 BC.

Homeric or Heroic Age..............1300—1200 BC.
   (The age that Homer wrote about)

Seige of Troy ....1200 BC.

Dark Ages.........................1200—1750 BC.
(Dorian Invasion)

Probable period Homer lived ....840 BC.

Probable period Hesiod lived ....750 BC.

Persian Wars........................550—490 BC.

Golden Age of Greece.................50—400 BC.

Decline of Greek Freedom ....400—300 BC.

Hellenistic (Greek) Dispersion ....332—146 BC.
Alexander the Great's Empire divided into six parts:
Macedonia, Greece, Thrace, Asia Minor, Babylonia, Egypt
Greece and Macedonia become provinces of Rome146
BC.

Historical Background

The Greeks proudly claim their heritage from the ancient Mycenaeans, who had absorbed the Minoan culture of the island of Crete. Minoan culture had dominated the Aegean (Greek) world from about 1600 to 1400 BC., and the Mycenaean from about 1400 BC. to 1200 BC. For about 450 years after the northern Indo-European Dorians had conquered the Mycenaeans, and then after that sailed the Mediterranean and conquered the island of Crete, Greece passed through a Dark Ages (1200-750 BC.). This was a period of destruction of temples, purposeless pillage of villages, and general disintegration of an advanced and wealthy civilization that had developed, among other skills, architecture, writing, record-keeping, metallurgy, shipbuilding, and surgery.

For several hundred years after the destruction of the Mycenaean civilization, with no unifying government, the people in small hamlets built walls at their outermost areas to protect themselves from marauders. Unlike the vast stretches of desert of the Mesopotamian Tigris-

Euphrates, or the Egyptian Nile rivers, which had made an unexpected raid all but impossible, the mountainous Greek landscape lent itself to surprise enemy attack.

In spite of the difficulties, a new civilization struggled out of the destruction of the Mycenaean and Minoan cultures. As H.G. Wells wrote, "The Greeks did not grow a civilization of their own; they wrecked one and put another together upon and out of the ruins."[88]

The different cultures of the two most important city-states, Athens and Sparta, were the result of the part each played during the Dark Ages. Sparta, which had become the homeland of the barbaric Dorians, was dedicated to military pursuits; Athens, which had resisted the Dorians, became a refuge for Mycenaeans fleeing the invaders, bringing with them the remnants of a higher civilization.

Athens

A Brief Historical Background

Swelling with refugees, or "outlanders," the city of Athens established an exclusionary social system, reserving the privileges of citizenship to a small, elite minority. This was referred to as a democracy, every citizen having a right to vote. However, excluded from citizenship were slaves, freedmen, "outlanders," and women.

> . . . even the Greek born in the city, whose father had come eight or ten miles from the city beyond the headland, was excluded . . . Pericles, a great Athenian statesman . . . had established a law (451 BC.) restricting citizenship to those who could establish Athenian descent on both sides . . . Thus . . . the citizen formed a closed corporation, ruling . . . a big population of serfs, slaves, and 'outlanders' . . . and if one desired the protection of the law, one sought a citizen to plead for one. For only the citizen had any standing in the law courts.[89]

Athens developed one of the highest cultures as yet known in the western world, combining peak achievements in philosophy, poetry, sculpture, drama, art, and architecture. The Golden Age of Greece, (500-400 BC.) produced intellectuals whose works are studied worldwide today for their skills in reasoning and their understanding of human nature. Among numerous other Greek men of history are Pericles, the great statesman; Socrates, Plato, and Aristotle, philosophers; and Aeschylus, Sophecles, Euripedes, and Aristophenes, playwrights.

The Athenian Empire, which had subjugated several adjoining city-states, could boast, not only of intellectual and artistic strength, but of military strength as well. The Greek-Persian wars (499-479 BC.) caused Athens to build a considerable navy. Then, as she grew in military power, she controlled the waterways around her shores. "No vessel might sail the sea without her consent . . . the process became more and more irksome as the pride and wealth of the subject cities grew."[90]

The increasingly suppressive Athenian policy led her neighbors to seek help from warlike Sparta. Sparta demanded that Athens grant independence to all Greek cities in her empire. But Pericles, the statesman, "persuaded the Athenians to reject this demand and Sparta declared war," (432 BC.).[91] Thus began the Peloponnesian Wars.

Sparta and her allies defeated the Athenian Empire in 404 B.C., but the wars weakened both Sparta and Athens. Though Athens rose to power again in 370 BC., and created the Second Athenian Empire, she never regained the glory enjoyed in the Periclean Golden Age.

Philip of Macedonia, and later his son, Alexander the Great, reduced Sparta and Athens and all Greece to a dependent status where they remained for the rest of Classical Antiquity. Under the rule of Alexander's chieftans, the period of dispersion of Greek culture began throughout Macedonia, Thrace, Asia Minor, Babylonia, and Egypt.[92] Worn out and submissive, Greece was easily overcome by Rome and became one of the provinces of the Roman Empire in 146 BC.

Religion

Mount Olympian Gods and Goddesses

Gods	Goddesses
Zeus	Athena
Apollo	Artemis
Hephaestus	Hestia
Ares	Aphrodite
Dionysus	Hera

A pantheon of gods and goddesses plays an active part in Greek history, epic poetry, and in the social and moral customs of the people. In addition to the Mount Olympian gods and goddesses, there are a multitude of lesser deities. Each city-state and each home worshipped a specific god and goddess, whether of Olympian origin or not. "The center and summit of the city was the shrine of the city god; participation in the worship of the god was the sign, the privilege, and the requisite of citizenship."[93]

The epic poems of Homer and Hesiod are the source book of Greek religion. And like religion and mythology generally, Greek myths shaped the attitudes of its people, though the myths as related by Homer and Hesiod are interpretations of much older Minoan myths.

When the northern Dorians conquered Crete, destroying that Minoan culture, as well as the Mycenaean culture, they supplanted the more matriarchal Minoan religion with their own patriarchal mythology. In Crete, which "was most repeatedly thought to be matrilineal and possibly matriarchal,"[94] the principal deity had been female. The Dorians, who were patrilineal and patriarchal brought their principal deity, Dyaus-Pitar, meaning literally God-Father. Dyaus-Pitar later became known in Greece as Zeus and later in Rome as Jupiter.[95] ". . . the gods of Olympus entered with the . . . Dorians, overlaid the Mycenaean . . . dieties and conquered them as their worshippers were conquered . . . Homer, Hesiod, and

91

the sculptors helped the political ascendency of the conquerors to spread the cult of the Olympians."[96] "The sex of the deity was determined by the sex of those in power."[97]

Where the Minoan goddesses were compassionate and powerful, those who were brought into the Olympian pantheon are changed. Hera becomes a nagging, suspicious wife, Athena a cold, manly daughter, Aphrodite a silly sex object. Artemis is of little importance, and Pandora, though not of the Olympians who in pre-Hellenic form had, previous to the Dorian invasion, brought abundance of gifts from the Earth Goddess, later brings evil and trouble and is a dangerous source of problems. "The prototypes later evolved into the wicked witch, the cruel step-mother, and the passive princess, etc., of our fairy tales."[98] Demeter (who is a very old deity and was an established mother-goddess on the islands and the mainland) survives, but she is not included among those on Mount Olympus.

The Minoan gods and goddesses were eventually replaced by the gods and goddesses of Mount Olympus. Zeus, ruler of the Olympian gods, throws his Minoan father, Chronos, into the ancient Hell, and proceeds

. . . almost every local goddess as his consort. Each valley, isle and cove seemed to have a local manifestation of a female goddess whom Zeus supplanted whether by marrying or having intercourse with her, dropping children all over Greece until descent from Zeus came to be a way of authenticating heroes and founders, much as some old American families claim descent from the pilgrims on the Mayflower.

By the time of Hesiod (poet) in the eighth century B.C., male dominance, which some have questioned in Homer, was no longer in doubt. Women once again, as they were in ancient Israel, were looked upon as a source of evil. In his *Theogony*, Hesiod tells

the story of Pandora . . . The misogyny of Hesiod was
further underlined by his emphasis upon the fact that
it was from Pandora that the 'deadly race and tribe of
women' descended who were always troublesome to
men.[99]

Through his poetry, Hesiod explains how Zeus
establishes his patriarchal government on Olympus,
becomes the father of the Hours, the Fates, the Muses,
and the Graces, denying any power to females. He even
takes away women's power to bear children when he
himself gives birth to Athena through his head.[100]
"Because she herself was born of man, Athena is able to
affirm that the father is the true parent of any child."[101]
Later, Aristotle reinforces this myth when he scientifically
reasons that only the father is the parent of a child.

The gods in Hesiod's poetry enjoy a variety of
activities. "Among the gods there are no virgins, and
sexual promiscuity (heterosexual and homosexual)
including rape—was never cause for censure even among
the married ones."[102]

In contrast, three of the five Olympian goddesses are
virgins. Athena is a warrior, judge and giver of
wisdom, but she is masculinized and denied sexual
activity and motherhood. Artemis is huntress and
warrior, but also a virgin. Hestia is respected as an old
maid. The two nonvirginal goddesses come off no
better; Aphrodite is pure sexual love, exercised with a
pronounced irresponsibilty. Hera is wife, mother and
powerful queen, but she must remain faithful and
suffer the promiscuity of her husband.

The goddesses are archetypical images of human
females as invisioned by males.[103]

The mythical story of the rivalry between Athena and
Poseidon is reflective of the way women were treated in
Greek life. In the myth, the men all vote for Poseidon and

the women for Athena. As there was one more woman than there were men, Athena won the contest. The men wanted to diffuse the anger of the god, Poseidon, and so they punished women threefold: ". . . they were to lose their vote; their children were no longer to be called by their mother's names; and they themselves were no longer to be called after their goddess, Athenians. Obviously, this myth mirrors a shift in the social organization of Athens."[104]

Male/Female Relationships—
Homeric or Heroic Age (1300-1200 BC.)

Though conquered by the Dorians, the Greek city-states held on to their legends of long-past glories in the *Iliad* and *The Odyssey*, epic poems attributed to Homer who probably lived about 850 BC. These poems glorified the heroic deeds of the Mycenaeans of about 1300 BC.—people who lived three hundred years before the poems were conceived. Memorized and told and retold from generation to generation for hundreds of years, the poems were not written down until around 500 BC. The Homeric poems give historians some idea of the social customs of the time Homer is thought to have lived.

These lengthy tales recount the heroic deeds and tell of the status of women and the relationship in the family of the father to his children. ". . . the father is supreme: he may take as many concubines as he likes, he may offer them to his guests, he may expose his children on the mountaintops to die, or slaughter them on the altars of the thirsty gods."[105]

Marriage, by purchase, is monogamous only for women. "The Homeric wife is as faithful as her husband is not."[106]

Women are not confined to the home in Homeric Greece as they are later in the Golden age. They may go outdoors and move about freely and discuss serious concerns with men.

Among the Homeric Greeks, cattle was the basis on which a girl's value was based when negotiations were underway for her purchase as a bride. As the Greeks became more and more interested in property and owned more cattle, a girl's value increased because she could bring cattle to her father when he sold her as a bride. Also, as the value of property increased, girls were more frequently allowed to live, rather than being exposed to die as infants.[107]

Male/Female Relationships—
Golden Age (480-399 BC.) Athens

By the time of the Golden Age, women's status, as represented in the laws, the Greek drama, philosophy, and the history of the period, had suffered markedly. As mentioned before, in Athens, only persons born in the city, of parents who were citizens, could become citizens. A male citizen could marry only a citizen-woman, that is, a woman whose father was a citizen and whose mother was a citizen-woman, though she had no privileges of citizenship. Her title simply meant that she was a daughter of a citizen and later could be the wife of a citizen. If a male citizen married a non-citizen woman, he would lose his citizenship.

To ensure the pureness of Athenian citizenship, the activities of citizen-women were severely restricted. A citizen must be sure that his wife's child was his. "She could not be trusted to this herself."[108]

In Athens there were five classes of women: citizen-women who stayed home and had children—the only women who could give birth to citizens; Hetairae, who were educated courtesans with whom men conversed and shared ideas; prostitutes and concubines; lower class and "outlanders;" and slaves. ". . . in Athenian Greece, 80 percent of all women were slaves . . ."[109]

Demosthenes, orator and statesman said, "We have hetairae for our delight, concubines for the daily needs of our bodies, wives in order that we may beget legitimate children and have faithful housekeepers."[110]

As in the Homeric period, marriage in the Golden Age was arranged by parents. Romantic love, considered by the Greeks to be a form of madness would almost never be a reason for marriage. Usually a girl married at 15 or 16 to a man fifteen or twenty years older than she was. The age difference itself served to subjugate women.[111] Her duties were ". . . to remain inside and to be obedient to her husband. If she went out at all it was to religious functions and funerals. She received no education."[112] At marriage the girl passed from the home and service of those who had reared her into the service of those who had not.[113] She worshipped the gods of her husband's family. Men were free to visit prostitutes and to take concubines.[114] But citizen-women were monogamous and were restricted to their homes. They spent most of their lives in the women's quarter of the house, either in the back of the house or upstairs and away from windows. No male ever visited the women's quarters, nor did a woman appear when men visited her husband. Citizen-women did not go shopping because business transactions were considered too complicated for women and because it was believed she needed to be protected from the eyes of strangers and from dealing with men.[115]

Any discussion about the necessity to protect women refers to women of the upper classes. Of the five classes of women, it is only the citizen-women who were secluded in their homes. Courtesans, prostitutes, lower classes, and slaves were free to come and go, unveiled and unchaperoned. The citizen-woman, whose main purpose was to give birth to pure Athenian-blooded citizens, could not go shopping, but her female slaves could.

The husband of an adulterous or raped wife was legally compelled to divorce her.[116] The chance of her giving birth to a child, not fathered by a citizen, was too great.

A woman's main purpose was to have children, particularly males. A family without children was not necessarily a family.[117]

. . . after a girl was married, infidelity was punished with the most terrible disgrace. Her husband was compelled to send her away. No man could marry her again; for if anyone ventured on such a course, he was thereby disenfranchised . . . If she appeared in a temple anyone could tear her dress off, and maltreat her to any extent . . . provided he stopped short of killing her . . . Restrictions of the most stringent nature and punishments the most terrible were employed to keep the citizenship pure.[118]

Men ate alone, or with other men. Wives did not go out to dinner in other houses with their husbands and they were excluded from eating with their husbands when they were entertaining male visitors in their own home. As some women were never seen it had to be proved by law that they existed.[119]

Athenian women were taught to spin and weave. "She was not allowed to see, hear, or ask anything more than was absolutely necessary. She should not appear in public."[120]

Citizen women were perpetually under the guardianship of a man, usually the father, or if he were dead, the male next-of-kin. Upon marriage a woman passed into the guardianship of her husband in most matters, with the important limitation that her father or whoever else had given her in marriage, retained the right to dissolve the marriage.[121]

The Athenians were protective of their women. A woman's dowry was to remain intact throughout her lifetime and to be used for her support, neither her father, nor her guardian, nor her husband, nor the woman herself could legally dispose of it. Upon marriage, the dowry passed from the guardianship of the father to that of the groom. The groom could use the principal but was required to maintain his wife from the income of her dowry, computed at 18 per cent annually. Upon divorce, the husband was required to return the dowry to his ex-wife's guardian, or pay interest, and with her dowry intact, she would be eligible for remarriage.[122]

97

"If a man had the misfortune of having only female children, it was arranged for the girls to be married to their nearest agnatic relative (a father's brother, that is, her uncle) in order to re-establish the family in the next generation."[123]

In both Athens and Sparta male homosexuality was an accepted practice, though in Sparta it was a sin after a male was over 35 years old.[124] "The chief rivals of the Hetairae are the boys of Athens." Love between males was considered to be more noble than love between man and his inferior, woman.[125]

After the age of six, boys were brought up by men and had virtually no association with females their own age as they grew up. And "In married life, men seldom find mental companionship at home; the rarity of education among women creates a gulf between the sexes, and men seek elsewhere the charms that they have not permitted their wives to acquire."[126]

Pomeroy notes that males came of age at 18; but that females never did.[127] Women could not buy or sell land, could not make contracts, or bring legal action. Property was bequeathed only to males. A widow could not inherit her husband's property. All of the Greek laws about women became part of ". . . the basis of that Roman law which in turn has provided the legal foundation of Western society."[128]

But, as though the laws were not enough to keep women in subjugation, philosophy told them that they were inferior. Aristotle, one of the greatest philosophers of all time, whose teaching about scientific reasoning endured for centuries as fact, taught that females were inferior to males. He justified his reasoning by referring to the natural world. In all nature, he said, the male was stronger, larger, more agile, and more advanced. He said also that women, because they were passive, should be under the rule of their husbands. He believed that men had more teeth than women and that human reproduction was caused only by the male.[129] The female, he said, was only the vessel and because females were inferior they were unfit for freedom or for political action.[130]

Even physiological error enters into her legal subjection, for just as primitive ignorance of the male role in reproduction tended to exalt women, so the male is exalted by the theory popular in Classical Greece.[131]

In essence, Aristotle maintains that woman is a mutilated or incomplete man, a thesis that has enjoyed a long and persistent history culminating in Freud's theories about women.[132]

That women seemed to have understood their position appears clear in Euripedes' play, "Medea," when Medea complains:

We women are the most unfortunate creatures. Firstly, with an excess of wealth it is required For us to buy a husband and take our bodies A master, for not to take one is even worse. And now the question is serious whether we take A good or bad one; for there is no easy escape For a woman, nor can she say no to her marriage. She arrives among the new modes of behavior and manners, And needs prophetic power, unless she has learned at home, How best to manage him who shares the bed with her. And if we work out this well and carefully, And the husband lives with us and lightly bears his yoke, Then life is enviable. If not, I'd rather die. A man, when he's tired of the company in his home, Goes out of the house and puts an end to his boredom And turns to a friend or companion of his own age. But we are forced to keep our eyes on one alone. What they say of us is that we have a peaceful time Living at home, while they do the fighting in war. How wrong they are! I would very much stand Three times in the front of battle than bear one child.[133]

"All in all, in the matter of sex-relations, Athenian custom and law are thoroughly man-made, and represent an Oriental retrogression from the society of Egypt, Crete, and the Homeric Age."[134]

"In the time of Homer, the position of women is dignified and free; by the time we reach the Golden Age of Pericles, women are cloistered slaves."[135]

Sparta

A Brief Historical Background

Unlike Athens which was a large, sprawling city, Sparta, which means "scattered," was a cluster of mountain villages. The capital, Sparta, encircled by mountains, needed no walls. It is famous for the Spartan Code which is attributed to Lycurgus, a lawgiver, who lived around 800 BC., but who may actually be a mythical person.

Under the code, the ruling class known as Spartans reduced the people in all the area under their rule to either Helots, or Perioeci; the former were slaves, the latter were freemen who engaged in industry and practiced art, both activities denied to the ruling Spartans.

The historian, Durant, asks, "How could thirty thousand citizens keep in lasting subjection four times their number of Helots:" He suggests that it could only have been done by abandoning the pursuit and patronage of the arts, and turning every Spartan into a soldier ready at any moment to suppress rebellion, or go to war.[136]

The Spartans waged war and became the leading city-state of Greece until Athens assumed that position after the Persian wars. Rivalry between the two city-states erupted in the Peloponnesian War, ending with Sparta's defeat of Athens in 404 BC. Sparta later suffered defeat at Thebes and after about two hundred years, along with the rest of Greece, became a province of Rome in 146 BC.

All people in Sparta existed to serve the city-state. The purpose of a Spartan man's life was to wage war; the purpose of a Spartan woman's life was to bear strong, future warrior sons.

Marriage for Spartans was virtually mandatory. Bachelors were ridiculed. No sickly Spartan girl was allowed to marry for fear she would weaken the Spartan line.

When a girl was born she was inspected by a group of old men who determined if she would remain alive. They could expose her to die if they wished. If she were said to be fit to live she was trained vigorously in physical pursuit, throwing the javelin, wrestling, racing, etc. to make her body strong for child-bearing.[137]

Just as the Athenians covered their women up to the eyes and hid them at home lest they should excite the concupiscence (lust) of their friends, so Spartans stripped theirs of covering and sent them into the marketplace so that their health and physical suitability might be marked by all potential fathers.[138]

Spartan girls, unlike Athenian girls, married later, usually at nineteen or twenty, and most often they knew the boys they were marrying because they belonged to the same group or social set. Partners within a "set" could be exchanged after marriage.

Nonetheless, husbands were somehow freed from any passion of jealous possessiveness of their wives, because it was held to be honorable for a free Spartan to share with any of his equals in the begetting of children. A middle-aged man with a young wife would introduce a younger man of good presence and breeding to his wife, and, if the wife approved and was pleased with him, the older man would happily accept as his own the offspring of such a temporary union. Similarly, a man might sleep with a woman for whom he had conceived a special admiration, her husband consenting. Thus, by reasons of this simple code of behaviour, those bugbears of the modern world—bastardy, adultery, divorce, and prostitution—were quite unknown. Furthermore, such was the social freedom enjoyed by married women, who, even as children inherited estates on an equal footing with their brothers that they were frequently able to run two households with a separate husband in each. Strangely enough, only one case is reported by the historians of a man running two households and having two wives.[139]

Spartan men led regulated lives, ate with men only at a men's dining room and were often away on military missions.[140] Spartan women, though they did not have the vote, and were still not equal with men, were better off than Athenian women. It is probable that women in Sparta had more control over their wealth, and it seems almost certain that they had more freedom. Athenian men resented Spartan women's freedom. Aristotle claimed that Sparta failed because Sparta did not control its women.[141]

Because the emphasis on child-bearing was to produce strong children from strong parents, married or not, there were few family ties, no adultery, no illegitimacy, and no need for divorce. Yet for all its emphasis on breeding a strong people, Sparta died out, leaving history the names of a few Spartan kings, but no names of notable Spartan women.

Women in Greek History

Women in Ancient Greece were subjugated, and literature "from the poets to the playwrights was essentially misogynistic."[142] The poet, Archilochus, called women the greatest evil that God had ever created, and the poet, Hipponax, said woman brings man happiness for two days, ". . . one when he marries her, the other when he buries her."[143]

The goddesses of earlier times on Crete, when women had a higher status, were replaced either by male gods or by more submissive goddesses, setting the tone for the position of women in Greece. It would seem that the thrust of laws, literature, and religion would prevent women from achieving anything. And for most women that was probably the case. For, in a society that rose to intellectual and artistic supremacy, the names of women are not mentioned as legislators, philosophers, sculptors, or dramatists. Yet, in spite of the repressive attitude about them, some women broke through to history.

The Pythagorean Society was founded by its teacher, Pythagorus, about 550 BC. His reputation for "his willingness to receive women as well as men into his schools," brought hundreds of men and women to study the curriculum of geometry, arithmetic, astronomy, and music.[144] "A list of women philosophers published in 1765 lists twenty-eight Pythagoreans . . ." among them, Theano, who may have been Pythagorus' wife, and Perictione.[145]

A list of women poets, famous in their time, is headed by Sappho from the island of Lesbos, who was the head of a girls' school there and is credited with inventing the personal lyric style of poetry.[146] Sappho was celebrated as "one of 'nine terrestrial muses' . . ."[147] The other eight who were at the time as important, but whose names have become obscure are "Erinna, . . . called by the ancients the equal of Homer . . ." Myrus, Myrtis, Corinna, Praxilla, Telesilla, Nossis, Anyta, Gorgo, Andromeda, Danophila. Boulding notes that where origin is known, none came from Athens.[148]

Among the Hetairae, a class of women, educated and free to associate intellectually and socially with citizens is Aspasia. The companion of Pericles, she is credited with having taught Socrates the art of rhetoric, and having trained some of the Athenian orators. She may be better known not for her intellectual accomplishments, but for her charm. Pericles divorced his wife and took Aspasia as his sole mistress whom he would have married except if he married a non-citizen-woman he would have lost his citizenship, the result of a law which Pericles himself had initiated many years previously. As a special privilege, when Pericles was ill, the legislators granted citizenship to his son by Aspasia, which was a breach of Athenian law.

Hetairae could attend the Academy of Learning and "participate in lectures and discussions on an equal footing with men. Two of Plato's best-known pupils were Lasthenia of Mantua and Axiothea."[149]

Hetairae offered citizens a companionship that their secluded, uneducated wives could not. They even went to war as cooks, nurses, and "companion(s)-in-arms," though it was the Hetairae's slaves who probably did the menial work.[150]

Plato wrote of the Hetaira, Diotimi, that Socrates learned from her (though she may have been a fictional character in Plato's *Dialogues*.) A list of the hetairae, companions to the great men of the Golden Age of Greece follows:[151]

Aspasia	Pericles
Leontium	Epicurus
Danae	Epicurus
Glycera	Menander
Metanaira	Isocrates
Herpyllis	Aristotle
Archeanassa	Plato
Lais(1)	Aristippus
Lais(2)	Diogenes
Lais(3)	Demosthenes
Phrybe	Hyperides

While none of the Greek women mentioned here directly influenced the course of history for their country, as did a few women in Egypt, nevertheless, educated Greek women, at least indirectly, influenced the world around them.

. . . the women scholars from the various Greek city-states who congregated in Athens influenced the entire Mediterranean world for centuries to come, particularly the urban cultures of Alexandria, Constantinople, and Rome, and later Moslem centers of scholarship. The thread of influence was broken for the Western Christian world with the decline of

Rome. With the rediscovery of antiquity in the early Renaissance, numbers of books were written about these lady scholars and poets of Greece. However, little of the original writings of these women survived the various library burnings of Christian and Moslem zealots.[152]

Rome

Historical Periods

Primitive Rome—up to 753 BC.
Rome Under Kings—753-509 BC.
The Republic—509-27 BC.
The Empire—27 BC.-476 AD.

Brief Historical Background

The plains of Italy were inhabited by men and women for 30,000 years before Christ. After 10,000 BC., a toolmaking culture endured until around 6000 BC., and then about 2000 BC. Northern Italy was invaded by tribes from Central Europe who moved south, pastured cattle and sheep, cultivated the soil, and made implements out of bronze.

About 1000 BC. they learned the use of iron and spread their culture over most of the peninsula. It is from these Villanovas a they were called, that the language and arts of Umbrians, Savines, and Latins come. However, around 800 BC. they were subjugated by the Etruscans who ruled Rome for only about 100 years, leaving their imperishable mark on the culture, principally in their pottery and other artifacts.

It is not clear how the city of Rome was founded. It and all its records were burned to the ground by the Gauls in 390 BC., but the myth of its founding holds strong, and the date is always given as April 22, 753 BC.

The myth tells the story of Numitor, who held the throne of Latium's capitol. Amulius wanted the throne and so he killed Numitor's two sons and required Numitor's only daughter, Rhea Silvia, to become a virginal priestess for the goddess, Vesta. But Rhea fell asleep and Mars, overwhelmed by her beauty, seduced her and gave her twins. Amulius demanded that the twins be drowned, but instead they were placed on a raft, drifted ashore, and were later suckled by a female wolf.

She-Wolf of the Capitol, c. 500 B.C. Bronze, approx. 33½" high. Musei Capitolini, Rome.

106

The Twins, Romulus and Remus, grew up, killed Amulius, and set out to build themselves a kingdom on the hills of Rome. The myth further explains that in order to get wives for their new kingdom, the Romans, Romulus and Remus, invited the neighboring Sabines to a party, seized the Sabine women, and drove off their husbands, and in the morning married the women.

When their husbands eventually returned, armed for battle, the women, now pregnant, asked for peace, saying they had lost one set of husbands and didn't want to lose their new husbands. Thus the Sabines joined the Romans (or Latins), and together with the Etruscans comprised the three original tribes of Rome.

Under a succession of kings, (753-509 BC.), Rome built a great state and set the stage for future social organization. The citizenship of Rome was restricted to males 15 years or older who were not slaves or aliens, and who were descendents of, or had been adopted into one of the first three tribes.

Each of the three original tribes was divided into groups of families, all in each group descendents of the same male ancestor. The leader of a group of families was called a *pater*. The leaders joined together to form the Senate. The population was divided into three major groups; the patricians from the descendents of Roman citizens; the plebians who were freemen having no political power in the early years; and the third group, the slaves.

Rome became a republic, according to a legend, deposing its king, Tarquin, after Tarquin's son, Sextus, raped his kinsman's wife, who then stabbed herself in shame. The outcry against Tarquin prompted the Romans to give power, not to a king for life, but to two consuls for one year, and to a Senate composed of patricians.

The period of the republic, (509-27 BC.) was marked at first by the struggle between the patricians and the plebians, ending with the plebians being given the right to vote, although elected offices could only be won by the patricians. The plebians also requested written law which resulted in the famous Law of the Twelve Tables written in 449 BC. A few years later, restrictions were further relaxed and plebians were allowed to marry patricians, and by 300 BC. all restrictions were ended, except the privilege of taking part in some religious rituals which were a requirement before one could hold public office. Plebians were unable to advance in government or Roman society.

During the period of the republic, especially from 200-30 BC. Rome conquered its neighboring communities, eventually unified what is now Italy, and expanded its holdings all around the Mediterranean Sea, engaging in plunder, bringing home slaves and riches. Rome became commercial where it had previously been agricultural. Its growing merchant class become more interested in wealth than in distinction by ancestry. Wealth soon became the basis for citizenship.

As more and more money was needed to maintain the tremendous military machinery, taxation was increased, at the same time that riches were being amassed by aristocrats and merchants. The rich grew richer, prices and unemployment rose, and the poor grew poorer, restless, and threatening to the stability of Rome. The Roman circus was set up partly to amuse the rich and partly to distract the discontented poor.

Rome's boundaries had grown beyond its ability to rule from a distance. Discord over power-control of Rome erupted into several civil wars, especially after the inauguration of the Roman Empire, which officially dates from 27BC.-476 AD. The fourth and the last civil war was fought between Octavian, Caesar's nephew, and Antony. After Antony gave Roman provinces in Egypt to Cleopatra's children, he was removed as commander of the Eastern forces and defeated by Octavian in 31 BC. With Cleopatra he later committed suicide.

Because the vastness of the growing empire increased the difficulties of administration, it was divided into four prefectures, Gaul, Italy, Illyrium, and the East. Barbarians threatened its borders, and people, discontented within its boundaries became a ready force to defeat authority.

Often known for its brutality inflicted on its conquered people, Rome became the world center for brutality as a performing art. The mass murders in the Circus Maximus provided sensational enjoyment for the spectators, to entertain the rich and to keep the poor from thinking about their problems.

In the vast marble colosseum—greater than any American football stadium—the death struggles of the gladiators, the mangled bodies of the charioteers, whetted the people's appetite for excitement and thrills.

The Empire was dying, and the Roman Games—ruthless, brutal, perverse—were the emotional outlet for the discontented mob. Feats of strength and skill no longer pleased. Men were pitted against wild beasts, professional swordsmen against unarmed prisoners. The Emperor Trajan gave one set of games that lasted 122 days during which 11,000 people and 10,000 animals were killed.[153]

The duelists in gladiatorial combats were usually mixed to avoid monotony; heavy-armed fought against light-armed . . . They might end in a draw, or a man who was clearly losing could appeal for mercy; it was then up to the magistrate running the show, and he generally followed the crowd's wishes. They waved handkerchiefs or turned their thumbs downward if they judged the pleader had fought bravely and deserved to be spared.[154]

At the same time that the Empire was expanding beyond its control, the new religion of Christianity was taking hold. Millions of hitherto pagan Romans were converting to Christianity, until finally pagan Rome became Christian Rome in 325 AD. when the Roman Emperor Constantine converted to Christianity. The Empire, which had been divided into four parts, was reunited, then split, reunited, and finally divided again, permanently between East and West. The West continued to fight for its existence in spite of internal disruptions, but German tribesmen broke through the Roman lines in 376 AD. Soon other barbarian tribes followed, including the Visigoths, Vandals, Suevis, Burgundians, Ostrogoths, Lombards, and Franks. The Visigoths sacked Rome in 410 AD., the vandals in 455 AD., and the peninsula now known as Italy, weakened and ready to be vanquished, was defeated by a little known barbarian general, Odovakar, King of Heruli, in 476 AD. The Eastern Roman Empire continued until 1450.

Western civilization was born in Sumer, about 2500 BC., and was halted, at least temporarily, with the fall of the Roman Empire. Because it had appeared invincible, and had lasted longer than any other empire, it has been studied exhaustively to determine the cause for its collapse. To attempt an easy analysis here would be presumptuous. Gibbon wrote six volumes to explain *The Decline and Fall of the Roman Empire.* Following are a few reasons often projected:

1. The government extended its forces too far and provided little "home rule" in the conquered territories.

2. There were too many excesses—human sacrifices were for "fun and games." Rome eventually suffered a "soul sickness," from which it needed to escape.

3. There were not enough rewards for being a good Roman as compared to the rewards offered by Christianity. For a government to last it has to offer rewards and punishments. Roman government offered punishments, too many, compared to Christianity. Christianity offered the reward of Everlasting Life After Death. Immortality of the Soul was more enticing than anything the Romans had to offer. It made suffering and martyrdom tolerable for the Christians who gained in numbers.

4. The Roman Empire was ripe for destruction. There were too many extremes between rich and poor, which opened the way for invasions.

5. The plague weakened the military strength, the fear of disease and of barbarians destroyed the determination to survive as an empire.

6. Farms were laid to waste because of the barbarian invasions.

Religion

Greek Mt. Olympian Gods	Roman Gods
Zeus	Jupiter
Apollo	Apollo
Hephaestus	Vulcan
Ares	Mars
Dionysus	Dionysus

Greek Mt. Olympian Goddesses	Roman Goddesses
Athena	Minerva
Artemis	Diana
Hestia	Vesta
Aphrodite	Venus
Hera	Juno

The earliest Roman divinities were the fearsome Etruscan gods, Mantus and Mania, "master and mistress of the Underworld each with an executive horde of winged demons."[155] Then there was the goddess of fate, Lasa or Mean, who carried a sword and snakes, and finally Lares and Penates who represented the home and crops.

Etruscan ritual culminated in the sacrifice of sheep, a bull, or a man. Human victims were slaughtered or buried alive at the funerals of the great. The Etruscan appears to have believed that for every enemy slain he could secure the release of a soul from hell . . . The belief in hell was the favorite feature of Etruscan theology.[156]

As far back as 496 BC. the goddesses and gods of Asia and Greece came to Rome. One of the earliest dieties, when life was primarily agricultural, and religion was concerned with raising crops, was the goddess, Ceres, who was later assimilated with the Greek Goddess Demeter. Ceres was one of the most important deities. All of the Greek gods and goddesses of Mt. Olympus were merged into Roman religion, most of them under different names.

The Romans had early absorbed the Greek gods . . . assimilating Zeus to Jupiter, Hermes to Mercury, Athena to Minerva . . .[157]

In the days before the monotheism of Judaism, Christianity, and Islam, people in the known world worshipped whatever deity gave them the most comfort. This is still true in many places, in India for instance, where a family may worship the god Shiva, or Vishnu, or other gods or goddesses.

In addition to the worship of individual gods or goddesses, Romans subscribed to three religious institutions: the vestal virgins, the Sibylline oracles, and the emperor, who was Rome's spiritual leader. Vestal virgins were selected from girls six to ten years old to keep the fires burning in the sacred hearth of the goddess Vesta. They were pledged to virginity and service for thirty years and in return were given special privileges. "The nearest equivalent in Rome to the old high priestess roles of the Eastern empires would be the vestal virgins."[158]

The lives of Vestals were severely regulated, but in some respects they were the most emancipated women in Rome . . . In the laws of the Twelve Tables 'she was to be freed from the power of her pater

112

familias' . . . they were the only women permitted to drive through the city of Rome in a two-wheeled wagon, which conferred high status on its occupants . . . 'and an attendant cleared the way for them'[158A]

"If any of them was found guilty of sexual relations she was beaten with rods and buried alive."[159]

Historians record from 483 on, eighteen Vestals. "Of these, eleven were accused of misconduct, seven were executed, one hanged herself, and three were acquitted."[160] It was believed that the welfare of the state depended on their performances and on their virginity . . .

In early Rome there probably had been only one Vestal serving at a time, for potential childbearers could not be reserved for the service of religion. But in historical times there was a college of six Vestals who varied in age.

The prosecution of the Vestals is a specific example of the firmly established principle of Greek and Roman thought connecting the virtue of women and the welfare of the state.[161]

The Sibyls, wise priestesses of the god Apollo, were prophetesses, responsible for creating the books of divinely inspired answers to worldly questions. "In major crises, the government confessed to learn the pleasure of heaven by consulting the Sibylline Books."[162] The books were consulted only for major decisions, by the sacred priests, or *augures*. It is not known what the books contained, for none of the original nine survives.

The populace of Rome was expected to worship their emperor because he was considered at least partly a god. Elaborate rituals accompanied this worship, including burning incense before his statue, which the Christians refused to do.

Other ideas gradually evolved to fill the need for personal religious involvement which seemed to be lacking in Roman religious life, namely:

Epicureanism, a Greek philosophy which was imported into Rome, taught that the pursuit of pleasure was valid as long as it did not injure the body or spirit of oneself or of others.

Many rich Romans used this philosophy as the justification for self-indulgence. The Epicurean period in Rome, 30 BC. to 90 AD. is one of debauchery, and also of the beginning of the decline of Rome.

Stoicism, also a Greek philosophy, though very stern, proclaimed

> . . . that man is here not to enjoy the pleasure of the senses, but to do his duty without complaint or stint . . . Educated Romans grasped at this philosophy as a dignified and presentable substitute for a faith in which they had ceased to believe, and found in its ethic a moral code completely congenial to their traditions and ideas.[163]

It is understandable that in a period of decline, when slaughter for pleasure, and other excesses, were becoming repugnant, that a philosophy which proscribed duty over pleasure would have been attractive to people who were worried about the future of their empire.

The cult of Cybele, the Great Mother goddess from Asia, offered another perspective on life.

> Various versions of the death of Attis . . . retell the story of the dying son/lover. An interesting factor in the accounts of Cybele and Attis is that this version of the religion of the Goddess was eventually brought from Anatolia to Rome. It was celebrated there in great processions and festivals until AD 268 and embraced by such emperors as Claudius and Augustus. We can only guess at the influence this had on the Christian religion that was developing there at

that time. Roman reports of the rituals of Cybele record that the son, this time as an effigy, was first tied to a tree and then buried. Three days later a light was said to appear in the burial tomb, whereupon Attis rose from the dead, bringing salvation with him in his rebirth. Cybele was always closely identified with the Goddess Rhea, who was known as the mother of Zeus . . ."[164] In time of crises, Romans called on oriental deities for help. For instance, when the Sibylline Books foretold that Hannibal, who in 205 BC. was going to attack Italy by marching his elephants over the Alps, would be defeated if the goddess Cybele were brought from Asia Minor to Rome, the Senate imported a black stone said to be the incarnation of the Great Mother and after ceremonies centering around the stone, Hannibal left Italy.

The cult of Isis held the hope of immortality, Isis was

. . . the ideal wife and mother, her appeal was to both men and women, but particularly women, who had few friends in the traditional Greek or Roman pantheon . . . In her worship there were priestesses as well as priests . . . she was the all-powerful queen of heaven, earth, and the underworld, giver of health, beauty, love, abundance, wisdom. Time and again decrees were passed banning her worship, but it always returned.[165]

By AD. 200 Isis temples had spread from Rome to France, Holland, and England."[166]

Mithraism, the third of the Eastern religions, was based on Mithras, the god of truth and light, who probably had Persian beginnings. It was a vigorous religion, and for men only, emphasizing combat. "Mithraism throughout the Third Century AD. was Christianity's most serious rival."[167]

So it is clear, Rome had many deities and philosophies to choose from.

From the east came not only Cybele, Isis, Mithras, mystery cults, astrology, and magic, but also the religion that was eventually to absorb and supplant them all—Christianity. It offered a Savior who did not belong to a remote past but whose teaching and miracles were within living memory.[168]

Jesus of Nazareth was, at first, considered by the Romans to be merely an irritating political rebel. But as the years went by and more and more of Christ's disciples preached the Christian doctrine throughout the Roman empire, the Romans began to take the religion as a serious threat.

The Jews had existed in the Roman Empire, coining their own money and being exempt from military service, living in relative peace with their non-Jewish neighbors, ". . . for Rome left freedom of religious matters to her subjects."[169] And for some 30 years after the crucifixion of Christ, it was probably difficult for the Roman government to distinguish between Judaism and Christianity. But by the time of Nero, 64 AD., the government was well aware that for them there was a new disturbing, and threatening religion from a group who refused to respect the Roman government.

The Christian revered his bishop, even his priest, far above the Roman magistrate; he submitted his legal troubles . . . to his church authorities rather than to the officials of the state.[170]

The Christian doctrine of non-violence was a real problem to an empire which thrived on war and was having difficulty keeping soldiers in the army.

Roman persecution of the Christians was at first sporadic and local. But by the time the empire was aware of all of its problems, and when unity was needed, persecution of Christians became a governmental act.

116

Emperor Diocletian, in 303 AD. issued orders intended to break up the church. A later edict in 313 by Emperor Constantine reversed Diocletian's and gave more religious freedom to Christians. The government then changed its intent and restored all pagan gods, nationalizing their temples. However, they reversed that too, later legislating those gods out of existence.

Christianity in its earliest years, the religion of the slaves and the poor, became a religion for anyone from any walk of life. Its doctrine was infectious and any Roman emperor had to take into account the numbers of Romans who had converted to the new religion if he was concerned with popular support. Only 20 years after Diocletian's persecution edict, Emperor Constantine converted to Christianity in 323 AD., making Christianity the state religion, proclaiming the empire, The Holy Roman Empire. "By his aid Christianity became . . . the mold for fourteen centuries of European life and thought."[171]

The last goddess temple was closed about 500 AD., and Christianity, well-established by about 400 AD., had all but put an end to the worship of Greco-Roman gods and goddesses.

Male/Female Relationships

Women enjoyed a higher status under the Etruscans, around 800 BC. and descent was traced from the mother.[172] But after the city of Rome was established, "Rome itself was very much a man's world. Its government was run by men, for men, and its history was written by men, for men."[173]

In a civilization where the myth of its founding was based on the kidnapping and rape of the Sabine women, respect for women was not very high. According to the myth,

. . . the Romans treated the young women, mostly Sabines, with great delicacy for the night. The next morning the captives were awakened to hear a lecture

117

by Romulus on the superiority of the marriage institution which he proposed for his new state. A woman, he explained, was to be under the absolute power of her husband, and if she was unfaithful or took to drinking (an activity which might lead to unfaithfulness), she would be punished. The sole judges of her activities were to be her husband or her male relatives. However, if a wife observed decorum, respected her husband, and bore him children (preferably male), she was to be regarded as mistress of the house during her husband's lifetime, and he would keep his interference in the household to a minimum.[174]

After Rome's founding, Roman citizenship was based on descendency from original inhabitants.

A Roman citizen could marry only a woman who was the daughter of a Roman citizen. Marriage with any other was impossible . . . It was for this reason that such care was taken of the purity of Roman women, and such a broad distinction was drawn between the conduct of a man and a woman.[175]

The Roman family structure was based on the *pater familia*.[176] This was a complex close-knit family organization which gave the oldest male, the father of the total family, absolute power. "In civilized Greece and Rome the father is in total control of his wife and children, the line of descent is from father to son, the mother's brother has vanquished."[177]

The father alone could decide which of the newborn children should live. He had power over his wife, his children (even when fully grown), their wives and children, his slaves and his children's slaves.

Everything a woman had was under a male guardian, first her father and then her husband. A girl brought a dowry into the marriage, though the dowry was always under male guardianship. Girls who could not raise a dowry could become concubines.

Once married, which could be as early as twelve years old, females were under the control of their husband's father. A woman was a perpetual minor. She could not vote nor testify in court. A man could sell his wife, or kill her. She had no legal rights over his children.

Roman history supplies many instances of the despotism which husbands exercised over their wives. The slightest indiscretion was sometimes punished by death, while men might do what they liked without hindrance. 'If you were to catch your wife,' was the law laid down by Cato the Censor,' in an act of infidelity, you would kill her with impunity without a trial, but if she were to catch you, she would not venture to touch you with her finger, and indeed she has no right.'[178]

However, the Roman women were better off than Greek women. Roman wives ate with their husbands, though the women sat while the men reclined. Roman wives received the friends of the husbands and ate with them. They could walk about outside with freedom, unveiled, and many Roman girls, as early as 485 BC. were educated. Only boys were given personal names. Girls were usually given feminized names of their fathers. For instance, a daughter of a man named Claudius would be named Claudia. If he had two daughters, the second daughter would also be named Claudia, referred to as the younger, or Claudia II.

During the period of expansion of the Empire, known as Imperial Rome, 200 BC. to 30 BC., law became more favorable to women. This was at the time when wealth that came from conquered lands became the basis for citizenship, replacing descendency from the original tribes. And, as it was also in other civilizations, the power of the father declined as the power of the state rose.

Though they had no direct power, women in Rome could exercise indirect power. In 195 BC. women publicly demonstrated *en masse*, in front of the Forum and persuaded the Senators to repeal the law passed by the law-maker, Oppius, in 215 BC., forbidding women "to use gold ornaments, varicolored dresses, or ride in chariots." The historian, Livy, quotes general Cato, who fought the repeal:

> If we had, each of us, upheld the rights and authority of the husband in our own households, we should not today have this trouble with our women. As things are now, our liberty of action, which has been annulled by female despotism at home, is crushed and trampled on here in the Forum . . . Call to mind all the regulations respecting women by which our ancestors curbed their license and made them obedient to their husbands; and yet with all those restrictions you can scarcely hold them in. If now you permit them to remove these restraints . . . and to put yourselves on an equality with their husbands, do you imagine that you will be able to bear them? From the moment that they become your equals they will be your masters.[179]

Nevertheless, the times were changing, and the Oppian law and other laws restricting women were repealed. Emperor Hadrian eventually took the life and death privileges away from the father and gave it to the courts. Emperor Antoninous "forbid a father to sell his children into slavery . . . The Roman woman gained new rights as the man lost old ones . . ."[180]

There were some wealthy Roman matrons who had inherited from their husbands or fathers—wealthy fathers who gave their daughters dowries that their husbands could not meddle with.[181] This changed the hold that men had over women and led the men to say that women were too free.

Marriage was not against a woman's will, though courtesans, prostitutes and actresses could not marry.

The Roman marriage contract was a part of a civil ceremony that had nothing to do with religion. It was not until Christianity that religion was introduced into the marriage ceremony.

In the period known as Epicurean Rome, (30 BC. to 90 AD.), freedom for women in Rome was greater than it had been at any time before. In this period of extreme pleasure-seeking, Roman women developed a reputation for having numerous adulterous affairs and for refusing to have children. All this when the Roman army was shrinking. Because the government needed more troops, it offered incentives for childbearing, and special privileges for women who had three or more children.[182]

In 28 BC. Emperor Augustus called the Senate together and scolded those who had not married. Candidates for public office were given precedence if they had children, and Julius Caesar offered more land to fathers who had more children.[183]

Childlessness and divorce were subject to fines, though infanticide was commonly practiced—exposure being the most common method.

Adultery came under the state's jurisdiction, rather than the husband's. An adulterous wife was to be banished and her property confiscated. Augustus's laws required a husband to divorce an adulterous wife. If he did not, he would be prosecuted. Probably as a backlash to permissiveness, strict laws were enacted to counter the sexual license. Emperor Augustus "exiled both his daughter and his granddaughter for illicit intercourse and forbade their burial in his tomb."[184]

Emperor Constantine punished women for rape, depending on whether or not they had been willing. "If the girl had been willing, her penalty was to be burned to death. If she had been unwilling, she was still punished, although her penalty was lighter, for she should have screamed and brought neighbors to her assistance."[185]

Whether or not the strict laws against adultery succeeded in curtailing adultery is not known. But it is known that the laws to encourage the birth rate did not work and the population continued to decline. Romans were probably beginning to suspect that their Golden Age

121

was coming to an end. The future did not look good and many Romans were reluctant to bring children into a bleak world (a reaction not uncommon during other historical periods.) Also, the Christian Church which was gaining converts, valued celibacy highly.[186] A large family "came to be regarded almost as a disgrace, a proof of lasciviousness."[187]

Women's activities of the social class below that of Roman matron included waitresses, retailers, prostitutes, butchers, fisherwomen, stonecutters and brickmakers. Though women were patronesses of guilds, "there is no evidence that women were permitted to belong to the profession of craft guilds of men, even when they worked in the same occupation."[188]

Women also worked as gladiators. "Arena girls were trained in special gladiator schools around Capua near Naples . . . Often a nobleman throwing a sumptuous feast would rent a pair of gladiatrixes to duel when dinner was over."[189]

Because Christians believed in the Resurrection, they turned away from the Roman practice of cremation. Women who had been healers became embalmers. It was exclusively a female occupation.[190]

Women learned to become political and to speak out, though in one instance, in 42 BC., when women spoke out in protest at the treatment of widows, the women were punished. Their husbands had been killed and these wives were taxed to the point of poverty. Hortensia spoke out against this injustice. She won her case and the practice ceased.

Roman slaves, as in some other civilizations, could own property, save money, and buy their freedom. They could also buy other slaves. When a male slave bought a wife, she became the personal slave of her husband, yet both were actually the property of her husband's master. Children of slaves took the status of their mothers. If they were born after she was freed, they were freeborn, but they were not legitimate unless her husband was also freed.[191]

"Compared to Athenian women, roman women were liberated, but compared to Roman men they were not."[192]

Yet Roman women, while they couldn't hold political office, could and did wield power. They were

> . . . involved with their culture and were able to influence their society, whereas the Athenian women were isolated and excluded from activities outside the home. Roman women dined with their husbands and attended respectable parties, games, shows, and even political gatherings . . . Roman women had access to money and power, and their fortunes were linked to those of the state. As men prospered, so did women.[193]

All testimony about the status of women is from men. In ancient times conditions for women were not good, but in ancient Rome women had greater freedom than they did in Greece though they were not as respected as they were in Egypt.

As was true in previous civilizations, women contribute the most to a civilization when it is first developing. At the civilization's height, women's sphere seems to decrease as men's expands, and women become restricted. In practice, the virtue of the state appears to abide in the virtue of its women—as for instance in the Vestal Virgins. As the civilization declines, the freedom of women is often blamed for the downfall of the country. Rome is the prime example.

> Women who attempted to challenge the old ways were a threat to Rome, regardless of the fact that the mythological old ways had never really existed. Since the Roman experience has been so influential, it means that whenever women attempt to change their status to work for equality, part of the mythology they have to fight is the burden of the fall of Rome, a story written for the most part by men and with a male view toward the female sex.[194]

One of the first stories of Roman women's achievement, though mythical, emphasized a woman's virtue. It tells of the time (in the second Punic War, 218-201 BC.), when the ship carrying the symbol of the Great Mother to Rome ran aground. The Romans were desperate to have the goddess's statue in Rome because the prophecy claimed that her presence would defeat Hannibal's attempt to conquer Rome. Yet no Roman could move the grounded boat. Claudia, in wanting to prove her virtue, said if her chastity were pure, the boat would follow her. She walked to Rome and the boat followed,[195]

Rome's favorite woman is *Cornelia*, who was a writer, the wife of a plebian, and later the widowed mother of two emperors who ruled from 162-121 BC.

> She deliberately educated these two sons (out of a total of twelve offspring) to lead a reform movement of the plebians against the patricians. Both sons died in the ensuing social unrest, but Cornelia remained a major international figure, 'visited by men of affairs and men of letters who came from near and far to pay her honor and discuss with her philosophy, letters and the times.' Ptolemy wanted to share the crown of Egypt with her, but she . . . refused remarriage.[196]

> When the second of her emperor sons was killed, "The Senate forbade Cornelia to wear mourning for her son."[197]

Hortensia, in 42 BC., was the leader of 1400 women who forced their way into the Forum to protest their male relatives' being condemned to death and the widows then being taxed into poverty. Hortensia's speech was successful. The number of women taxed was reduced to 400.[198]

Livia Drusilla, "sometimes referred to as the 'Founder of the Empire,' succeeded "in getting her son Tiberius crowned as emperor," and signed public documents with him, acting as a ruler until he 'moved his court right out of Rome to get away from her," though the "Senate was about to heap honors on her."[199]

Agrippa assisted her husband, Germanicus, on his military campaigns. When he was poisoned by his enemy Piso, Agrippa retaliated by publicly accusing Piso, a dangerous thing for a woman to do at a time when women were ordered not to speak out. Piso committed suicide, but when Agrippa became powerful she was banished by Emperor Tiberius ". . . to a little island of the Campanian coast, where she maintained her reputation to the last by starving herself to death."[200]

Arria, wife of Paetus, who stressed among other virtuous wives, that a wife ought not to outlive her husband, especially if he were a victim of political persecution. When her husband, in 45 AD. was ordered to commit suicide by Emperor Claudius, Arria ". . . plunged the dagger into her own breast to set an example, and spoke her celebrated last words, 'It does not hurt, Paetus.'[201]

Helena, later named St. Helena, was Emperor Constantine's mother, concubine of Constantine's father, who had left her as he had been ordered to do by Emperor Diocletian. She was a Christian and must have exerted her religious influence on her son who became the first Christian Roman emperor in 323 AD.

One of her most memorable contributions to later history was to see the possibility in special sites in the Holy Land as pilgrimage destinations for Christians. She established church foundations at a number of such sites.[202]

Early Christianity

Christianity appealed to the people in the Roman Empire because, among other things, it was an alternative to the worst side of the Roman way of life. In the face of Roman cruelty—lions tearing people apart in the Circus

Maximus for the entertainment of spectators—Christianity offered the solace of a life after death. In contrast to the Roman freedom of adultery, Christianity offered moral righteousness. As the rich became richer, acquiring more slaves, more landholdings, and more power, the poor became powerless and poorer. But Christianity offered hope in the midst of despair. People were told that it was easier for a poor person to get into Heaven than it was for a rich person. And the day of judgment was coming.

Jesus of Nazareth preached a non-violent philosophy at a time when the Roman world was sick of violence. People were ready for a philosophy which offered a new meaning to life. They were told that the Kingdom of God was coming to replace evil with goodness, and those who accepted the new belief would have life everlasting.

Boulding pictures the first early Christians:

> Visualize a growing nucleus of women and men living in a community and traveling around with Jesus, holding meetings, visiting synagogues, talking with people on the streets. These are working-class people who do not have to observe elaborate social taboos. Jesus himself was very easy and at home with women from all backgrounds, as with men. He was bringing together a new family for a new society, and sex was just not relevant. Nobody was antisex, they were all 'beyond' sex . . .

> It is not difficult to imagine this cheerful band, full of anticipations about the new time. But what kept them going after Jesus' death? The women were the first who were sure they saw him return, then the men also saw him. This shared conviction would greatly intensify the feelings of togetherness of the group. They all flocked to Jerusalem to 'see what would happen.' It is explicitly mentioned that there were both women and men among the 120 (the number named in the story in Acts 1:15) who met each day in a second-story apartment in the city. All this built up to a gathering on the fiftieth day after Jesus' death when

people came together with special expectancy. The account in Acts tells us that tongues of fire appeared over the heads of the gathered women and men, and they spoke 'with tongues.' Peter said a few words at the end of the gathering;'

'And it shall come to pass in the last days, saith God, I will pour out of my Spirit upon all flesh: and your sons and your *daughters* shall prophesy: . . . And on my servants and on my *handmaidens* I will pour out, in those days, of my Spirit; and they shall prophesy.' (Acts 2:17-18) (Italics Boulding's).

Think of what it meant for women who had lived the old Judaic pattern of subservience to men to have been part of this group. For them the Age of the Holy Spirit had indeed already started.[203]

In the beginning, Christianity was a challenge to a concept of priesthood as well as to the subjection of women. When specific religious assignments were necessary, they were a dangerous burden rather than a privilege, given the level of persecution in the second and third centuries.[204]

Dangerous or not, women assumed a full role in the new religion.

The earliest communion rituals were freely participated in by everyone, with no distinction as to special authority or status of any individuals. This denial of special priesthood roles was especially scandalous to their fellow-Romans. It was bad enough for men, but that women should participate too![205]

Typical of an institution in its beginnings, Christianity opened its ceremonies to women, not only as followers but also as leaders. And as a fledgling group it was criticized by the establishment.

The very women of the heretics, how bold! who teach, argue, perform exorcisms, promise cures, baptize. Their ordinations are inconsiderate, trivial, changeable . . . Thus today one is a bishop, tomorrow another.[206]

In his wanderings, Jesus was joined by people in all walks of life and by "kindly and pious women."[207] His attitude about women was different from the prevailing Jewish attitude about women. ". . . he made no derogatory comments and showed no contemptuous attitudes about them."[208] ". . . indeed he may have been history's first 'feminist.'[209]

Christianity Within Judaism

Living to themselves in relative peace and in religious freedom, the Jews had been exempt from Roman persecution. "The immunity granted by the government, and the contempt of the populace combined to secure freedom for the Jewish religion."[210]

Christianity, which grew out of Judaism, enjoyed the same kind of religious freedom for many years and was almost indistinguishable from its parent-religion.

"Until 70 AD., Christianity was preached chiefly in synagogues and among Jews."[211] The apostle Paul, ". . . visited first the Jewish communities and then preached to the Gentiles."[212] Christianity's break with Judaism was inevitable as long as Christianity insisted that Jesus was the Son of God. To the Jews, Jesus was a man, a prophet in a long line of prophets, and to say that he was a divinity was, to the Jews, blasphemy. But though they were offended by the Christians' referral to Jesus as the divine savior and though they resented his authority in speaking in the name of God, nevertheless, when Jesus was seized by the Romans and when he was condemned, ". . . quite clearly the condemnation did not have the approval of the Jewish people."[213]

Christianity a Threat to Rome

In time, Romans recognized that Christianity was a threat to the empire. It preached pacifism at a time when the Roman army needed recruits, and also, contrary to the Roman belief that religion and religious ceremonies should be a part of government. Christianity preached that its doctrine was supreme over any government. Christians who refused to worship the emperor and the gods of Rome were called "atheists." They were also called "communists," because of their communal living and their sharing their possessions with each other, or giving up their material goods. But the real test of whether or not they would be persecuted depended on their willingness to worship the emperor. Those who did not were imprisoned, or punished further, sometimes to the point of death.

> The law had exempted the Jews from emperor worship, and the Christians, at first confused with the Jews, were granted the same privilege. But the execution of Peter and Paul, and the burning of Christians to light up Nero's games, turned this mutual and contemptuous tolerance into unceasing hostility and intermittent war. We cannot wonder that after such provocation the Christians turned their full armory against Rome—denounced its immorality and idolatry, ridiculed its gods, rejoiced in its calamities, and predicted its early fall.[214]

Development of Church Authority

In spite of massive persecutions by the Romans, Christianity gained converts, though in its first years there were so many different sects it would have been difficult to determine what exactly a Christian was. As time went on the movement became unwieldy. The Church saw that it must set up some guidelines for membership by determining church canon law, by establishing church doctrine, and by setting up its organizational authority.

At some point, generally thought to be around 180 AD., the books of the New Testament were determined to be authentic and inspired and therefore were church law, often called canon law. Then in the third century, the structure of the church was established in Rome, bishops were recognized as the final arbiters of Christian doctrine, and the pope became its recognized leader.[215]

With church laws, known as canons, with doctrines, and with an established power structure, women's roles within the church were subordinated, whereas in Christianity's beginnings women worked with equality alongside men. As there was an urgency for converts to get ready for the Kingdom of Heaven, which was promised soon, people turned to the celibate life, believing that spiritual union with Christ transcended any sexual union on earth. "Because of this sense of urgency of the end times, a new and radically equivalent role of women and men together in Christ was forged."[216] But when the end had not come, there was a "spiritual slowdown and a hardening of the attitude about women, and the new equivalence between men and women suffered."[217]

> As the patterns of the larger society took over, men's authority roles became more evident . . . While women retained the role of deaconnesses for some centuries, they were excluded from the priestly role as soon as it was developed.[218]

But the role of deaconness was not an important role in the church hierarchy.

> The legal status of deaconnesses in the first few centuries seems to have been that of ordained servants and nothing more . . . Saint Ignatius of Antioch in 117 AD., was the first to mention a stratification in orders according to bishops, presbytyrs, and deacons, male

and female . . . deaconnesses were cautioned not to give quick answers . . . not to preach in holy places . . . not to serve at the altar . . . Whatever ministries were initially assigned to women were apparently removed with every succeeding century . . . deacons could excommunicate deaconnesses.[219]

One fear of having women in church leadership is man's fear of menstruating women. As Broderson, a student of canon law writes in his study, "I must . . . emphasize that the biological fact of menstruation is the main obstacle to women's participation in liturgical functions: one always shied away from it with fear. The demand for cultic cleanliness won out against the deaconness."[220]

Pious women were, however, left with a few alternatives. They could join a nunnery and live a life of prayer; they could live as canonesses and minister to social needs; or they could establish religious centers for women, which many did.

Early Church Leaders

The first great church leaders listed in the *Encyclopedia Americana* are four men who "early stood out," and who wrestled with the intellectual problems of the church. They are Paul of Tarsus (Saint Paul), (10?-64?), Tertullian of Carthage, (160?-230?); Origen of Alexandria, (185?-254?); and Augustine of Hippo (Saint Augustine), (354-430). The Encyclopedia states that their beliefs profoundly affected the church.[221]

All four men were gravely concerned with the Fall of Man, believed to be the result of Eve's tempting Adam, based on the Judaic Old Testament's Adam and Eve myth.

"Yet the connection between sex and the Fall, which so intrigued and even obsessed the early Christians, had not really been central to the thinking of the Jews. Men in the Old Testament were patriarchal and powerful, and often guiltlessly enjoyed the services of several wives and concubines."[222] But with the early leaders of Christianity a sense of sexual shame was introduced. Sex was seen as being responsible for the corruption of body and soul.

Paul died a martyr's death in Rome. Referred to as the founder of Christian theology, he had written many epistles to his followers which "were preserved . . . until gradually they entered into the subtlest theory of the Church . . ."[223]

Paul wrote:

> Women should keep quiet in church. They must take a subordinate place. If they want to find out anything they should ask their husbands at home, for it is disgraceful for a woman to speak in church. . . . A man ought not to wear anything on his head in church, for he is the image of God and reflects God's glory, while woman is a reflection of man's glory. For man was not made from woman, but woman from man; that is why she ought to wear upon her head something to symbolize her subjection.[224]

As was mentioned before, women had played an important part in the early days of the church. Paul had apparently objected to this.

> . . . whatever his reasons, Paul explicitly objected to this new turn, and his reactionary efforts in the matter of women succeeded in setting the tone for thinking about women that would be continually reinforced in the intellectual and practical tradition in the West for the next two thousand years.[225]

Paul's influence is mentioned again and again. As the church became stronger in the Roman Empire, Paul's writings had great influence on the subordination of women. Some writers today believe that his writings are used to deny women access to the priesthood and power within the church in the 1970's and 1980's.

Tertullian, the second man listed in the Encyclopedia, was desirous that every woman should wear a veil or else all men would be put in peril by the sight of her.[226] Tertullian pictorially denounced the Romans, referring to the Day of Judgment:

> How vast the spectacle will be on that day! How I shall marvel, laugh, rejoice, and exult, seeing so many kings—supposedly received into heaven—groaning in the depths of darkness!—and the magistrates who persecuted the name of Jesus melting in fiercer flames than they ever kindled—against the Christians![227]

Equally descriptive when he spoke of women, Tertullian "addressed women in the coarsest terms as 'the gate by which the demon enters,' and told them that 'it is on your account that Jesus Christ died. He condemned all Christians who became soldiers, artists, or state officials; all parents who did not veil their daughters."[228]

Origin, another early church leader, at seventeen, after his father was beheaded as a Christian martyr, adopted a strict ascetic life, fasting, sleeping only a little, wearing no shoes. In a zealous desire to avoid sexual temptation he castrated himself. Many men followed his example of castration in order to lead a life free from women's temptation, though by the fourth century, the church forbid castration.

For over twenty years he wrote hundreds of books on Christian theology before he was persecuted in 250. His writings brought Christianity to a full-fledged philosophy.

Augustine (Saint Augustine) who converted to Christianity later in life and confessed all his earlier sins, professed that "men at their birth are tainted with original sin . . . from the transgression of the first man, Adam," a philosophy which was formally adopted although in modified form . . . by the church.[229]

Summarizing Christian attitudes, Seltman, in his book, *Women in Antiquity*, wrote

> . . . in a small volume which is devoted to the study of women in the ancient world one must face the fact that the opinions of the Church Fathers, whose ideas

replaced the teachings of Christ, appear to have been for women as dismal as they were unfortunate. For men, on the contrary, the church, like Islam, carried much that was advantageous, for Christendom and Islam made available emotions, states of mind, and political conditions by which men could profit, in which they could revel, and through which power could be won and justified.[230]

Church Power

The Church adopted many things from Rome, including the stole, the garments of pagan priests, incense, holy water, the Latin language, burning candles, architecture, and Church canon law was based on the structure of Roman law.

As the Roman Empire disintegrated in the wake of barbarian invasions, plagues, and the lack of trust in their emperors, people turned more and more to the Church, not only for spiritual guidance but for what had previously been governmental functions including taxation, imprisonment, and education.

In about four hundred years Christianity had grown from a small, unpopular sect to a massive, sustained movement. Roman governmental administrators were soon replaced by Church bishops as the source of power.

As the barbarian races settled and became Christian, the Pope began to claim an overlordship of their kings. In a few centuries the Pope had become . . . the high priest, censor, judge, and divine monarch of Christendom; his influence extended in the west far beyond the utmost range of the old empire . . .[231]

For most of the Medieval Period, Church power in Central Europe was the greatest power.

In summary, again, as it had been with the stages in the development of civilizations, so it was also with the development of Christianity: women contributed the most and were treated with equality in Christianity's beginnings. When Christianity was securely established, men reserved the important functions for themselves, conferring power, privileges, and prestige on men, subordinating and restricting women.

Notable Women in Early Christianity

Thecla—An Apostle who traveled with Paul.

> St. Thecla of Ioconium was a historical personage and according to the Catholic Encyclopedia she was accepted as a 'bona fide Apostle' by the early Church and is still accepted as such in the Eastern Church. She was a companion of Saint Paul, who ordained her as a preacher of the Gospel and an Apostle of Christ. A book called the Acts of Paul and Thecla was widely read in the first four Christian centuries and even as late as 590 it was referred to as an authentic document of the apostolic age. It is now included among the Apocrypha.
>
> No one questioned its authenticity, even though Tertullian had attempted to cast doubt upon it in the third century, until it was barred from the official canon of the New Testament in AD. 367. Seventeen years after that date, however, Saint Jerome, 'the most learned of the Latin fathers,' still vouched for its authenticity as well as for the undeniable historicity of Thecla herself, the female Apostle.[232]

In addition to the fact that she was an Apostle, she typified the power of virginity which the early Church praised.

> Among the female martyrs, the favorites were virgins who preferred burning pitch, the rack, and the hot iron, to sexual intercourse. Such virginity was said to have miraculous powers; typically, when a hungry lion was turned loose upon Thecla in the arena, he stopped short and then licked her feet in humble admiration of her purity.[233]

Other women of whom we have only a little information include:

Lady Fabiola—"Founded a hospital and is said to have revolutionized health care in Rome."[234]

Paula and her daughter **Eustachium**—Formed a convent after going to Jerusalem with St. Jerome.[235]

Pelegia—" 'Passed' as a hermit in a cell on the Mount of Olives and was widely venerated as Pelagius. It was not discovered until her death that she was a woman."[236]

Eugenie—". . . a Greek and Latin scholar whose studies led her to Christianity in the third century and who cut her hair and entered a monastery as a man. Many years later, after she had long served as abbot, her sex was discovered . . ."[237]

Women who were founders of communities for religious women known in history because their brothers mentioned their names:[238]

St. Augustine's sister—name unknown.

Theobisia—Sister of Gregory.

Macrina—Sister of St. Basil who is claimed "to be the author of the Rule of St. Basil supposed to be the first formally enunciated monastic rule; her brother took it over from her when he founded his monastery several years after she founded hers."[239]

Marcella—Sister of St. Ambrose, "founded a convent on her own estate."[240]

Florentine—Sister of two bishops.

Marguerite—Sister of Honoratius.

Chapter 3

THE MEDIEVAL PERIOD—
400 to 1400 AD.

Brief Historical Background

The medieval period, also known as the Middle Ages, spans about one thousand years. The early part of this period, up to about 800, is often called the Dark Ages— "dark" referring to the lack of cultural development. People who were fighting wars or defending themselves, or simply trying to survive famine or the plague had little time for the writing of literature, or developing art, music, philosophy, or other activities usually associated with leisure that comes with the safety of living in established, secure societies.

To back up for a moment, Emperor Constantine, in 330, had transferred the capital of the Holy Roman Empire from Rome eastward to Constantinople, believing the capital in the East would be easier to defend. His successor, Emperor Theodosius, in 395, divided the Empire into Eastern and Western districts for the purpose of strengthening it. But the division did not help to fortify the Empire against its enemies: the opposite happened. The empire had become too vast to defend. The agricultural Western Empire was besieged on the north and the west by different tribes. A map below shows the routes of the various tribal people who attacked the Western Roman Empire.

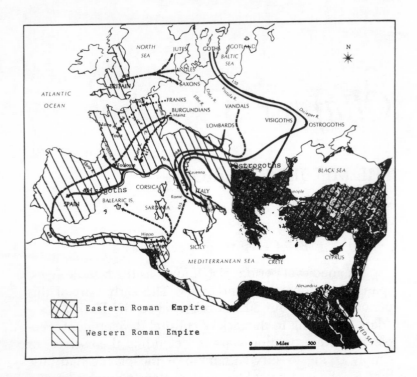

Routes of the Germanic Migrations

The Germanic tribes of Visigoths, Burgundians, Vandals, Ostrogoths, Lombards, Franks, Angles, Saxons, and Jutes overran the Western Roman Empire from the fourth to the sixth centuries. Most of these Germanic tribes were later displaced by the Huns.

The Eastern Empire was smaller, more centralized, and easier to defend. It became a fortress defending the Western Empire many times from invasions on its eastern borders. When the tribal people realized they could not break the Eastern Empire, they concentrated on the west.[1]

Tribes overran western Europe, wrecking towns, destroying what little trade there was, killing and pillag-

138

ing. It was a period of several hundred years of violence followed by epidemics of bubonic plague, famine, and a lack of security in the future.

> Our histories of these times are very imperfect; there were few places where men could write, and little encouragement to write at all; no one was sure even of the safety of his manuscript or the possibility of its being read. But we know enough to tell that this age was an age not merely of war and robbery, but of famine and pestilence . . .[2]

When the tribal king, Odovakar, sacked Rome in 476, Western Europe considered that the head of the Christian world was the emperor at Constantinople. This left each area in western Europe with its own problem.

In England, for instance, Rome had withdrawn her troops because they were needed at home. Before the Romans had occupied Rome, England was a conglomerate of tribal people and after the Romans left there were continual tribal migrations from Europe to England. There were Picts, Norsemen, Celts, Gails, Scots, Saxons, Angles, and Jutes. In 577 the Teutons arrived from Germany and took command of Angleland, or England.

At this point Christianity in England was diminished by the Germanic pagan gods and the legends of King Arthur's attempts to save Christianity from the heathens inspired Christians.

In Ireland, with the help of a woman known as St. Brigid, Patrick, an ordained priest, successfully resisted the pagan druids. Ireland eventually converted to Catholicism.

France, once known as Gaul, was overrun by Franks, Visigoths and Burgundian kings. Clovis, the king of most of Gaul, conquered the surrounding territory, was converted to Christianity by his wife, Clothilde. Clovis moved his capital to Paris and died at the age of forty-five. "Queen Clothilde, having helped to make Gaul, France, came to Tours after the death of her husband and served there in the Church of St. Martins . . ."[3]

Spain was captured by the Visigoths of Gaul who ruled it until the Moslem Moors captured it in 713. The Visigoths forgot their Germanic language and spoke a transformed Latin which became Spanish. Christians struggled against Moslems for control of Spain until the capture of Toledo in 1036 by Alfonso VI of Castile who absorbed Moslem culture into Christian Spain.

In Italy, Odovakar of the Heruli tribe which had conquered Rome was in control of Italy. In 488, Theodoric's forces came from the Eastern Roman Empire in Constantinople, combined his army with the Ostrogoths against Odovakar, finally taking possession of Southern Italy and Sicily. Theodoric kept the Ostrogoths as military police, gave them land, ransomed back Romans, and gave Romans the best of any land distribution. He repaired much of the damage done by the barbarians and he protected the Church. But the Gothic wars were to be fought again. In fact, Rome was captured five times.

In Fourth Century Rome there were 175 holidays in the year; ten with gladiatorial contests; sixty-four with circus performances; the rest with shows in the theaters. The barbarians took advantage of this passion for vicarious battle by attacking . . . while the people were absorbed at the amphitheater or the circus.[4]

The last Gothic War in Rome, in 553, was fought by the Eastern Emperor, Justinian, who had hoped to "drive barbarism back to its lairs and restore Roman civilization to all its old expanses . . ."[5] He had wanted to "recapture Africa from the Vandals, Italy from the Ostrogoths, Spain from the Visigoths, Gaul from the Franks, Britain from the Saxons." Justinian defeated what barbarians there were in Italy, but at such a cost that "only ruins bore witness to Rome's ancient grandeur . . . Rome would not fully recover from that victory till the Renaissance."[6]

Though Justinian fought many wars in his attempts to unify Europe once again under the Roman Empire, he did not succeed. And he is known in history, not so much for his wars but for his law code which laid the groundwork for the social structure which became known as feudalism.

Justinian saw the necessity for keeping people on the agricultural lands which they had deserted when the barbarians overran the countryside. Part of the Justinian Law Code read:

> . . . a freeman who had cultivated a tract of land for thirty years was required, with his descendents to remain forever attached to the land . . . A serf who ran away . . . could be reclaimed like a runaway slave . . .[7]

Though it had seemed that Justinian might have been able to restore the Empire, in fact, when he died, he left the treasury empty. His lieutenants had lost the lands which he had reclaimed. Syria, Palestine, Egypt, Africa, and Spain were abandoned to the Arabs; Italy to the Lombards; within a century after Justinian's death, the Empire had lost more territory than it had gained.[8]

> . . . Western Europe, in the sixth century was a chaos of conquest, disintegration and rebarbarization. Much of the classic culture survived, for the most part silent and hidden in a few monastaries and families. But the physical and psychological foundations of social order had been so disturbed that centuries would be needed to restore them. Italy . . . the land that had given order to half the world suffered for five centuries a disintegration of morals, economy and government.[9]

For several hundred years waves of tribal people continued to invade Central Europe, terrorizing peasants, clergy, and nobles, making any kind of business arrangement unreliable. As late as 876 a lease for a rural neighborhood in Luca stated that rent was to be suspended if the heathen returned and destroyed house and produce.[10]

Peasants attempting to fight the invaders were massacred. Feudal lords who depended on the produce of the land were impoverished as their soil was reduced to untilled wastelands.[11]

Population which had declined at the end of the Roman Empire, continued to decrease. Even the most important towns had only a few thousand inhabitants. And what few people there were in scattered towns had difficulty communicating. The old Roman roads fell into disrepair, bridges were down and were not repaired. People lived in frightened isolation.

Local Christian princes assumed that their duty was to make Christianity secure against the pagans. Emperor Charlemagne (768-814) tried to unite the Christians against the tribes and to convert barbarians to Christianity. He gave them the choice between baptism and death, and ". . . had 4500 Saxon rebels beheaded in one day."[12]

Charlemagne, one of the greatest medieval kings, worked diligently to increase knowledge in a period when the style of living was war and plunder. He brought books and teachers into his kingdom, but after his empire collapsed, the desire for knowledge—a desire which he had helped to create—lost out to the desire for security and increased landholdings.

By the time of Charlemagne, people from Gaul south were being Christianized. But beginning about 800, northerners from what is now Denmark, Sweden, and Norway, launched attacks on the countries to the south of them in Europe. These "pagans to the north, . . . were for nearly a century and a half to afflict the west . . ."[13]

They attacked from Russia to Britain, navigating rivers into the interiors with their sixty-five foot vessels. When the waters were too shallow or dangerous, they carried their boats on land. In 890, the Northmen by-passed Paris in this way.[14] For a hundred and fifty years, no area, either coastal or in the interior, was free from the fear of a raid by the Norsemen, or Vikings. Wherever they went they spread terror.

The Vikings behind Valkyries were heavenly maidens who carried slain warriors from the battlefields to Valhalla. Here we see 5 Valkyries attending two knights.

In time, the communities to be sacked learned to buy "from the marauders the promise to discontinue their ravages at least for the time being."[15] This meant that the Norsemen would return again and again for money. The princes who were buying-off the Norsemen, collected this money from their subjects and from the church, draining money from the West toward Scandinavia.

Gradually the Norsemen were subdued. They either became Christians, or they assimilated into the territories they had conquered, or they were too often defeated by the local princes who had become stronger. "By about the year 930, the continent had become practically free from the nightmare menace of the Northmen . . . the practice of extended raids disappeared."[16] Security and hope for the future developed, population increased, and, with the greater use of horses, communication improved.

The Christian Church which had survived Roman persecutions and then hundreds of years of tribal invasions, competed with pagan gods for converts and eventually became the overriding power of the medieval period. Either by threat of death, or by choice, tribal people converted to Christianity. Their pagan religion proved to be no match for the more organized Christian Church.

> More than one seafarer from the North on returning from his warlike cruises, brought home the new religion almost as if it were part of his booty. The two great Christianizing kings of Norway, Olaf son of Tryggvi and Olaf son of Harald, had both received baptism—the first on English soil in 994, and the second in France in 1014—at a time when, as yet without kingdoms, they were leaders of Viking bands.[17]

By the year 1000, the tribal invaders had been assimilated into the institutions of western Europe, that is, into feudalism, Catholicism, and into agricultural and town life.

At the beginning of the medieval period, Europe was overrun by many tribes. By the year 600, except for Italy, all of Western Europe was in the hands of Germans with pagan gods. Yet by about the year 1000, the Christian Church had succeeded in converting the conquerors. That it did so at times by fear and torture cannot be denied. But the idea of Christianity was the powerful force of the medieval period. The popes had hoped for a united Europe as the Roman Empire had been at its peak, but that did not happen.

What did occur was a reordering of the social structure from barbarism to feudalism, to a system of nations which evolved civil and canon laws, jury systems, habeas corpus, and some representative government in Spain, France in its Estates-General, and the Parliament of England.

The medieval period saw the further development of guilds, and the cultivation of social manners in chivalry. It saw the beginning of universities, the building of massive Romanesque and Gothic cathedrals and castles, and from the Crusades the development of trade with the East and the beginning of adventure that led to the explorations of Columbus and Magellan. The period that began with confusion, illiteracy, fear, and despair, ended, in spite of the Inquisition and the witch-hunts, with hope, excitement, wealth, a desire for learning, and the beginning of confidence in the future.

Feudalism

Life in the early medieval period was uncertain and dangerous. "Neither the State nor the family any longer provided adequate protection. The village community was barely strong enough to maintain order within its own boundaries and the urban community scarcely existed."[18] Barons, or Lords who ruled over territories where boundaries changed with each new battle could not protect the peasants who lived nearby.

The peasants were easy victims for wandering robbers. Defending themselves, or hiding in the forests, they had little time to tend their crops or animals. Yet everybody, Lord and peasant alike, needed the food that could be grown if there were time and protection to take care of the land. And the Lord always needed additional military assistance. The necessity of the rulers for food and for military help during attack, and the necessity of the peasant for protection, led to a medieval governmental institution known as feudalism.

Feudalism was a system of the powerful man securing the support of subordinates who bound themselves to him in service, in exchange for military protection and land to grow crops. The peasant, under feudalism was called a serf and his position was that of a free man, though actually he had little freedom. He was given a piece of land to grow food, which he and his family could eat, or he could sell the surplus, except for a tenth which he had to give to his Lord.

In addition to the taxes or rents the serf must pay for the use of the land, he also owed his Lord

> . . . many days of unpaid labor . . . Some lords required three days weekly through most of the year, four or five days a week in plowing or harvest time; additional labor days, paid only by meals, might be exacted in emergencies. This obligation lay upon only one male in each household. The serf was obliged to grind his corn, bake his bread, brew his beer, press his grapes, at the lord's mill, oven, vat, or press, and pay a small fee for each such use. He paid a fee for the right to fish, hunt, or pasture his animals, on the lord's domain. His actions at law had to be brought before the baronial court, and cost him a fee varying with the gravity of the case. He had to serve at call in the Baron's regiment in war. If the baron was captured, the serf was expected to contribute to the ransom. He contributed also the substantial gift due to the lord's son on being made a knight. He paid the baron a tax on all products that he took for sale to market or fair. He could not sell his beer or wine until the lord had had two weeks' prior time to sell the lord's beer or wine. In many cases he was obliged to buy a prescribed quantity of wine yearly from his lord . . . He paid a fine if he sent a son to higher education or gave him to the Church, for thereby the manor lost a hand. He paid a tax, and required the

lord's consent, in case he or his children married a person not belonging to his manor, for then the lord would lose some or all of the offspring . . . If the peasant died without issue residing with him, the house and land reverted to the lord . . . If his heir was an unmarried daughter, she could retain the holding only by marrying a man living on the same manor.[19]

Within the feudal system, besides the Lord and the serf, there were household warriors called vassals. These men, usually knights who had gone through lengthy training in the art of tournament fighting, swore military allegiance to the Lord in exchange for land known as a fief.

The vassal-Lord relationship ended with the death of either, meaning the fief usually became the vassal's free and clear upon the death of the Lord. But the serf-Lord relationship was hereditary. That is, when a serf died, the Lord, through his control of the land, still retained rights over the serf's widow and her children.

The Lord's vassals might be served by their own vassals, and also by squires who were sons of nobility not yet knighted. Lords, vassals, squires were all skilled in tournaments (lists) with swords (lances) where they fought (tilted) in competition with each other or in actual battle against neighboring noblemen, or against an enemy king. All of these men owed allegiance to the king, ready to do battle.

For, of all the problems besetting the governing classes in those days, the most urgent by far was not that of administering the country or a private estate in time of peace, but that of procuring the means to wage war. Whether public or private, whether undertaken light-heartedly or in defense of life and property, war was for many centuries to be regarded as the normal thread of every leader's career . . .[20]

Lords held court in their fortified castles, served by knights who were trained to "defend the Church, protect the poor, make peace in his province, and pursue the infidels . . . to all women he was to be a guardian, saving their chastity; to all knights he was to be a brother in mutual courtesy and aid . . ."[21]

The knight's son was seldom brought up in his father's house. He was entrusted to his father's lord. There he performed "the duties of a page, received instruction in the arts of hunting and war, and later in courtly manners."[22]

Because the kinship ties were weak, it is suggested that the feudal interdependence of serfs, vassals, and Lords was necessary.[23] But "whoever owed obedience was obliged to give financial help to his chief or master in case of need; the serf, the so-called 'free tenant of a manor, the subject of a King, and finally the vassal."[24]

Chivalry and Courtly Love

Chivalry, a mannerly way of treating women, grew out of feudal knighthood. When chivalry is mentioned today it is usually in relation to something like a man's opening a door for a woman, or holding her chair while she is being seated at a dinner table. These gestures come through history from the medieval period. In reality, a woman can open her own door, so the act is one of ceremony, not necessity. But the chivalric gestures of the medieval period indicated an awareness of women not acknowledged before. Women were seen as a class to be protected and knights were sworn to guard women's chastity. But in these cases, as in most references to protecting women, even today, the ones referred to are upper class women. In medieval times serfs were treated just slightly better than slaves, while the noble women were treated with exaggerated courteous gestures.

Among the people of the Lords' courts, the princes, vassals, squires, princesses, and high-born ladies, there developed a style of love peculiar to the medieval period, known as courtly love. Knights and other young men of noble birth, some of whom were musicians and poets, wrote, sang, and dedicated their poetry to the high-born ladies of the courts.

The knight who wrote poetry and sang his songs to a lady-love was called a troubador. He would declare his love to a woman of noble birth, years older than he was, and already married. The woman's husband, rather than being jealous of the attention to his wife, was flattered that she was the object of the troubador's poetry. And the troubador considered himself more noble because of his love for a high-born lady. He would endeavor to think of her constantly, and dedicate his sword-tilting tournament to her, most likely while he wore her handkerchief in his arm band.

Courtly love did very little to raise the status of women because it touched so few. The knights were protectors of women, but this applied to only a small class of aristocratic women. Most women remained unprotected. And though in courtly love women were regarded as superiors to their lovers, in marriage they were actually inferior to their husbands. Courtly love changed literature through the poetry that was written in the name of love, more than it changed life.

The following pages tell of one man's joy and his agonies in the pursuit of courtly love.

The Service of Women

On Sunday, April 25, 1227, crowds gathered at every crossing along a road on the Italian mainland near Venice, to watch an extraordinary procession pass by. It had been thoroughly advertised in advance by a messenger bearing an open letter to all the knights of Lombardy, Austria, and Bohemia. The letter stated that on April 24 the goddess Venus would arise from the sea near Venice and start the next day to travel north to Bohemia, breaking lances with every warrior who would meet her in the lists. Whoever tilted with her would gain a gold ring and great honor with ladies; whoever failed to meet her would henceforth be shunned by all lovely ladies; and whoever first unhorsed her would win all the horses of her retinue.

The cavalcade of the putative deity, when it finally hove into view, was worth the wait. First there slowly rode by a dozen squires, extravagantly dressed in white; then came two maids-in-waiting, also gorgeously got up, followed in turn by half a dozen musicians, festively sawing and blowing away; finally there appeared on a luxuriously caparisoned horse a husky man-sized figure attired in an outrageously ornate white gown, a heavy veil, a pearly headdress, and waist-length pearl-bedecked braids. Even in the credulous Middle Ages, none but fools and louts supposed this to be a real goddess, nor even a real woman; indeed, it was an open secret, not particularly meant to be kept, that inside the finery, the pearls, and the braids, was none other than Ulrich von Lichtenstein, knight errant, jouster of great prowess, Minnesinger of some talent, and devoted admirer of an unnamed lady for whose love he was undertaking this superb arduous, and all but impossible task. The curious poor watched and cheered, noblemen saluted gravely, the ladies, informed by gossip of Venus' real identity, hastened to kiss him warmly at every halt, and impatient knights-at-arms sent their men to him with invitations to combat.

Ulrich accepted every challenge, and by his own reckoning (which may, of course represent some degree of hyperbole), broke the incredible total of three hundred lances as he fought his way to Vienna in the course of the next five weeks. In those combats, he succeeded in unhorsing four of his opponents, and was never himself unhorsed. It was a notable performance; throughout the world of Austrian chivalry his name and fame spread greatly, and lords and ladies spoke admiringly at many a dinner table of the magnitude of the love that could have inspired such service and produced such a record of performance in the lists. And what was the purpose of these immense exertions and this very considerable expenditure? To win for Ulrich the unutterable joy of being allowed to see and speak to the nameless lady face to face, and possibly be favored with a kiss.

To understand this singular state of affairs, let us learn something of Ulrich's life up to that point. He had been born about AD. 1200 in the hilly, fertile Austrian province of Steiermark, or Styria. His father must have been a member of the lesser nobility, for although Ulrich never possessed any great titles or vast fiefs, he grew up within castle walls, was knighted after a suitable apprenticeship, and led an active life in the service of his feudal overlords. His signature on certain existing documents indicates that for his successes as knight-errant and jouster, he eventually won the position of high steward of Steiermark, and later on, also became a marshal and a justice of the province. At the height of his fortune he owned not only the cast of Lichtenstein, from which he took his name, but two others and considerable land. According to a fairly recent scholarly German monograph these and other documentary details indicate that he was a reasonably clever, energetic, and purposeful medieval politician and landowner.

But of all of this Ulrich never bothered to say anything in his autobiography, which is the principal source of information on his life. It runs to a wearying thirty thousand lines of narrative verse plus numerous added lyric poems, which is surely room enough for everything, but he devoted it entirely to the only subject that seemed important to him—courtly love. Its very title is the story of his life: *Frauendienst*, or the service of woman. *Frauendienst*, dictated by the illiterate knight in later life to a scribe, is not a work of fiction, even though the aging man-at-arms may have yielded to the delights of exaggeration or been tricked by the distortions of memory. Nor is it a work of satire, though *Don Quixote de la Mancha*, not written until more than three centuries later, could have been directly patterned upon it. *Frauendienst* is one man's personal testimony—the actual record of his life as he lived it under the domination of courtly love.

When he was a mere lad of five, says Ulrich, he first heard older boys saying that true honor and happiness could come only through serving a noble and lovely woman; he was deeply impressed, and began to shape his childish thoughts in that direction. Even at that tender age it was perfectly clear to him that such service, the keystone of courtly love, could be undertaken only for a woman one could never marry. True love had to be clandestine, bittersweet, and beset by endless difficulties and frustrations; by virtue of all this, it was spiritually uplifting, and made a knight a better man and a greater warrior.

The subject evidently dominated the thoughts of the boy, for by the age of twelve he put away childish things and consciously chose as the lady of his heart a princess. In every way, it was a perfect choice; she was far too highborn for him, considerably older than himself, and, of course, already married. He became a page in her court, and conscientiously cultivated his feelings of love until they commanded his whole being. He adored her in total secrecy, and trembled (inconspicuously) in her presence. When he saw her hands touch the petals of flowers he had secretly placed where she would see them, he was all but in a faint. And when she washed her hands before dinner, young Ulrich would sometimes filch the basin, smuggle it off to his room, and there reverently drink the dirty water.

Five years of this went by; his love affair progressed no further, however, since being totally unworthy of the lady he dared not even tell her of his feelings. At the age of seventeen he therefore took himself off to the court of Margrave Henry of Austria, to raise his status; there he studied knightly skills for five more years, and at last was made a knight in 1222, during the wedding festival of the Duke of Saxony. By a marvelous coincidence, his ladylove, whom he had not seen but religiously dreamed of during those years, was one of the guests at the wedding, and the very sight of her so moved him that he immediately took a secret vow to devote his newly won knighthood to serving her. This decision filled him with melancholy and with painful longings, a condition which apparently made him very happy.

That summer, feverish and flushed with his infatuation, he roamed the countryside fighting in numerous tourneys and winning many victories, all of which he ascribed to the mighty force of love within him. At last, having compiled an impressive record, and feeling worthy to offer the lady the tribute of his devotion, he persuaded a niece of his to call on her and privately tell her of his desire to be an acknowledged but distant, respectful admirer of hers; he even got his niece to learn and sing for the Princess a song he had written. (Ulrich was already a competent Minnesinger—the German equivalent of the troubadour—as were many young noblemen of breeding.)

The heartless lady, unmoved by his ten years of silent devotion and his recent feats of valor, sent back a cruel and pointed reply; she considered him presumptuous, was scornfully critical of the high-flown language of his quite inappropriate offer, and for good measure, took the trouble to let him know that he was too ugly to be considered even in the role of a very distant admirer. For it seems (and the lady was specific) that the unhappy young knight had a harelip.

Undaunted—perhaps even inspired by this obvious proof that she had actually noticed him—Ulrich promptly undertook a journey to a famous surgeon and had his lip repaired. Considering the techniques of medieval surgery, this must have been both excruciatingly painful and quite dangerous; indeed, he lay feverish on a sickbed for six weeks. News of this, plus a new song he wrote for her, softened the lady's heart, and she sent word that he might attend a riding party and enjoy the rare privilege of speaking with her for a moment, if the opportunity should arise. And it did, once, when he had the chance to help her down from her horse, and could have uttered a sentence or two of devotion; unfortunately he was tongue-tied by her nearness and could say nothing. The lovely lady, considerably put out, whispered to him that he was a fraud, and gracefully indicated her displeasure by ripping out a forelock of his air as she dismounted. Not in the least angered by this, Ulrich reappeared the next day, this time found his voice, and humbly begged her to permit him to be her secret knight and to allow him to fight for her and love her. She accepted his service, but under the very minimum conditions, granting him no "favor" whatever—neither embrace, kiss, nor word of promise, and not so much as a ribbon to carry in his bosom. Ulrich, nevertheless, was filled with joy and thankfulness for her kindness, and sallied forth, tilting about the countryside with anyone who would break a lance with him, and composing many a song to his ladylove which his secretary set down for him since writing was not a knightly accomplishment. The messages and letters that passed between him and the Princess at this time conveyed, in the one direction, her condescension, coldness, and criticism. But this was exactly what was expected of her in the situation, and he found each new blow a delicious pain; it even sounds somewhat as though a large part of his pleasure lay in observing his own noble constancy under duress. If so, he must have had a thoroughly agreeable time for the next three years.

At the end of that period, Ulrich petitioned her forthrightly through a go-between to grant him her love, at least verbally, in return for his faithful adoration and service. The Princess not only sharply rebuked the go-between for Ulrich's unseemly persistency, but expressed her scorn that Ulrich had falsely spoken of losing a finger fighting for love of her. Actually, he had suffered a finger wound which healed, but an incorrect report had reached her. When the go-between related her scornful message, Ulrich paled for a moment, then resolutely drew out a sharp knife and ordered his friend to hack off the finger at one blow. This done, the knight had an artisan make a green velvet case in which the finger was held by gold clasps, and sent her the special poem about the matter. Deeply impressed by this evidence of her power over him, she returned word that she would look at the finger every day from thenceforth, a message which, incidentally, he received as he did all other communiques from her—on his knees, with bowed head and folded hands.

Determined now to earn her love by some stupendous feat, Ulrich conceived the scheme of the jousting-trip from Venice to Bohemia in the disguise of Venus. He went to Venice and there had seamstresses make a dozen white gowns to his own measurements; meanwhile he sent off a messenger with the open letter announcing the event. The northward march began on schedule on April 25, and concluded five weeks later, during which time Ulrich shattered an average of eight lances every day, made the notable record already mentioned, and acquired great glory and honor, all in the cause of love and for the sake of the Princess he so faithfully adored. All this being so, it comes as something of a shock when one reads Ulrich's own statement that in the midst of this triumphal *Venusreise* he stopped off for three days to visit his wife and children. For the fact is that this lovesick Galahad, this kissless wonder, this dauntless knight-errant, had long had a wife to lie with when he had the urge, and a family to live with when he felt lonely. He himself speaks of his affection (but not his love) for his wife; to love her would have been improper and almost unthinkable. Like the other men of his class and time, Ulrich considered marriage a phase of feudal business-management, since it consisted basically of the joining of lands, the cementing of loyalties, and the production of heirs and future defenders. But the purifying, ennobling rapture of love for an ideal woman—what had that to do with details of crops and cattle, fleas and fireplaces, serfs and swamp drainage? Yet, though true love was impossible between husband and wife, without it a man was valueless. Ulrich could therefore unashamedly visit his wife during his grand tour, proud of what he had been doing and certain that if she knew of it, she too was proud, because *Frauendienst* made her husband nobler and finer.

Having completed his epochal feat of love service, Ulrich waited for his reward, and at long last it came: the Princess sent word that he might visit her. Yet he was to expect no warm welcome: she specified that he must come in the disguise of a leper and take his place among lepers who would be visiting her to beg for alms. But of course this monstrous indignity fazed the faithful Ulrich not in the least; nor did he falter when she knowingly let him, disguised in his rags, spend that night in a ditch in the rain; nor was he outraged when the next night he was finally allowed to climb a rope up the castle wall to her chamber, only to find it lit by a hundred tapers and staffed by eight maids-in-waiting who hovered about her where she lay in bed. Though Ulrich pleaded urgently that they all be sent out, she continued to be coyly proper, and when she began to see that this patient fellow really was getting stubborn at last, she told him that to earn the favor he would have to prove his obedience by wading in a near-by lake. She herself assisted him out the window—and then, bending to kiss him, let loose the rope, tumbling Ulrich to the ground, or perhaps into a stinking moat. (It is worth remembering at this point that this painful incident was not recorded by any enemy or satirist of Ulrich, but by himself, his purpose being to make clear the extent of his suffering for love and his fidelity in the face of trials.)

Even such torments cannnot go on forever. The cruel Princess next ordered Ulrich to go on a crusade in her service, but when she learned that he joyfully and obediently received the direct command from her, she suddenly relented, bade him rather stay at home near to her, and finally granted him her love. What an outpouring of thankful verse then! What a spate of shattered lances, dented helmets, broken blades, humbled opponents! For having won her love, Ulrich was magnificent: this was the height of his career as a knight. Regrettably, it is not clear in the *Frauendienst* just which of her favors she so tardily vouchsafed after nearly a decade and a half, but in the light of other contemporary documents concerning the customs of courtly love, one can be fairly sure that she permitted him the kiss and the embrace, and perhaps even the right to caress her, but if she gave him the final reward at all, it was probably on extremely rare occasions. For sexual outlet was not really the point of all this. Ulrich had not been laboring nearly fifteen years for so ordinary a commodity; his real reward had always been in his suffering, striving, and yearning.

The proof of this is that it took him nearly fifteen years to win her love, and to become idyllically happy—but that condition once achieved, lasted only a brief two years. For at the end of that time, the Princess wounded him in some fashion so cruel that he could not bring himself to name it, even long after. Perhaps she had accepted the service of some other knight, or even granted her love to another: what is probably more to the point, Ulrich's quest had ended when he won her, and in the peculiar psychology of courtly love, most of the magic had vanished with the pain. Whatever the cause of his break with her, at any rate, he formally quitted her service after all the years of loyalty, wrote a series of bitter songs against womankind, and permitted his affair and his break with her to become a matter of aristocratic gossip.

But for him the absence of love was an intolerable spiritual impoverishment. Soon he discovered another perfect lady; in her service he made another mighty tour, this time in the get-up of King Arthur; the new lady, too, eventually granted her love and was a source of increasing spiritual power. And then she, in turn—well, let us be brief about it: Ulrich continued this kind of thing for most of his long life. Even in his reflective years, looking back with perspective on it all, he could write of his harelip, his torn out forelock, his chopped-off finger, his transvestite mumming, his leper's rags, his tumble into the moat, all in a tone of self-admiration. For, to the end, he considered that love, the finest thing in his life, had made him a true Christian and a model knight.[25]

Chivalry and courtly love touched the lives of upper class women only. But the troubador love poems provided the first women-centered poetry the world had yet known, and they brought back to the world a reawakening of an appreciation for literature. The medieval poetry and courtly love songs were the beginning of a flood of literature which would follow into the Renaissance and the modern period.

Religion

The Christian Church, established by Emperor Constantine in 325 as the state church of the Holy Roman

Empire, competed with pagan religions and eventually overpowered them. In the early medieval years, life on earth was a day-to-day struggle for survival. But Christianity offered the believer something to look forward to— a life-after-death in heavenly paradise. Pagan religions could not compete against such a promise.

While Christians disagreed with each other on many issues, and slaughtered each other over their differences, they agreed on one thing: the pagan temples should be closed. "Those who disobeyed would forfeit their property and their lives."[26] The last goddess temple was closed in 560.[27]

The Church grew in numbers and it also grew in wealth. And as it became rich, it became corrupt.

A church that was actually a European superstate, dealing with the worship, morals, education, marriages, wars, crusades, deaths, and wills of the population of half a continent, sharing actively in the administration of secular affairs, and raising the most expensive structures in medieval history, could sustain its function only through exploiting a hundred sources of revenue.[28]

After about the year 800, all communities in the Christian Roman Empire were required to pay a tithe of ten percent of their produce or their income to the local church. The church also obtained large land-holdings, and other valuables such as jewels which were given to religious Christians. "It was not unusual for a cathedral, a monastery, or a nunnery to own several thousand manors, including a dozen towns or even a great city or two."[29]

Most of the people in western Europe looked to the church to be a model. The monks who lived stark lives of work and prayer were looked up to as the true embodiers of Christianity. When there were stories of drunkenness in the monasteries, the ideal was lost and reform was vital.[30]

Christian monks and nuns took on the responsibility for most of the early medieval education. They are credited with saving and copying most of the literature from Antiquity that survived the invasions. Whatever education there was during the early medieval years was largely through the work of the church.

The Crusades 1096-1250

While the church was strong in some places it was weak in others. When news of Christians being persecuted by Moslems and Turks in Jerusalem reached Pope Urban II in 1070, he toured central Europe and assembled a vast army to rescue the Holy Land from the infidels. To serfs and vassals who would join him on a Crusade he promised freedom for the period of the war. He promised a protection to the lords of their estates: citizens, he declared, were exempt from taxes, debtors didn't need to pay interest, and prisoners were set free if they would all join the Crusade. Thus the first of seven Crusades to the Holy Land was launched. Some bands of crusaders, on their way to the East, tortured Jews, raping and killing and leaving a trail of blood and spoilage as they went, declaring, why wait until they reached Jerusalem when they could destroy non-believers on their way.

Rich and poor joined the march across Europe, the rich on horseback, and the poor on foot, but it was said that only the rich came back. The defenseless poor were slaughtered or taken captive as slaves. The rich, if captured, could ransom their own freedom. The Crusades, from the First in 1096, to the Seventh in 1250, except for brief periods, did not secure the Holy Land for Christianity. The Christians at that time were the barbarians, invading the much more advanced Islamic civilization without success. The remnants of each Crusade straggled home in defeat. "The power, prestige of the Roman Church was immensely enhanced by the First Crusade and progressively damaged by the rest."[31] "The First Crusade was an occurrence like the discovery of America; the later ones more and more like a trip across the Atlantic."[32]

160

They did, however, unify the spirit of western Europe and firmly established that Christianity was a mighty spiritual force, though its power might have suffered by the Crusades. Whatever else they did, the Crusades changed the course of history in Europe.

> War does one good—it teaches people geography. The Italian merchants who throve on the Crusades learned to make good charts of the Mediterranean; the monkish chroniclers who accompanied the knights received and transmitted a new conception of the vastness and variety of Asia. The zest for exploration and travel was stirred; . . . Christian physicians learned from Jewish and Moslem practitioners, and surgery profited from the Crusades.
>
> Trade followed the cross, and perhaps the cross was guided by trade. The knights lost Palestine, but the Italian merchant fleets won control of the Mediterranean . . . The Crusades had begun with an agricultural feudalism inspired by German barbarism crossed with religious sentiment; they ended with the rise of industry, and the expansion of commerce, in an economic revolution that heralded and financed the Renaissance.[33]

Crusaders had embarked from Italy for Jerusalem and returned to land in Italy again on their way home. In Italy they bought goods and supplies on their way to Jerusalem, and on their way back home they brought oriental spices, silks, and crafts which they traded at Venice, Genoa, and other Italian cities. Small shops in Italy expanded into large merchandising centers. Money circulated and a new social class of merchants developed.

Before the Crusades, the class structure included the clergy, the peasants, and the nobles. After the Crusades, and with the growth of towns, the merchant class began to exert power in town government. This merchant class became known as the *bourgeoisie*. The Crusades opened up trade routes, established a merchant class, and with the circulation of money, introduced a sense of prosperity. Italian merchants became patrons of the arts, giving money to struggling artists and a new era of cultural appreciation was started, leading to the Renaissance.

The Virgin with Apostles, apse mosaic from the cathedral of Torcello, eleventh century.

The Cult of the Virgin Mary

In the medieval period, hope and fear were part of the people's spiritual life. Hope that after death a person would have everlasting life in heaven, and fear that if one didn't live by church doctrine, the punishment would be everlasting damnation in hell. God was seen as a punisher, and Christ as a judge.

In the need for a more sympathetic symbol, people turned to the Virgin Mary, who represented compassion, forgiveness, and mothering. She was not considered a divinity, but she was worshipped as a goddess. The Emperor Constantine, after 325,

Thad ordered the destruction of all goddess temples throughout the empire and had sternly forbidden the worship of Mary, 'fearing Her worship would over-shadow Her son.'[34]

The populace of a recovering Europe could no longer accept the stern picture of a god, damning the major-ity of creatures to hell; and of their own accord the people softened the terrors of the theologians with the pity of the Mother of Christ . . . Just as the stern-ness of Yahveh had necessitated Christ, so the justice of Christ needed Mary's mercy to temper it. In effect the Mother—the oldest figure in religious worship—became . . . the third person of a new Trinity . . .[35]

The Cult of the Virgin Mary was a small part of early Byzantine Greek-speaking Christianity and later it was a movement in Western Europe in the Age of Charlemagne around 800. But the 12th century inter-est in Mary was intensified as a reaction to the strict authority of the church. The Cult spread rapidly. Peo-ple made pilgrimages to the Virgin's shrines and made claims for her healing.

Her popularity came from the people, not from the fathers of the church who had been generally hostile to women and who had preached against women as temptresses to sin. "It was the people who created the fairest flower of the medieval spirit, and made Mary the most beloved figure in history."[36]

Rich and poor adored her, prayed to her, and worked side-by-side to build huge cathedrals to her, or at least to include within the cathedrals a Lady Chapel which they reserved as a shrine to the Virgin Mary.

Theodora and Attendants, apse mosaic from San Vitale.

". . . the interesting thing is that women as a whole benefited so little from this emphasis upon Mary. In fact the very opposite tended to happen."[37] In primitive cultures when women were worshipped as goddesses, it was their fertility that was blessed: Mary worship idealized the opposite of fertility—virginity.

The emphasis on virginity tended to create in many minds an almost hysterical aversion to the state of matrimony . . . Though she was a mother figure, she was also an immaculate mother figure who not only remained a virgin but had herself been conceived without sin, which, in medieval terminology, meant without intercourse. Women might be the same sex as Mary but they were also the same as Eve, and it was as Eve that women kept reminding the religious man of his sinfulness, of his desire to have sex. Lust itself was a sin, and sexual intercourse, except for the purpose of procreation, was regarded by the church as a sin equal to murder and heresy . . . With such fear of women engrained in the clergy, it was perhaps inevitable that the clergy would condemn them, while at the same time admire them through the Virgin.[38]

". . . the medieval Cult of the Virgin . . . underlined the weakness, inferiority, and subordination of real females."[39] Mary could not serve as a model for women because her perfection isolated her from humanness.

Interesting that it was at the height of Mary worship in the thirteenth century that the Church required priests to be celibate. Ordinary, earthly women could no more compare with the perfection of the Virgin Mary, than they could live up to the "ideal" of women as they were glorified in the troubador love songs of courtly love.

THE INQUISITION—
1230-1400

Though Christianity had demonstrated its strength as a unifying force in the waves of the Crusades, it was worried that non-believers on European soil were gaining strength and it set out to eliminate heretics. A heretic, condemned by the church, was seen as representing Satan and was to be treated as one guilty of treason. Their property was to be confiscated and they were to be burned at the stake.

Because Pope Gregory IX believed that heresy was increasing and might divide the Church, in 1231 he launched the official Inquisition, sending out *inquisitores* to question and judge suspected heretics. Sometimes the use of torture elicited confession. ". . . those who confessed and repented, even at the foot of the stake, were given life imprisonment, the obdurate were burned to death in the public square."[40]

A person could be accused of heresy for a number of things including reading the Bible in their own language. During the first several hundred years of the medieval period, Latin was the language of scholars and churchmen. But as more people learned to read and write in the language of their own country, whether it was in Spanish, German, French, English, or other languages, they began to read the Bible printed in their own language, known as "in the vernacular." But reading the Bible "in the vernacular" caused problems for the church. Theologians said

. . . if every man interpret the Bible according to his own light, and make his own individual brand of Christianity, the religion that held up the frail moral code of Europe would soon be shattered into a hundred creeds, and lose its efficacy as a social cement binding natively savage men into a society and civilization.[41]

The church decreed that no one could have either the Old or the New Testament in their possession whether it was in Latin or in the vernacular.

The rules of the Inquisition were that no one was to argue with a heretic. Heretics were given the opportunity to accept Christianity. If they did not, they were condemned.

The person who accused a heretic was to remain anonymous, and accusing heretics could be profitable because ". . . the estate and chattels of heretics were confiscated, to be divided in varying proportions among the monarchy, the informer, and the church."[42] In spite of the repression of the Inquisition, a variety of religious organizations, the Beguines, Bogomiles, Waldenses, Paterines, and Cathari evolved and denounced the wealth of the church. The most threatening to the church was probably the Cathari who were especially numerous in France. At first the Catharist priests held religious debates, but in time, destroying Catharism was one of the main objectives of the Inquisition.[43]

Heer, in his book, *The Medieval World*, notes that "women of noble birth became prominent as patrons of religious heterodoxy," which is defined as opposed to the usual beliefs or established doctrines. As a consequence, in the Inquisition ". . . the worst humiliations were heaped upon women, the much-hated, much-feared and much-courted women of the South."[44]

Women were tired of the masculine ascendency, they disliked being chattels in the marriage market and the objects of monkish suspicion and contempt. Looking for a way to escape from this oppression they found it in education of the mind and of the spirit. Courtly culture and Catharism both flourished under the protection of noble ladies, above all the noble ladies of Provence. (France)[45]

The methods of the inquisitors, including torture, were adopted into the law codes of many governments; and perhaps our contemporary secret torture of suspects finds its model in the Inquisition even more than in Roman law. Compared with the persecution of heresy in Europe in 1227 and 1492, the persecution of Christians by Romans in the first three centuries after Christ was a mild and humane procedure. Making every allowance required of an historian and permitted to a Christian, we must rank the Inquisition, along with the wars and persecution of our time, as among the darkest blots on the record of mankind, revealing a ferocity unknown in any beast.[46]

After Queen Isabella and King Ferdinand appointed the first inquisitors, the Inquisition in Spain reached the height of its fury against converted Jews who might have reverted back to Judaism, Moors who might have fallen back to Mohammedism, and Christians who might have become heretics. Following is a description of the inquisition process:

At first the procedure was simple: those condemned to death were marched to the public plaza, they were bound in tiers on a pyre, the inquisitors sat in state on a platform facing it, a last appeal for confessions was made, the sentences were read, the fires were lit, the agony was consummated. But as burnings became more frequent and suffered some loss in their psychological power, the ceremony was made more complex and awesome, and was staged with all the care and cost of a major theatrical performance. When possible it was timed to celebrate the accession, marriage, or visit of a Spanish king, queen, or prince. Municipal and state officials, Inquisition personnel, local priests and monks, were invited—in effect required—to attend. On the eve of the execution these dignitaries joined in a somber procession through the main streets of the city to deposit the green cross of the Inquisition upon the altar of the cathedral or principal church. A final effort was made to secure confessions from the condemned; many then yielded, and had their sentences commuted to imprisonment for a term or for life. On the following morning the prisoners were led through dense crowds to a city square: imposters, blasphemers, bigamists, heretics, relapsed converts: in later days, Protestants; sometimes the procession included effigies of absent condemnees, or boxes carrying the bones of persons condemned after death. In the square, on one or several elevated stages, sat the inquisitors, the secular and monastic clergy, and the officials of town and state; now and then the King himself presided. A sermon was preached, after which all present were commanded to recite an oath of obedience to the Holy Office of the Inquisition, and a pledge to denounce and prosecute heresy in all its forms and everywhere. Then, one by one, the prisoners were led before the tribunal, and their sentences were read. We must not imagine any brave defiances; probably, at this stage, every prisoner was near to spiritual exhaustion and physical collapse. Even now he might save his life by confession; in that case the Inquisition usually contented itself with scourging him, confiscating his goods, and imprisoning him for life. If the confession was withheld till after sentence had been pronounced, the prisoner earned the mercy of being strangled before being burned; and as such last-minute confessions were frequent, burning alive was relatively rare. Those who were judged guilty of major heresy, but denied it to the end, were (till 1725) refused the last sacraments of the Church, and were, by the intention of the Inquisition, abandoned to everlasting hell. The "reconciled" were now taken back to prison; the impenitent were "relaxed" to the secular arm, with a pious caution that no blood should be shed. These were led out from the city between throngs that had gathered from leagues around for this holiday spectacle. Arrived at the place prepared for execution, the confessed were strangled, then burned: the recalcitrant were burned alive. The fires were fed till nothing remained of the dead but ashes, which were scattered over fields and streams. The priests and spectators returned to their altars and their homes, convinced that a propitiatory offering had been made to a God insulted by heresy. Human sacrifice had been restored.[47]

"The medieval Inquisition achieved its immediate purpose. It stamped out . . . Catharism in France, . . . restored south Italy to orthodoxy, and postponed for three centuries the . . ." Protestant Reformation.[48]

WITCH-HUNTING—

1400-1800

The medieval period ends with the beginning of the witch hunts which spanned three hundred years. Though men, along with women, were condemned as witches, "evidence indicates that the proportion of women to men who were burned alive from about 800 to 1800 was as much as ten thousand to one."[49]

While belief in witchcraft had been almost universal, history being filled with reliance on the supernatural to explain an event or prophesy the future, in the medieval period, nearing the end of the Inquisition, the church looked at the practice of witchcraft as related to Satan.

Women who had been known for their abilities to heal, to use herbs and potions to cure illnesses, became suspect.

> Forecasting, poisoning, and healing thus became inextricably mixed. But when the suspicion started to descend the social ladder, the large group of middle- and lower-class women herbalists and healers began to be caught in the net."[50]

But accusing someone of witchcraft was not limited to pointing to women healers. Anyone who was deviant, who did not conform to social expectations could be accused of being possessed by the devil. Women were burned alive for

> . . . threatening their husbands, for talking back or refusing a priest, for stealing, for prostitution, for adultery, for bearing a child out of wedlock . . . for scolding and nagging . . .[51]

It is easy to see that whatever else witch hunts did, they kept women in line.

> We read in the old chronicles of women in the last weeks of pregnancy being burned until the heat burst their bellies and propelled the fetus outward beyond the fire at its mother's feet. We read of little daughters of burnt women being forced to dance with bare feet one hundred times around the still glowing embers— in order to 'impress upon them the memory of their mother's sins.' And all of this in an age when the only law of the land was the law of the church, when civil courts were merely the agents of the Christian hierarchy.[52]

The trial of nineteen year old Joan of Arc . . . though formally a prisoner of the Inquisition, began in 1431. She was charged by her English captors with heresy, a crime punishable by burning to death at the stake, but her English jurors accused her of witchcraft. She was a sorceress, they said, because she would not acknowledge that the church had more authority than the "voices" which had led her to bring a French army to victory over the English.[53]

"Several popes commissioned agents of the Inquisition to deal with witches," but the full fury of witch hunting was not reached until the Renaissance under the auspices of Catholics and Protestants . . ."[54]

Male/Female Relationships

Laws of the Barbarian Tribes

Ideas in the early medieval period about how males and females should relate to each other came from three sources: St. Paul's Christian values; the Roman idea of male guardianship over females; and from the Germanic tribes' concept of authority in the family. As most of western Europe by the year 600 was held by the Germanic barbarians, the civilization that evolved was a combination of German and Christianized Roman.

This book has already explored attitudes about the sexes among the early Christians, and also ideas within the concept of the Roman "pater familia." But the barbarian pagan tribes' ideas on such social customs as marriage, divorce, inheritance, etc., differed from the Christians; and the Romans; and from each other in some respects.

Until Roman law was revived in the eleventh century, Europe was "governed by Gothic and Burgundian codes and the kindred laws of the Franks."[55]

In general the northern tribes put more restraints upon women than tribes to the south, where the Burgundian and Visigothic codes, owing partly to Roman influences, show a greater liberality with regard to matters of inheritance, property, and guardianship.[56]

In France, or Gaul, the Salic Franks brought their German language, and pagan gods, and laws which were favorable to men. The Salic Law

. . . kept women under perpetual wardship of father, husband, or son; it made death the penalty for adultery by the wife, but asked no penalty of the adulterous male; and it permitted divorce at the husband's whim . . . but the most famous clause read: 'of Salic land no portion of the inheritance shall go to a woman.'[57]

Among the Riparian Franks different penalties existed for murder, depending on the worth of the victim.

. . . the penalty for killing a free woman between the age of puberty and her fortieth year at 600 solidi, while the death of a young girl cost 200. The code estimated 600 solidi, to be the equivalent of 300 cattle or fifty male horses, and so severe was the penalty that provisions were made to pay it in installments extending over three generations.[58]

The Burgundian law code, about 500 AD., made it clear that when a woman married, her property became her husband's and he had power over her. If he should die, she would have guardianship over her children. If there were no son, a daughter could inherit from her father or mother. Even if a daughter should enter a convent, she would inherit equally with her brothers. If she had sisters and she died, her sisters would inherit her property. Her brothers inherited her property only if she had no sisters.[59]

Burgundian girls were purchased in marriage, the father receiving the bride price, or wittimon. If her father was dead and she had no brothers, her uncle and sisters received equal shares in the bride price. When there was no father, brother, or uncle, the mother received the bride price and shared it with the nearest relative.[60]

As for leaving one's spouse, the Burgundians spelled out the penalties:

If any woman leaves (puts aside) her husband to whom she is legally married, let her be smothered in mire.

If anyone wishes to put away his wife without cause, let him give her another payment such as he gave her for marriage price, and let the amount of the fine be twelve solidi.

If by chance a man wishes to put away his wife, and is able to prove one of these three crimes against her, that is, adultery, witchcraft, or violation of graves, let him have full right to put her away: and let the judge pronounce the sentence of the law against her, just as should be done against criminals.

But if she admits none of these three crimes, let no man be permitted to put away his wife for any other crime. But if he chooses, he may go away from the home, leaving all household property behind, and his wife with their children may possess the property of the husband.[61]

On adultery the Burgundian law stated that both man and woman should either be killed, or the relatives of the girl could deliver her into slavery, or her family could be paid a price and the man could go free.[62]

The law codes of the Visigoths of the fifth and sixth centuries were most favorable to women.

Let sisters have an equal share with their brothers in their parents' inheritance. If a father or a mother should die intestate, sisters shall succeed without any hindrance to the inheritance of their parents' wealth, sharing it equally with their brothers.[63]

Saxon and Thuringian laws were stricter than Burgundian laws. In 785, they set the rules of guardianship:

If any man die and leave a widow, let his son by another wife be her guardian; failing him, let the brother of the dead man be guardian, and if he had no brother, then the nearest of the husband's kinsmen.

When a man dies leaving no sons but only daughters, the inheritance shall go to them, but the guardianship over them shall pass to their father's brother or nearest kinsman.

If a widow with a daughter remarries and has a son, the guardianship over the daughter goes to the said son; if, however, having a son, she then marries and has a daughter, the guardianship over the daughter goes not to the son by her first marriage but to the father's brother or nearest kinsman.[64]

As for marriage, if a girl of the Saxon or Thuringian tribe married without the consent of her father or a male guardian she lost the right to inherit.

Though the Burgundian and Visigothic law codes allowed females to inherit property, the Saxons did not.

On the death of the father or mother the inheritance goes to the son, not the daughter.

When a man has a son and a daughter and the son marries, has a son, and then dies, the inheritance belongs to the son's son, that is to the grandson, not to the daughter.[65]

Among the Northmen, the Vikings, marriages were through purchase, and if a girl married against the will of her parents her husband became an outlaw, and could with legality be slain by her family. If a husband did not have good reason when he wished to divorce his wife, her family could kill him.

Either mate might divorce the other for dressing like the opposite sex—as when the wife wore breeches, or the man wore a shirt open at the breast. A husband might kill with impunity—i.e., without provoking a blood feud—any man whom he caught in illicit relations with his wife.[66]

Medieval Ideas About Women

Ideas from the Church affected the way men and women related to each other. "The theories of churchmen were generally hostile to women."[67] In about the year 400, Augustine, the Bishop of Hippo, "denied that women had souls." In the sixth century, this was actually debated at the Council in Macon. "It was the Celtic bishops from England who saved the day for half the human race at that council."[68]

One of the great leaders of the Christian church, and considered ". . . the church's most authoritative thinker,"[69] was Thomas Aquinas, a monk who later became a saint. He wrote 21 volumes of his *Summa Theologica* addressed to Christians, defending the Christian doctrine.

Thomas Aquinas relied on Aristotle's reasoning to prove his position on politics, religion, logic, metaphysics, theology, psychology, and ethics, including the ethics of the subordination of women.

Aristotle, the Greek philosopher who lived from 384-324 BC. had been considered a great scientist. For about fifteen hundred years his "scientific" opinions were accepted, among them that the female is a defective male, and that, in human reproduction the woman is merely the vessel, holding the embryo which is totally the male's. Also, because the female is passive, he asserted, and the male is active, the female is not fit for freedom or political action.[70]

Thomas follows Aristotle in his view that the male is ordered to the more noble activity, intellectual knowledge, whereas the female, although possessing a rational soul, was created solely with respect to her sexuality, her body, as an aid in reproduction for the preservation of the species. Thomas also follows Aristotelian biology in his assertion that the girl child represents a defective human being, the result of an accident to the male sperm, which was thought to contain the complete human being *in potentia* and to reproduce by nature the likeness of its origin, that is, another male. This finality of the female as a mere instrumentality, an aid to reproduction, is the only explanation Thomas can offer for the existence of a "second sex," since for any other activity—work or play—man would have been better served by a male helpmate.[71]

In addition to the barbarian laws, and the church's acceptance of Aristotle's views on the superiority of males over females, the medical views of the medieval period also contributed to the belief in the inferiority of females. "Galen (AD. 131-201), one of the greatest biologists of antiquity, was the principal authority in the medical schools of medieval and Renaissance Europe."[72]

He wrote:

The female is more imperfect than the male. The first reason is that she is colder. If, among animals, the warmer ones are more active, it follows that the colder ones must be more imperfect . . .

Just as man is the most perfect of all animals, so also, within the human species, man is more perfect than woman. The cause of this superiority is the [male's] superabundance of warmth, heat being the primary instrument of nature . . .[73]

176

Marriage, Divorce,
Childbearing, Wife-beating

The early age of marriage and the method of arranging marriage contracts, established females as property to be used to the best advantage of their fathers or male guardians. That is not to say that fathers didn't love their children, but that the overriding reason for a father or a feudal lord to marry off a girl was to increase landholdings.

Mainly because of the feudal laws of inheritance, marriages were arranged extremely early. If a father, a serf, should die and leave an unmarried daughter, the Lord would have the right to arrange for her marriage to someone the lord would want to inherit the fief. "Weddings were often arranged and sometimes solemnized when children were in their cradles. A father took the earliest opportunity of marrying his child in order that the right of marriage might not fall to the lords."[74]

Innumerable examples might be quoted. In the great Berkeley family, Maurice, the third Lord Berkeley (b. 1289), was at the age of eight married by his father to Eva, daughter of Lord Zouch, who was about the same age, and was by her made father of a son before he was fourteen. Maurice, the fourth lord (b. 1338), also married at the age of eight to a daughter of Hugh Despenser of the same age; and the next lord Thomas (b. 1366), married at the age of fourteen to Margaret de Lisle, aged about seven.[75] Then, too, there were marriages of considerable age differences.

. . . The Duke of Berry, that avid collector of art works and castles, was forty-nine when he took twelve-year-old Jeanne de Boulogne for his second wife. There is no suggestion that such a marriage was regarded as indecent . . . No attempt was made to shield the young from sexual knowledge or to delay sexual experience. Modesty was enforced for girls, but no illu-

177

sions were held about their innate purity or monogamous instincts. Marriage was hallowed but adultery was omnipresent. In the upper classes, where marriages were arranged, invariably with a political purpose, boys and girls were married from the age of eight. The formal arrangement would become a physical one as soon as that was biologically possible. Thus, a young duke or prince might be a father at thirteen. The princess Isabeau, married to the dauphin who was later to be Charles VI, had had three pregnancies by the time she was sixteen.[76]

Because the fiefs which the lord loaned or rented, or gave to his vassals and serfs were inheritable, the lords had strong reasons to control marriages. The principle of guardianship

> . . . degenerated in the end to blatant commercialism. Kings and barons—kings especially—vied with each other in giving or selling the hands of orphan sons or daughters. Sometimes, threatened with the prospect of an unwelcome husband, a widow would pay in hard cash for permission to refuse him."[77]

The marriage ceremony itself took on religious significance after the year 1268 when a religious ceremony was necessary to make a marriage legal. Marriage became a holy sacrament between a man, a woman, and God, and for a person to marry an unbaptized person might mean being an outcast from the church.

Even though the Church blessed marriage, it "permitted wife beating . . . in the thirteenth century, the 'Laws and Customs of Beauvais' bade a man beat his wife 'only in reason.'[78] Wives were subjects of their husbands and must obey them. Failure to do so could bring his wrath upon her. "Disobedient wives were liable to correction by force. Canon law specifically allowed wife-beating, and judging . . ." by many sources, "such punishments were practiced in the highest circles."[79]

178

Wife beating, at the church's instigation, had become so popular by the fifteenth century, that even a priest was moved to protest. Barnardino of Siena in 1427 suggested in a sermon that his male parishioners might practice a little restraint in the punishment of their wives and treat them with at least as much mercy as they treated their hens and their pigs.

Many stories of wife beating provided humor for the villages. And daughters were advised by their fathers as in the case of Geoffrey de la Tour de Landry who instructed his daughters by telling him the story that follows:

> Here is an example to every good woman that she suffer and endure patiently, nor strive with her husband nor answer him before strangers, as did once a woman who did answer her husband before strangers with short words; and he smote her with his fist down to the earth; and then with his foot he struck her in her visage and brake her nose, and all her life after she had her nose crooked, the which so spoiled and disfigured her visage after, that she might not for shame show her face, it was so foul blemished. And this she had for her language that she was wont to say to her husband. And therefore the wife ought to suffer, and let the husband have the words, and to be master, for that is her duty.[80]

Provided a husband did not kill or cripple his wife, he was free to exercise punishment without the law intervening, for ". . . it is legal for a man to beat his wife when she wrongs him—for instance, when she is about to surrender her body to another man, when she contradicts or abuses him, or when she refuses, like a decent woman, to obey his reasonable commands."[81]

Women had no recourse in the courts because the law approved of wife beating. And in addition, "Civil law ruled that the word of women could not be admitted in court, 'because of their frailty.'" The law even prohibited those ladies who were born into the nobility and of course all others, from representing their own estates in England and in France.[82]

When the church entered marriage, it forbade divorce. Under the early Christians, divorce had been permitted for certain reasons including a woman's barrenness or religious differences, or if a husband was a prisoner of an enemy. In the years after 1268, only separation or annulment were permitted within the Church, and those were granted only if the marriage had not been consummated, or if one partner could prove heresy, adultery, or cruelty. Even so, as annulment meant that neither party could remarry, and if there had been children, they would be considered bastards.[83]

Under feudalism a serf

> paid a tax and required the lord's consent, in case he or his children married a person not belonging to his manor, for then the lord would lose some or all of the offspring; on many estates permission and fee were required for any marriage at all. In scattered instances we hear of the *jus primae noctis* or *droit du seigneur*, whereby the lord might claim the 'right of the first night' with the serf's bride; but in almost all cases the serf was allowed to 'redeem' his bride by paying a fee to the lord . . . If a peasant died without issue residing with him, the house and land reverted to the lord . . . If his heir was an unmarried daughter, she could retain the holding only by marrying a man living on the same manor.[84]

The following diary, written by an Italian merchant Gregorio Dati, who was born in 1362, tells his story of marriages to four women and the births of his children:

> . . . My beloved wife, Bandecca, went to Paradise after a nine-month illness started by a miscarriage . . . July 1390 . . .

I had an illegitimate male child by Margherita, a Tartar slave whom I had bought. He was born on 21 December 1391 in Valencia.

We [business associates] renewed our partnership on 1 January 1393 when I undertook to invest 1,000 [gold] florins. I did not actually have the money but was about to get married—which I then did—and to receive the dowry which procured me a larger share and more consideration in our company . . . I married my second wife, Betta, on 22 June . . . On the 26th of that same June, I received a payment of 800 gold florins from the bank of Giacomino and Company. This was the dowry.

On Sunday morning, 17 May 1394, Betta gave birth to a girl . . . On Friday evening, 17 March 1396, the Lord blessed our marriage with a male son . . . 12 March 1397, Betta gave birth to our third child . . . 27 April 1398, Betta gave birth to our fourth child . . . 1 July 1399, Betta had our fifth child . . . 22 June 1400, Betta gave birth for the sixth time . . . On Wednesday, 13 July 1401 . . . the Lord lent us a seventh child . . . On 5 July 1402 . . . Betta gave birth to our eighth child . . . After that my wife [Betta] passed on to Paradise. The [business] partnership is to start on 1 January 1403 and to last three years . . . I have undertaken to put up 2,000 florins. This is how I propose to raise them: 1,370 florins . . . are still due to me from my old partnership . . . The rest I expect to obtain if I marry again this year, when I hope to find a woman with a dowry as large as God may be pleased to grant me . . .

I record that on 8 May 1403, I was bethrothed to Ginevra, daughter of Antonio Brancacci . . . The dowry was 1,000 florins: 700 in cash and 300 in a farm at Campi.

On Sunday morning at Terce, 17 April 1404, Ginevra gave birth to our first-born son . . . Altogether

Ginevra and I had eleven children: four boys and seven girls.

After that it was God's will to recall to Himself the blessed soul of my wife Ginevra. She died in childbirth after lengthy suffering . . . God bless her and grant us fortitude.

I then took another wife, Caterina, the daughter of Dardano Guicciardini, on 30 March 1421 . . . The dowry was 600 florins.

Caterina, my fourth wife, miscarried after four months.

On 4 October 1422 . . . Caterina gave birth to a daughter . . .

On Friday, 7 January 1424, Caterina gave birth to a fine healthy boy . . .

20 March 1425, Caterina had another healthy and attractive child . . .

26 July 1426, Caterina had a fine little girl . . .

Monday, 18 August 1427, Caterina gave birth to a fine little girl . . .

2 June 1431, Caterina gave birth to a girl . . .

"At this point with about nine of his children still alive, he stops keeping his diary and dies in 1435."[85]

Inheritance

In the early medieval period in the Germanic areas, children sometimes took the name of either their father or their mother, or both. Even as late as the 1431 trial of Jeanne d'Arc, when she was asked her name by her judge, she answers that sometimes her name is Jeanne d'Arc and sometimes Jeanne Romee. Her father was Jacques d'Arc and her mother Isabelle Romee.[86] This practice was not typical of England, however,. In fact the law there used the loss of a maiden name to partly justify excluding a girl from inheriting property.

Because women lose the name of their ancestors, and by marriage usually are transferred into another family, they participate seldom in heirship with males. Bracton is bold to say, 'A woman is never called to succeed as long as there is a male,' but to this rule he subjoineth exception.[87]

In Milan, Italy, also, girls were excluded in inheritance for a different reason:

But the sister may ask for no share of her father's inheritance if her brother procures a decent match for her and gives her a dowry. Milan, 1216.

Married daughters or granddaughters may not inherit with the males; they must be content with their dowries. Venice, 1232.

If a woman has received anything from her brother, let her be content and let her not be able to inherit anything more.[88]

In Spain and France, women inherited with greater equality. Though there were laws which prohibited women from inheriting fiefs at the death of their fathers, mainly because they were considered incapable of bearing arms, it was eventually apparent that if a woman couldn't do all the work of the fief. "her husband could do it in her stead."[89]

As a consequence, many upper-class women in the medieval period had vast landholdings and were ". . . controlling the distribution of substantial amounts of capital through their wills, as well as in their daily lives."[90] So, though women by the laws of the land were not capable of inheriting land, many upper-class women did in fact do so.

Education

When Rome fell, its educational system was destroyed. For the first several hundred years of the medieval period, much of what education there was took place in the monasteries and convents. Then, with feudalism, a boy of noble birth was trained for knighthood in the castle of his father's lord. He was trained in courtly manners, and in the arts of war. Reading and writing were not taught as knightly skills.

Girls of noble birth were trained in courtly manners which included the accomplishments of playing chess, telling stories, singing and playing a musical instrument. "Their object was to fashion ladies who would shine in society."[91]

Girls could attend "song schools," "schools run by 'chantry' priests who were paid to say masses for the dead and who usually ran a school on the site."[92]

They were trained to keep husbands and to be good wives. Some works written on this subject were for noblewomen and some for women of all classes. Whatever the social class, these treatises "concern themselves with the attitude of the wife to the husband, and with religious duties, and devote much attention to instruction in Christian faith."[93] These written works express the idea that it is risky to teach females, and that only nuns should be educated.

> Barberino will allow a noble girl to read and write so that she should be able to govern her estates; but he debates whether daughters of ordinary gentlemen ought to be taught, and decides against it; and he forbids outright any learning for daughters of merchants or artisans. Phillippe de Navarre categorically forbids women to read or write, and the Knight of La Tour Landry will allow them only the knowledge of reading, so that women may read scriptures. all of them want to constrict women's minds as Chinese constricted their feet; the reason is the fear of their reading demoralizing romances and writing love letters.[94]

Phillippe de Navarre gave his reasons why women should not be taught to read and write.

Women should not learn to read or write unless they are going to be nuns, as much harm has come from such knowledge. For some men will dare to send or give or drop letters near them, containing indecent requests in the form of songs or rhymes or tales, which they would never dare convey by message or word of mouth. And even if the woman had no desire to err, the devil is so crafty and skillful in tempting that he would soon lead her on to read the letters and answer them . . .[95]

In spite of such opposition there is considerable evidence that upper class and merchant class women did learn to read, and many, also, learned to write although it was believed that it was less harmful if a woman was limited to knowing how to read.

Almost nothing is known about the education of a serf's children except that he had to pay his lord a fee if he sent his son to be educated. Girls were probably taught domestic skills at home.

> . . . it is certain that the overwhelming majority of peasant women or general domestic servants received no education at all . . . Jeanne d'Arc most famous of peasant girls . . . knew neither 'a' or 'b' . . .[96]

Girls who grew up in towns probably had a better chance of being educated than girls raised in the country.
By the twelfth century boys and girls of the upper-classes were educated either in nunneries, which accepted boys as well as girls, or boys were educated for Knighthood and girls "sent to the households of great ladies where they could learn breeding and no doubt acquire some intellectual attainment."[97] There was some apprenticeship training for merchant-class (bourgeoisie) of both boys and girls, and for the poorer classes, some elementary schooling.

However, in spite of the evidence for the existence of elementary schools in foreign countries and a certain amount of corresponding information for England, elementary education cannot have been widespread. such elementary schools as there were, doubtless served the petty bourgeoisie of towns, not the country folk or children of the lowest classes.[98]

Upper-class boys and girls were also tutored at home. One area of education that was a "must" for females was in learning something about family medicine. Since all doctors were men, and women were apparently embarrassed to discuss their feminine ailments with men, it was advised that they educate and treat themselves on family healing.

In the fourteenth century an English version of a treatise attributed to Trotula . . . is prefaced by a translator's explanation that as 'women of our tongue do better read and understand this language than any other, and every woman lettered read it to other unlettered and help them and counsel them in their maladies withouten showing their disease to man . . .'[99]

However, no woman could set up a healing practice without bringing great trouble on herself. Even the healing which she did in her own family could make her the subject of the witch hunts.

When universities were developed in the twelfth and thirteenth centuries, students, even in the universities for medicine and law, were considered part of the clergy.

Since women were prohibited from becoming clerics they were automatically eliminated from any possibility of attaining a university education . . . they were excluded from formal grammar schools which were regarded as preparatory schools for the university.[100]

Working-class families, that is, families of serfs, or families in business in the towns, needed their children to work for them. Most parents in the medieval period could not afford the luxury of giving their children an education.

Nunneries

Nunneries were available as rather expensive boarding schools for upper-class children, but their primary purpose was for the religious education or contemplation for women. When they were first built, they were administered by an abbess who was female. She was the ruler of the nunnery and the area around it, collecting taxes and settling disputes.

There were only two alternatives available to upper-class women: they could marry, or they could join a nunnery, also known as a convent or an abbey.

In order for a girl to enter religious, celibate life, her father had to give a dowry to the nunnery. Many girls entered this kind of life simply because there was nothing else for them to do, not because they were especially religious. But, as it required a dowry to enter, nunneries therefore included only women of the upper-classes. In the early Christian era and early medieval period, when women had formed their own religious orders, offering instruction in Christian doctrine, they exercised considerable leadership. Female participation in the early Christian church in conversions, baptisms, and instructions, was on an equal basis as men's participation. Nunneries which were in the early years dedicated to active religious life more so than a life of cloistered prayer, developed throughout western Europe on a par with the development of monastaries. "By 1300 Europe had as many nuns as monks."[101]

The seventh and eighth centuries saw the formation of double monasteries, one for women and one for men, side-by-side, often led by a woman, particularly so in Anglo-Saxon England.

These women were learned in scripture; they taught; they administered great religious houses; they missionized alongside the men, and without any hint in the sources that these public roles were improper for women. Their life was active; not as in the case with the later type of medieval female religious, wholly cloistered and contemplative.[102]

Germany became a center for women's monasticism and ". . . in the 1100's one hundred new Benedictine convents were established there . . . Though French convents spread more slowly and in england the Danish invasion in 800;s had brought monastic life for women almost to a standstill . . ."[103] But in Spain, Gueen Lenore founded ". . . a truly royal abbey."

The abbess was the absolute monarch of her sixty villages and could punish clergy for heresy and the king's officials for secular offenses. She also heard confessions. Monks vowed to the hospitals under the abbey's care took their vows of obedience directly to her. The most famous choir school of Europe developed there. The Spanish royal abbey, with the support both of king and pope, held on to its power longer than any other convent in Europe—right up to the 1800's.[104]

Boulding explains the shrinking of the size of the nunnery from about one hundred and fifty women to about twenty-five, to the changing economy of Europe which was moving from a barter economy to a cash economy. Presumably this would mean that if a father could dower his daughter to enter a nunnery by giving land or cattle, the nunnery could in turn barter with those for what it needed to survive. But when the convent needed money to support itself, and fathers didn't have money, their daughters could no longer enter a nunnery.

Other things contributed to the demise of the nunneries. Women had enthusiastically supported the Christian Church and had worked diligently for its acceptance and success. But when the church became firmly established as a political and religious power, it eliminated women from all but the menial tasks.

Abbesses not only had to contend with economic transitions; they had to contend with the determined efforts of bishops to reduce the autonomy of convents. The famous double monasteries of the eighth and ninth centuries, where monks and nuns both served under an abbess, declined in the tenth century under church pressure and were replaced by monasteries with dependent convents attached. Here the nuns 'served for monks by copying books and performing other services.'[105] It is obvious that nuns did not care much for this situation, because this type of dependent convent also disappeared by 1300. Women simply stopped applying to enter them.[106]

Just as women outside nunneries were expected to subjugate themselves, nuns inside these institutions were also expected to do the same. The literature written about how nuns should act is more concerned with women's weakness than with her spiritual soul.

The nun was to speak as little as possible for if Eve had not spoken, she would have not fallen. Even the sins mentioned seem peculiarly trifling and 'female', for example, the nun must be careful not to laugh, or break a dish, or soil her habit. The nun must be especially careful to guard her eyes and no man may look at her eyes without express permission.[107]

As nunneries came under male control, the abbess being responsible to an abbot or a bishop, religious women sought freedom in other less restricted groups.

What might be considered a woman's movement began as the result of the need for more freedom for women. This may have been a combination of a guild and a religious movement that ". . . began spontaneously in a

number of different locations." It was, as Boulding quotes
Colledge,

> that great and victorious revolt of pious women, eve-
> rywhere in Europe, against the reactionary traditions
> which would have condemned them in the cloisters as
> well as in the world to a role of subordination and
> silence.[108]

The Beguines are the women referred to here. The
movement was ". . . started by well-to-do women with
property in both countryside and city who built special
houses on the edge of cities for unmarried women workers moving into the cities." They combined religious worship with administering to the poor, setting up hospitals,
schools and "workshops for the poor."[109]

The Beguines respected the authority of the Church,
though "no men ever had authority roles of any kind in a
beguinage,"[110] they conducted sermons and heard confessions until they were forbidden to do so.

As the traditional nunneries were closing down, and
as the Inquisition grew and suppressed other groups,

> . . . a number of passionately devout and spiritually
> awakened women sought refuge in Dominican and
> Franciscan convents and in Beguinages . . . But there
> they often found themselves in little better case, and
> their position became increasingly difficult during the
> thirteenth and fourteenth centuries . . . Cast spiritu-
> ally and intellectually adrift, women were confronted
> with the closed ranks of a masculine society, governed
> by a thoroughly masculine theology and by a morality
> made by men. The other half of humanity came into
> the picture only when specifically feminine services
> were needed.[111]

Unlike the nuns in the nunneries, the monks in the
monasteries were trained and then sent out into the world
to serve kings, or bishops. Nuns were supposed to
remain, if not in the nunnery, at least not very far from it.

As stories of actions in nunneries and monasteries about drunkenness and personal vanity and other non-religious activity reached the bishops and popes, restrictions on these religious institutions were increased. In 1300 Pope Boniface VIII ordered nuns to stay inside the nunneries, but they were known to walk outside the walls anyway.

Whatever else may be said about them, ". . . even in the period of decline, nunneries were a boon for women of the Middle Ages."[112]

Work-Roles

The work roles of men and women who did not join nunneries or monasteries depended on the social class into which they were born. For upper-class women their responsibilities varied. Many upper class women in the earlier barbarian period, later in the courts of Charlemagne, (800) and all through the medieval period were responsible for important tasks. They were involved in politics, money-management, and border disputes. They founded religious, educational, and health centers.[113]

Women of the aristocracy could also take military training if they chose, and they often did. Among the outstanding aristocratic women warriors of the Middle Ages we find Matilda of Tuscany, who at fifteen rode beside her mother Beatrix and father Godfrey of Lorraine at the head of the Tuscan forces, to repel Norman invaders . . . Spain had several famous women warriors, including . . . the 'nun-ensign' Dona Catalina de Eraaus, who is said to have turned the tide of many a battle by appearing as the soldiers were getting ready to fight . . . Eleanora de Arborea of Sardinia took the field after her brother's murder and successfully suppressed a domestic rebellion, then went on to defeat the king of Aragon in battle . . . The heroines of the defense of Vienna in 1554 were a three-thousand-woman army which fought in three regiments under Forteguerra, Piccolonimini, and Fausti.[114]

191

English princesses assumed their responsibilities in their teens.

One striking feature of their lives is how early they began their public responsibilities. It is almost impossible to imagine ten-to-fifteen-year-old girls in Western societies having the necessary training and self-discipline to undertake roles the princesses took for granted. The success of the medieval princesses in their diplomatic roles is all the more remarkable when one considers that nearly every one of them had to make her home in a foreign country and function in a language not her native tongue, with a set of customs alien to her own upbringing. There was no running home to mother. Not a single one of these princesses was considered outstanding in her own time or later. Nonetheless, these women often performed key functions that history ascribes to their less capable husbands, due to the convention of recording history in terms of reigning kings.[115]

Noble women at home, though subject to their husbands, had the responsibility of home management.

When the nobility of Europe went forth to do battle it was their wives who managed their affairs at home, superintended the farming, interviewed the tenants, and saved up money for their husband's next expedition. A good and loyal wife was the best and strongest support a man away on a crusade or a war could leave behind.[116]

The lord's lady needed to know feudal law in case her husband's rights were invaded, she had to supervise everything that was made in the castle, from the bread to the materials spun for clothing. She had to know how to preserve meat and fowl in the days before refrigeration and she had to supervise the dairy.

In addition to all this, she needed to be ready at any time in her husband's absence to defend the castle walls, for her husband's enemies might very well choose the time of his absence to overtake his castle. "Annals of the Hundred Years War glitter with deeds of warlike ladies."[117] One historical account from 1461 relates how the King came to take Bokenham castle when Lord Knyvet was away.

> The King sent nine commissioners and an escheator to take it, expecting only formal legal proceedings, but when they entered the outer ward they found the drawbridge raised and John Knyvet's wife Alice appeared in a little tower over the inner fort of the bridge, keeping the castle with slings. parveises, fagots, timber and other armaments of war and assisted by William Toby of Old Bokenham, gentleman, and others to the number of fifty persons, armed with swords, glaives, bows and arrows and addressed them as follows: 'Maister Twyer ye be a Justice of the Peace. I required you to keep the peace, for I will not leave possession of this castle to die therefore and if ye bring to break the peace or make any war to get the place of me, I shall defend me, for liever I had in such wise to die than to be slain when my husband cometh home, for he charged me to keep it.' The forces of the law retired in confusion.[118]

In the manor house—the home of men lower than the lord, homes of "stewards, squires and other gentry," women

> . . . supervised a considerable domestic work force, including many women laborers, in the care of domestic animals and poultry, production of butter and cheese, butchering of livestock for table and market, care of the kitchen garden, food preparation and preservation, spinning, weaving, and sewing. Besides

these activities she supervised the marketing of everything produced over and above family needs and
oversaw storage in the manor warehouse. She was
expected to run a school for the village children, . . .
When her husband was away at wars or in the city or
at court on business, which could be for long periods
of time, she had to be able to manage the entire
estate . . .[119]

Serfs or peasants, male or female, worked on the
lord's land or around the manor house, as their parents
had before them and their children and grandchildren
would after them. Women worked as hard as men and in
addition they maintained their own cottages or huts.

The work of the serf was probably the hardest physical work for both men and women. On the fields women
worked right alongside men in ploughing, planting,
weeding, reaping, binding, threshing, winnowing, and
they also sheared sheep. All of this in addition to bearing
children, spinning wool to make clothing for her husband
and children. Langland poetically describes the work
roles of husband and wife living as serfs in the medieval
period.

His coat of the cloth that is named carry-marry His
hood full of holes with the hair sticking through His
clumsy knobbed shoes cobbled over so thickly
Though his toes started out as he trod on the ground,
His nose hanging over each side of his hoggers, All
splashed in the puddles as he followed the plow, Two
miserable mittens made out of old rags, The fingers
worn out and the filth clotted on them, He wading in
mud, almost up to his ankles, And before him four
oxen, so weary and feeble, One could reckon their
ribs, so rueful were they, His wife walked beside him,
with a long ox goad, In a clouted coat cut short to the
knee, Wrapped in a winnowing sheet to keep out the
weather.[120]

Work roles for men and women who had moved in from the farms to the cities to work in factories that became numerous at the end of the medieval period, often lived in one-room tenements, rose at dawn and worked until after dark. Women who had babies took them with them, or farmed them out for care. "Another alternative was infanticide, and the rates of infanticide continued high throughout the Middle Ages. Children who survived to the age of five or six went out to work on their own or with their mothers."[121]

In England the specialized crafts were protected from women entering them. For instance, women who were glasscutters and gemcutters, whose husbands had died, could not take on apprentices to learn the craft ". . . for the men of the craft do not believe that a woman can master it well enough to teach a child to master it . . ."[122]

When women enter the labor market they are often seen as taking jobs away from men. In England, in 1461, they were accused of "contributing to unemployment among weavers,"[123] Women's entry into some of the "more specialized crafts" was limited to wives and daughters of the masters. Yet women entered the labor market in the medieval period of necessity.

The appearance of women in the labour market in the Middle Ages was due to the same reason as their work today, i.e., it was necessary for the married woman to earn a supplementary wage and necessary for the single woman to earn a livelihood. In every class in western society marriage is a career, to which most girls aspire . . . but not all women could hope to marry,[124]

Women in the working class played a large part in the development of industry in the medieval period. They were

butchers, chandlers, ironmongers, net-makers, shoe-makers, glovers, girdlers, haberdashers, purse-

195

makers, capmakers, skinners, bookbinders, gilders, painters, silk-weavers, and embroiderers, spicers, smiths and goldsmiths among many other trades.[125]

When women were admitted to guild membership they "were not members on the same basis as were male artisans."[126] Then, too, town life was linked to guild association and voting rights were given to guild members who were head of households, which meant that the husband was given civic rights over his wife, though his wife was a hard-working business partner. Widows of the merchant class probably had more civic rights than married women as seems to have been the case throughout history.

Women were generally excluded from apprenticeship training, entering guilds as wives and daughters, and they were assigned the most menial and less-skilled tasks.[127] The salary of men and women differed too. In the fourteenth century in France,

. . . women's wages were set at three-quarters of the men's wages. By the fifteenth century it was one-half, and by the sixteenth still less.[128]

And as Boulding further points out,

The more women entered into the wage labor market, the more pronounced wage differentials became . . . The scholars of Toulouse in 1422 paid women grape-pickers half of what they paid the men, who only had to carry the full baskets back to the college cellar. The monks of Paris did the same. The women construction workers who worked side by side with men in building the college of Toulouse were paid less than the men who did the same kind of labor.[129]

The question has been asked, what was the feeling of men toward paid labor for women.

The reason occasionally given for barring employment of women was that work of a particular craft was too hard for them, but the main reason was the same as that which animates hostility to female labour today. Women's wages were lower even for the same work, and men were afraid of being undercut by cheap labour.[130]

Gradually women lost out in guild membership altogether in the craft and industrial work of the medieval period. Factory work began to replace work done in the home. "Prior to the Renaissance nearly everyone had to work hard, and the higher status of the women, the more responsibility they had."[131] But a tiny, do-nothing leisure class began to develop among women, which expanded in the Renaissance and will be discussed further, later.

As things changed from a barter to a money economy, and from church power to more state power,

> Women had to remain in their own niches inside declining religious bureaucracies while men filled the new secular bureaucracies of the state. The linking of higher education with training for the priesthood effectively barred them from preparing for entry into the new state machinery.[132]

In the knowledge explosion that occurred near the end of the medieval period, lists of scholars seeking answers to age-old questions and new possibilities, such as Thomas Aquinas, Vincent of Beauvais, Roger Bacon, Albertus Magnus, Duns Scotus, Bonaventura, and others, all clergymen, do not include any names of women because women were not allowed in the hierarchy of the church. Sometimes the best compliment women can have is for a man to say that women acted like men. Friedrich Heer in his book *The Medieval World*, sums up women's work-role contribution thus:

Women, feared by monks and theologians and disdained as the least valuable of all human material, contributed largely by their labours to both urban and rural economic life. Women worked in the fields and sometimes, as among the Germans, were responsible for the entire agricultural routine. Townswomen were active in a wide variety of trades and industries. The women of Paris are known to have engaged in more than a hundred different occupations. They worked as weavers, embroiderers and retailers; when their husbands died they carried on their businesses with resource and courage, proving themselves master craftsmen in their own right; they were teachers, doctors and merchants, capable of handling the large-scale affairs of foreign trade. In all these fields they acquitted themselves like men.[133]

In Summary

In the early years of the medieval period, women, rich and poor, worked unselfishly to get the Christian Church accepted in the barbarian world. As Boulding says, "Christian queens did not become pagans to please their husbands. It always went the other way."[134]

After reviewing the accomplishments of women in the early church, one wonders if Christianity might not have disappeared, as other struggling religions have throughout history, if it had not been for the dedicated Christian women.

At the beginning of the medieval period, women were involved in converting barbarians to Christianity all over Western Europe. However, at the end of the medieval period, when the church had firmly established its roots, women were excluded from important religious functions that had been taken from them and relegated to men. And the tortuous Inquisition fell more heavily on women than men because women had dared to criticize the church for corruption and had branched out into alternative Christian sects, stressing self-help and meditation.

Women were also the main targets of the witch hunts. As healers and dispensers of medicine they were accused of sorcery, and as people who dared to be different, many were accused, for that deviance, of being possessed by Satan. In the medieval period the main power was the power of the church which denigraded women.

In the secular world the laws of the Romans and the barbarians, the feudal system, the marriage, divorce, and educational customs, the guilds, the "scientific" ideas about women, all contributed further to the denigration of women.

The attempts to exalt women did not do so. The knightly custom of courtly love which "idealized" women, was artificial. Courtly love and the Cult of the Virgin Mary placed women on a pedestal, which serves the worshipper, and restricts the worshipped. As with Rome's Vestal Virgins, and Christianity's Eve, the virtue of the worshipper resides in the women worshipped. If the women "fall from the pedestal," it is as though the man's goodness has been tarnished and the women must therefore be punished. Pedestals are dangerous places to be.

Yet in spite of all of the forces working against them, medieval women were responsible in large part for the Christianizing and civilizing of Western Europe. Women administered to the plague-stricken in the towns and villages, they rode and fought in the Crusades. And though they were denied the privileges and the wages of men, they worked alongside men in the fields, the trades, and the guilds.

Women established nunneries, monasteries, hospitals, administered large land-holdings, successfully led armies of soldiers, and ruled as queens and empresses.

This is not to glorify women. But it does speak to women's ability to survive in the face of determined opposition, and accomplish important feats—especially if the arts of civilizing, educating, administering to the sick, and establishing businesses and trade are considered important.

Notable Women in the Medieval Period

In the Eastern Roman Empire

Pulcheria—The daughter of Emperor Arcadius, Pulcheria became the regent of the Eastern Roman Empire at the age of sixteen in 414, and ruled for thirty-three years. Her brother, Emperor Theodosius II, preferred to copy manuscripts. In all his reign, the Eastern Empire was peaceful, compared to the crumbling Western Roman Empire. Pulcheria chose her brother's wife, a Greek Christian scholar, Eudocia. Pulcheria was very religious, devoted her life to service, and was canonized by the Greek Orthodox Church after she died.[135]

Eudocia—Sister-in-law of Pulcheria and wife of Emperor Theodosius II, Eudocia served with Pulcheria to govern the Eastern Roman Empire. She helped to reorganize the University of Constantinople, was a writer and orator. She may have written the law codes attributed to her husband.[136]

Theodora [I]*—Wife of Emperor Justinian (527-565), she founded hospitals and convents and was active in politics, "made and unmade popes . . . Sometimes she countermanded her husband's order, often to the advantage of the state."[137]

Irene—The wife of Emperor Leo IV, she ruled the Eastern Empire for five years, from 775-780, after her husband's death and while her son, Constantine VI was under age. When her son came of age he exiled her, but then brought her back as an associate. She had him imprisoned and blinded so that she could rule. During this period, people who worshipped religious statues of Christ, Mary, or saints, or other religious objects were persecuted as Iconoclasts, turned out of their monasteries. When Irene ruled she "quietly ended the enforcement of Iconoclast edicts, permitted the monks to return to their monasteries . . ."[138] She brought together the leaders of the Church for The Second Council of Nicaea in 787, "lowered taxes, helped the poor, established charitable hospitals . . . people loved her but the army didn't like being ruled by a woman more capable than most men . . ."[139] Charlemagne wanted to marry her but she was deposed in 802, exiled to the Island of Lesbos where she scraped together a living as a seamstress. She was later canonized as a saint.[140]

Theodora [II]—She ruled from 842-856 as the widow of Theophilus when her children, Michael and Thecla were minors. Iconoclasm was a source of religious bloodshed at that time. She ". . . ended the persecution her husband had revived and was an able ruler."[141]

Helena—Wife of Constantine VII (912-958) whose husband turned the rule of the Eastern Empire over to her. "It was during her rule that Princess Olga of Russia came to Constantinople to be baptized and to cement Byzantine and Russian relations."[142]

Zoe & Theodora [III]—Zoe, wife of Romanus and later Constantine IX, with her sister, Theodora, governed the Eastern Empire from 1028-55 through the reigns of four emperors: Romanus III, Michael IV, Michael V, and Constantine IX. "Seldom had the empire been ruled better." The royal sisters discovered and reduced corruption in both government and Church, impartially sat as judges. When Zoe died in 1050 Theodora went into a convent and Constantine IX ruled. But when he died, the populace brought Theodora out of the convent to rule. They crowned her Empress, but she died one year later.[143]

Anna Comnena—The eldest daughter of Emperor Alexus I, she founded a medical school in 1083, was an historian and a doctor, a poet, philosopher, and a politician. She resented her brother John because he was born to the throne. She felt herself better qualified. She planned to have him assassinated, was detected, forgiven, and exiled to a convent where she wrote her father's history, *Alexriad*.[144]

In the Western Roman Empire

Placidia—At the same time that Pulcheria and Eudocia were administering the Eastern Roman Empire,

Placidia became regent of the Western Roman Empire and ruled for her son, Valentinium III from Rome for twenty-five years. In 414, knowing it would help smooth the relationships between barbarians and Romans, she married the king of the Visigoths, and when he was killed she married again.[145]

Amalswinthe—Daughter of Theodoric I, the first barbarian king of Rome, she ruled for two years as regent after father died, and she "reorganized the crumbling educational system of the Roman schools."[146]

In Alexandria

Hypatia—Non-Christian mathematician, philosopher, scientist whose works are listed in every history of science study. She was murdered in Alexandria in 415 at the age of thirty by Christian monks.[147]

In Ireland

St. Brigid—When Ireland became Christian in 558, it was largely because a monk named Patrick and a woman named Brigid had worked unceasingly to persuade the pagan Druids to convert. Brigid founded the Church of the Oak Tree which developed into a nunnery, a monastery, and a school. Noted for her brilliance at law, her influence lasts to this day.[148]

In Sweden

St. Birgitta—of Sweden (1303-1373) moved to Rome where she could expand her talents as a religious woman. She founded religious order for knights and wrote eight volumes of her *Revelations*, popular during her time in history. She was known as a healer, developed hospitals and orphanages in Sweden and in Rome. She founded an order for women known as Birgittine houses which spread over Europe and were cultural centers for upper-class European women. She was a politician who promoted marriages among the aristocracy which she believed would promote peace.[149]

In Poland

Jadwiga—(1371-1399). One of the many queens who helped to Christianize Europe, Jadwiga was crowned queen of Poland when she was sixteen. A religious woman, she was obliged by her marriage contract to help in the mass conversion of Lithuania. Though she, by peaceful negotiations contained "the dangerous Order of the Teutonic Knights," she was capable of successful military action and led her army when there were border disputes. She is at least partially responsible for the founding of the University of Cracow in Poland. "She died in child-birth at twenty-eight, and is still revered as one of the great rulers and great saints of Polish history."[150]

In Hungary

Elisabeth of Thuringia—was the daughter of the Hungarian king, Andrew (1207-31). She was married at the age of thirteen to a German prince, at fourteen she became a mother and at twenty a widow. After her brother-in-law "despoiled her and drove her away penniless," she devoted her life as a religious woman to the poor, taking in women with leprosy and tending their sores. She died at the age of twenty-four, but had become known, even throughout her teen years as a pious, unselfish woman who worked unselfishly among the poor.[151]

In England

Hilda of Whitby—who lived in the early 600's in England, built a double monastery, and took in both monks and nuns. It became a center for learning. She was on the council when "the highest religious body held council in Whitby."[152]

Bertha—Wife of King Aethelbert of King in 600's, Queen Bertha converted her husband to Christianity and when Pope Gregory was concerned that England was reverting to paganism. Queen Bertha worked to re-Christianize England.[153]

Aethelburg—Daughter of Queen Bertha. When she became wife of King Eadwin of Northumbria, she "brought a Christian cleric with her who baptised her husband; she also founded a double monastery, and churches in Northumbria."[154]

In Germany

Hrotsvita—A German nun, poet, and playwright who wrote six plays in Latin. She is considered one of the most gifted religious writers around the late 900's.[155]

St. Hildegarde—Lived from 1098-1178 and was the abbess of St. Ruper at Bingen. She had lived for most of her eight-two years as a Benedictine nun. Hildegarde believed that wealth and corruption in the Church was the result of masculine weakness and she said that women had to take more Church responsibility. She was referred to as "the Sibyl of the Rhine," because she was a visionary. She was also a poet, a scientist and a writer. She corresponded with popes and kings in Latine and published many visionary books, *Scivias*. Though she was one of the scholars of her time, she is also known for her great support in getting followers to join the Second Crusade.[156]

Herrad—Abbess of Hohenburg around 1100, and a scholar and writer who compiled an encyclopedic book for nuns, some of which survives today.[157]

In Italy

Theodelinda—Sixth century, wife of King Agilulf. She negotiated a treaty between the Lombards and the governor of Italy and made it easier for the Lombards to be converted to Christianity. Pope Gregory thanked her for her work.[158]

Clare—When Francis of Assisi was gathering his religious followers, Clare, a girl of the middle-class, joined him in 1212 and set up a sister house for religious women who took the vow of poverty, known as Poor Clares. This was an alternative to the upper-class monastic life. Clare wrote the rules for her convent and fought against the

Church and others, holding firm to the poverty vow. Francis relied on Clare in his decision-making. The women of the Poor Clares nursed the sick, helped the poor, and helped their brothers in the Franciscan monastery by cooking, mending, and making clothes. Clare communicated with queens and other important public women. She was canonized soon after her death.[159]

Catherine of Siena—(1347-1380). When the headquarters of the Roman Catholic Church was moved to Avignon, France, Catherine of Siena "threatened the popes with dire penalties if they refused to return to Rome." (Heer, 266) Catherine was a daughter of a working-class family, became a nun, whose destiny it was to "reform the papacy and she did in fact complete the task Birgitta (of Sweden) had set for herself, bringing back the pope from his 'captivity in Avignon." She was canonized after her death.[160]

Trotula—A teacher at the University of Salerno in the eleventh century, she wrote medical books including *The Diseases of Women and Their Cure*, and *The Compounding of Medicaments*. At the University of Salerno apparently there were quite a few women doctors, such as Trotula who came from the noble family of Ruggiero. But the profession for women was difficult because, "the Church, male doctors and universities united to disqualify women."[161]

In France

Clothilde—Married to Clovis, the king of the Franks in 493 and soon converted him to Christianity. Durant writes, "Queen Clothilde had helped to make Gaul, France." (Durant, 91) She founded hospitals and educational and religious houses for women. When her husband died she lived as a nun.

Caesaria—One of the first women scholars to found a convent in Europe, at Arles, France, in the early 500's.[162]

Radegunde—The daughter of a Thuringian tribal chief, she died in France in 587. Though at twelve years old she was married against her will to a Frank king who had kidnapped her, she remained strong and independent. A Christian, she founded a religious settlement at Poitiers and became a deaconess. She built a "fortress-villa to protect her two hundred nuns," was a peacemaker among Europe's kings and queens and was a "gifted writer and poet."[163]

Balthild—In seventh century France, she was the daughter of royal Anglo-Saxons. She was kidnapped as a child, made a slave, escaped and married King Chlodwig II. When he lost his mind she ruled France for the rest of his life and as long as her sons were minors. She forbid the sale of Christians as slaves in France, and helped to link the convents of France with those in England. She founded a monastery and because of her efforts many convents were opened, increasing the educational opportunities in Europe. She "generally turned a turbulent kingdom into a peaceful one."[164]

Eleanor of Aquitane—(1122-1202) She joined her lands in France to Henry II when she married him. In her fifty years as Queen of England, she bore ten children. Disgusted with Henry's adultery, Eleanor tried to return to her own kingdom in Aquitane, France, but Henry imprisoned her for fourteen years, threatening to confine her to a convent to get her lands in France, but he died before that happened.

Her courts in France and in England were virtually learning centers for courtly manners and customs which were copied all over Western Europe.

When her son John became king of England, Eleanor led military defenses for her son when his lands were threatened, though she was then eighty years old.[165]

Ermengarde—She was the Countess of Narbonne in the twelfth century. Though she married several times, her husbands were not interested in government. For fifty years she governed her lands and soldiers and led the French royalist party in southern France against the English. She fought numerous wars in defense of her territories, was a patron of troubadors, and a protector of the Church, and had great renown as an arbiter and judge in difficult cases of feudal law."[166]

Blanche of Castile—She served as Regent of France when her son Louis went on a Crusade, and in the first half of the thirteenth century during the persecution of the Jews, the Queen-mother treated the Jews with wisdom and quelled anti-semitism. She championed the poor when many people were imprisoned for failure to pay a special tax, and were dying from the prison heat. Blanche opened the prison doors herself, setting the prisoners free.[167]

Christine de Pisan—(c.1363-c.1431) Though born in Italy, she was raised in the French court. When she was young she was widowed and left to raise three children and to support her mother, which she did by writing, soon becoming very popular. While she was not a feminist she was concerned about women's educational situation and wrote manuscripts about the need for women to be educated. She also wrote manuscripts on military strategy, international law, and the political problems of France. "Her *City of Women* was the first history of women to be written by a woman."[168] All of this at a time when educating women was seen as a threat to men for it was believed that "Education would . . . heighten her natural depravity."[169]

Chapter 4

THE RENAISSANCE—
1400 to 1700

Brief Historical Background

The Renaissance appears in history almost as an explosion. For the approximate one thousand years of the Medieval period, the culture of the Western world had been relatively dormant. Primarily concerned with struggling for their existence against barbarians, plagues, taxation, and the Inquisition, people had little time left over for the arts, or for exploring philosophical or scientific ideas.

Then, during a period of about three hundred years, as though bottled up too long, creative energies burst forth in the fields of art, science, navigation, and theology. The magnitude of human endeavors is apparent in this list of *some* of the major figures of the Renaissance— men who changed art, drama, religion, science, the view of the earth and of the universe.

ARTISTS

Lorenzo Ghiberti

Donato Donatello

Sandro Botticelli

Tommaso Masaccio

Leonardo da Vanci

Jerome Bosch

Hans Holbein the
Younger

Albrecht Durer

Michelangelo
Buonarroti

Raphael Sanzio

Tiziano Vecellio
(Titian)

Antonio da
Correggio

Benvenuto Cellini

Pieter Bruegel the
Elder

Domenico
Theotocopuli (El
Greco)

Michelangelo da
Caravaggio

Peter Paul Rubens

Diago Valazquez

Rembrandt van
Rijn

Jan Vermeer

DRAMATIST

William
Shakespeare

THEOLOGIANS

Martin Luther

John Calvin

EXPLORERS

Amerigo Vespucci

John Cabot

Christopher
Columbus

Vasco da Gama

Ferdinand Magellan

SCIENTISTS

Nicolaus Copernicu

Galileo Galilei

Johannes Kepler

Isaac Newton

The world literally opened up to exploration when Christopher Columbus and others discovered water routes to new and old continents and changed the map of the world, and possibilities within it. Major inventions of the period opened up the universe. The telescope proved that the earth revolved around the sun instead of otherwise as had been believed since Antiquity. If the earth could no longer be considered the center of the universe how did that affect the importance of people on earth? The invention of the microscope revealed the existence of bacteria, a discovery necessary to conquer disease. Maybe ill health was not the work of demons in the body after all.

In Germany, the invention of the printing press opened limitless possibilities for all classes of people to learn to read—not in Latin, the language of the Church—but in their own language.

With all of this, the Renaissance world became "human-centered," rather than religion-centered as it had been in the Medieval period.

The crusades had opened trade between the Western and Eastern world and were largely responsible for bringing the Medieval period to an end in the 1400's. Florence, Italy, which lay on the route between western Europe and the Holy Land, grew in wealth as the crusaders stopped to buy goods to take with them to the Holy Land, and then, on their return, stopped to sell goods from the Eastern world.

The increased supply of money created a sense of optimism, and businesses in Florence prospered. Rich townsmen and popes paid artists to carve beautiful marble statues, build magnificent buildings, and paint masterful pictures. Art in the Renaissance began to reflect the new feeling of interest and confidence in the human spirit and in humanity in general, a philosophy which became known as "humanism."

For their models, the artists looked back in history to their ancient, proud beginnings. Artists, scientists, and philosophers studied Greek and Roman art, architecture, philosophy, logic, mathematics and science of Antiquity. Thus the Renaissance was a period of rebirth of the learning of Antiquity, beginning in Florence, Italy, where the moral and financial depression of the Medieval period first began to dissipate. The renewed desire for learning, the appreciation of beauty, and the restored sense of pride and confidence in man's achievements spread from Italy to Holland, and then eventually to all of western Europe.

The rise of the merchant class of people began to change the social structure of the Medieval feudal system which had hitherto consisted of serfs, vassals, lords, and the church. Also, the invention of gun powder marked the end of the feudal castle as the stronghold of powerful small kings. It was no longer possible to defend castle walls with bows and arrows against canons.

Small kingdoms joined together for mutual protection and eventually began to form into small nations, developing a sense of national pride that competed with Rome's demands that the church remain all-powerful. These merging kingships were more apt to challenge the authority of the distant popes than the small feudal territories had been.

At every step, as the Medieval period came to an end, the church lost ground. People were beginning to rely more on their confidence and their abilities than on what the church dictated.

The church's hope for re-establishing its old power by uniting Roman and Greek Catholicism was dashed in 1452 when the shrine of the Eastern Church, Hagia Sophia, in Constantinople was captured by the Moslems. From then on, the Roman Catholic Church was on its own in the Western world and could depend only on itself for prestige and power.

The European kingships in northern Europe, especially in Germany, became increasingly resentful of the Pope's authority. The Germans resented the large amount of German money which had to be sent from the churches in Germany to the Vatican in Rome. In their resentment they became more openly critical of certain church practices.

The most specific complaint was for the selling of indulgences, a practice of forgiving a person for his or her sins if that person contributed money to the church. A growing number of protesters wanted to reform the church, prohibit the selling of indulgences, reduce the pope's authority, eliminate the canonization of saints, and require the church to rely more on Scripture than on the authority of the pope. This reform movement was later referred to as The Reformation. It resulted in a breaking away from Catholicism and the establishment of Protestantism.

Religion

Numerous protest groups began to spring up. Among them were Lutherans, Calvinists, Anglicans, Anabaptists, Huguenots, Moravians, Quakers, and Puritans.

Lutherans

At the same time that the church was being criticized, a German monk, Martin Luther (1483-1546) was urging that people should be able to interpret the Scripture of the Bible for themselves. With the invention of the printing press and with Luther's translation of the Bible into the German language, reading the Bible in the vernacular became a possibility.

Luther also believed that priests should be allowed to marry and to have children. "By marrying and raising a family these ministers would shed the aura of sanctity that had made the priesthood awesomely powerful."[1]

The German princes welcomed the protest movement, and when it was clear that the church at Rome was not about to change, the Lutheran Church was established in Northern Europe, monasteries were closed, church property was taken over by the state and people who remained faithful to the Catholic Church were persecuted. Because Luther stressed the value of marriage, it could have been expected that the respect for women's position might have changed for the better with the Reformation. But the leaders of Protestantism said that because generally women were physically weaker than men, that was God's sign of male superiority. Even though women were important to the early reform movement, Luther

> . . . excluded women from the ministry on the grounds of preserving order and decency and because of the inferior aptitudes inherent in the female sex . . . Luther was willing to make an occasional exception . . . but any concessions to women were to be made on male terms by the men themselves.[2]

Calvinists

John Calvin, (1509-1564), the strongest reformer after Luther, was born and educated in France, but did most of his religious work in Switzerland. His was the doctrine of "predestination," in which he claimed that God appoints to each person perpetual happiness or perpetual misery. In Geneva, Calvin

> . . . was in effect a complete dictator of morals and his views on sex, love, and other pleasures became the code by which Genevans lived for the next century. It was punishable by fine or imprisonment to sing, to dance at weddings, to curse, to serve too many dishes at dinner, or to wear clothes of too extravagant a cut. Plays were banned, jewelry and other adornments discouraged, and elegant hairstyles made grounds for jailing. Sexual transgressions, however, were something else again . . . they merited as severe punishments as heresy: . . . adultery deserved death, sometimes by drowning, sometimes by beheading . . . Engagements were limited to six weeks' duration, for one did not dally or play at romance, but got down to cases . . .[3]

The Puritans transferred some of these severe attitudes into puritanism which they brought to North America.

Calvin held, as did Luther, that the subjugation of woman to man was part of God's law, and he said her ministry was the ministry of motherhood.

> . . . and this prevented her from assuming positions in the church which in turn deprived her of authority to preach publicly. Ultimately Calvin concluded that a woman should not be allowed to speak in church , to baptize, to offer, and could not claim for herself the function of any man, much less the priest.[4]

Anglicans

Because the Roman Catholic Church would not give England's King Henry VIII an annulment or a divorce from his first wife so that he could marry another woman, one more Protestant church was established. Henry's first wife had not given him a male heir. Though she had five children, only one child, a girl, had lived.

After waiting many years for the popes in Rome to grant the king's desire to marry Anne Boleyn, the English bishops withdrew from the authority of the popes, Henry divorced his first wife, married his second wife, and the Anglican Church of England was born. In addition to the birth of a new protestant church, the right to divorce under certain conditions was created. And something previously not allowed, was the right of divorced people to remarry. In Catholicism, even though married people might have separated, their marriage bonds remained as long as both spouses were alive.

In spite of this slight change in male/female marriage-divorce relationship, the Anglican view of women was hardly different than that of Lutheranism or Calvinism.

> . . . the Anglican writers with almost uniform monotony expounded the basic principle of male headship and credited men with superior understanding and reasoning. Women, on the other hand, were said to

have been so constituted that they required guidance, control, and protection . . . The good woman was the wife who was ever vigilant in conforming to the wishes of her husband . . . ready to obey, and always good humored. Any wife should be treated by a husband as he would a child, which a woman was at heart . . .[5]

Catholics

Among the Catholics there was no change in church attitude toward women in the 16th century. But at least one nun had the courage to write about the church's attitude toward her. St. Theresa of Avila (1515-1582) wrote, ". . . the very thought that I am a woman is enough to make my wings droop."[6] St. Theresa did not believe women's physical weakness was enough reason for their subordination.

When thou wert in the world, Lord, thou didst not despise women, but didst always help them and show them great compassion. thou didst find more faith and no less love in them than in men . . . We can do nothing in public that is of any use to thee, nor dare we speak of some of the truths over which we weep in secret, lest thou should not hear this, our just petition. Yet, Lord, I cannot believe this of thy goodness and righteousness, for thou art a righteous Judge, not like judges in the world, who, being after all, men and sons of Adam, refuse to consider any woman's virtue as above suspicion. Yes, my King but the day will come when all will be known. I am not speaking on my account, for the whole world is already aware of my wickedness, and I am glad that it should become known; but, when I see what the times are like, I feel it is not right to repel spirits which are virtuous and brave, even though they be the spirits of women.[7]

Minor Protestant Religions

Anabaptists

This small group "practiced complete equality of women and men in every respect, including preaching. Both Catholics and Lutherans persecuted them, and they lived hunted lives . . . they were always on the run. Elizabeth Dirks of Holland, an Anabaptist teacher was imprisoned, tortured and drowned in a sack."[8]

Huguenots

These seventeenth century protestants were in conflict with the French government, accused of trying to overthrow the king, persecuted, then given religious freedom which was later taken from them. Several noble women provided refuge for the Huguenots during the worst of the Catholic persecutions.

Moravians

This was a group which formed first in Bohemia, dedicated to pure scriptural reading. A seventeenth century Moravian minister, John Comenius, (1572-1670) believed

> . . . that neither sex should try to rule each other. He could see no good reason why women should be excluded from the pursuit of knowledge and argued that women were often endowed with a greater sharpness of mind as well as a capacity for knowledge than men. He also wanted them to be well educated since the more learning they had stuffed into their minds, 'the less will the folly that arises from emptiness of mind find a place.'[9]

Quakers

Founded in England by George Fox 1652, the Quaker religion, formally known as The Religious Society of Friends, rose up against state-dominated church and against church practices which they believed tended too much toward the Roman Catholic Church. Quakers take their beliefs from the Bible and believe that there is "that of God in every man," and that if one follows the Divine Spirit and righteous conduct one can find true belief.

"The homes of women became the first meeting place for Quaker worship, much as the homes of Roman women became the first place for Christian worship."[10] Women were preachers and when they were arrested for preaching and imprisoned, their children were cared for by other Quaker women.

The first Quakers to come to North America in 1656 were two women, Ann Austin and Mary Fisher who were imprisoned and deported. Quakers who arrived later were beaten and driven away. Four were hanged, one of them being a woman, Mary Dyer. Many later found refuge in Rhode Island and in Pennsylvania.

Puritans

The Puritans protested the Anglican Church of England's lavish church decorations and complicated church services. They set out to "purify" religion, relying wholly on Scripture, and abhorring decorations and any luxury.

The religion attracted a thrift-minded middle-class people. As they became more severe, King James I of England attempted to suppress them, but that only drew them closer together. They eventually emigrated to New England in 1620. The Puritan religion set the tone for social behavior in New England for many years after their arrival.

Church Effort to Regain Power

All of the religious disturbances of the early Renaissance created suspicion from one group to another and within groups. Church authority had been questioned, and in some places destroyed and replaced by new religions. The power of the church had been weakened by a revival of learning, and by a desire for power by men who put their nations' needs above Rome's demands. The church was nervous about its erosion of power.

As in any period of social tension, society seems to need a "scapegoat"—someone, or a group, on whom the ills of society can be blamed when the group in power feels threatened.

The defeat of the Greek Catholic Church at Constantinople had dashed the hopes for united church power. In addition, Protestantism was gaining ground. Church leaders believed that at least part of the blame must be put on Satan, and Satan was believed to do his work through witches. Most witches, it was also believed, were women.

Witch-hunts

The witch-hunts which started in the Medieval period were vigorously increased in the Renaissance. In the areas where the church retained its power, as in Italy, Spain, and Ireland, there were few witch trials. But in Northern Europe where church power was most threatened, witch-hunts abounded.

In 1484 Pope Innocent VIII wrote a church document called a church Bull, in which he lamented that two Dominican monks at the University of Cologne, Germany, had not been given full cooperation in their witch-hunts. These two monks, Jacob Sprenger and Henry Kramer "intensified their activities and . . . reaped a rich harvest of burnings."[12]

Sprenger and Kramer had both been Inquisitors when the church was conducting its search for heretics, or nonbelievers, so they were well qualified to search out witches. They listened to accusers, tortured and burned suspects, and wrote about it all in their book, *Malleus Maleficarum, The Witches' Hammer,* (meaning the hammer with which to strike witches.) The book, written in 1486, put all that was believed about witches into church writing.

Officially endorsed by the University of Cologne and avidly studied throughout Western Europe, it was scarcely ever out of print for the next two centuries. It went through nineteen separate editions by the eighteenth century, inspired the publishing of scores of similar works in other languages, and influenced the direction and content of nightmares, neuroses, accusations, trials, and burnings for at least two hundred years.

From actual testimony of witnesses and confessed witches, Sprenger and Kramer had learned that, by means of incantations and brews, evil-doing women could summon plagues of locusts to destroy a harvest or bring a hailstorm to ruin it, make men impotent or women frigid, induce abortions or dry up a mother's milk. They could see at a distance, fly at night, and leave a duplicate body behind to fool people; sometimes they could turn themselves into cats or other creatures; some of them turned men into animals and kept them at hard labor; and some kidnapped children, and roasted and ate them . . .

The Inquisitors explained at length why witchcraft was far more common among women than among men. Basically, woman is a weak, inferior creature; moreover, she is afflicted with insatiable carnal lust. This makes her easy prey to the advances of the Devil, who offers to satisfy her desires.[13]

People who did *not* believe in witches were accused of heresy. So, to speak out against the witch-hunts was dangerous. Objections could only be made anonymously. "Friedrich von Spee, a Jesuit poet and confessor of witches . . . described the methods of witchhunters. Since a defender of witches exposed himself to denunciation as a witch and death by fire, Spee's book was anonymously issued."[14] von Spee wrote:

Lest, however, further proofs against her should be lacking, the Commissioner has his own creatures, often depraved and notorious, who question into all her past life. This, of course, cannot be done without coming upon some saying or doing of hers which evil-minded men can easily twist or distort into ground for suspicion of witchcraft . . .

Without any scruples, therefore, after this confession she is executed. Yet she would have been executed, nevertheless, even though she had not confessed; for when once a beginning has been made with torture, the die is already cast—she cannot escape, she must die.

So, whether she confesses or does not confess, the result is the same . . . If she does not confess, the torture is repeated—twice, thrice, four times: everything one pleases is permissible, for in an excepted crime [i.e., one in which, by reason of its enormity, all restraints upon proceedings are suspended] there is no limit of duration or severity or repetition of the tortures . . .

If, now, any under stress of pain has once falsely declared herself guilty, her wretched plight beggars description. For not only is there in general no door for her escape, but she is also compelled to accuse others, of whom she knows no ill, and whose names are not seldom suggested to her by her examiners or by the executioner, or of whom she has heard as suspected or accused or already once arrested and released. These in their turn are forced to accuse others, and still others, and so it goes on: who can help seeing that it must go on without end?[15]

"Scarcely any of those who were accused escaped punishment . . . The children of those convicted and punished were sent into exile."[16]

The witch-hunts caused economic hardship. The executioners grew rich, farmlands were left untended by families who had been scattered by the persecution, and the people became impoverished. It was when the money for persecution dried up that the zeal for the witch-hunts died out.

The cost in human life is recorded in the town records all over Europe. Any action that did not have society's full approval was suspect. Joan of Arc wore men's clothing. "Such a form of deviant behavior could only be due to witchcraft."[17] Women who were the heads of their own families, independent by choice or necessity, were more severely subject to witchcraft persecution. "The majority of the witches were women, and many accusers were clergymen, though at the height of the burnings all kinds of male adventurers got into the act, collecting 'bonuses' for every witch they identified."[18]

When one witch-finder was imprisoned in London, "And upon the gallows he confessed he had been the death of above two hundred twenty women in England and Scotland, for the gain of twenty shillings a piece, and beseeched forgiveness. And was executed . . ."[19]

In the seventeenth century alone, 511 were tried in England and Scotland, 800 were tortured by one continental judge in 16 years; and in Wurtemburg 900 were burned in one year. In Geneva there were 500 burned in three months.[20] In 1631 Cardinal Albizzi on a trip to Cologne wrote: 'A horrible spectacle met our eyes. Outside of the walls of many towns and villages, we saw numerous stakes to which poor, wretched women were bound and burned as witches."[21]

Religion of the Renaissance in Summary

With the Reformation, Catholics were persecuted in Protestant countries and Protestants were persecuted in Catholic countries. The new religions which might have offered important roles to women in their church services, failed to do so. The best, it seems, that a woman could hope for in the Protestant religion was to become the minister's wife. Only a few minor religions allowed equality of participation between men and women, and that at risk of human life.

In short, religious attitudes toward women did not change much during the rise of Protestanism or the coming of Catholic reform. Protestantism by emphasizing the virtue of marriage had eliminated some of the clerical misogyny, but a woman, whether she was a Protestant, Catholic, Jew, or Muslim, was not to assert any authority over the male. She was clearly subordinate, even if by some chance she might even become a ruling monarch.[22]

Witch-hunts which began in the Medieval period lasted through the Renaissance. In this period of great artistic and scientific accomplishments there was a new sense of freedom and optimism in the Western World, and a desire for learning in which women were beginning to take an active part. Yet it is at this time that the massive, tortuous witch-hunts directed mainly against women—especially independent women—were accelerated.

Male/Female Relationships

Married life began early for girls in the Renaissance, usually at about age thirteen, with bethrothals earlier. As before the Renaissance, love had nothing to do with marriage. Among the lower classes, marriage was for carrying out household functions, cooking, making clothing, growing crops, raising children. Among the upper classes, marriage was for economic reasons—a man married the woman who could bring him the largest dowry, or marriage was for political reasons, for instance in the joining of one section of land with another to put the territory under one ruler—almost always the husband.

Parents wanted a girl married early as she would be subject to her husband and she should be married before she had ideas of her own. In Italy in the sixteenth century an unmarried seventeen-year-old daughter was a family disgrace.[23]

Marriage was a bargaining situation between the father and the future son-in-law. The husband considered himself an absolute owner—the wife considered herself her husband's servant. She was his "wife and subject." Her husband spoke to her with stick in hand.

> "A woman, a dog, a walnut tree, The More you beat 'em, the better they be."[24]

> ". . . many children and even infants were espoused in church ceremonies at the desire of parents who had struck a bargain . . . though it had to be ratified by actual marriage later on, only a few of the children when they grew up, dared to appeal for the release from the contract."[25]

In 1477, Anna Sforza, aged three, was affianced to Alfonso d'Este; she walked in the ceremony, but he, being newborn, had to be carried by a chamberlain. Not only the mighty arranged such marriages for benefit. A study made of the records of the English diocese of Chester in the middle of the sixteenth century shows a number of similar marriages among the children of obscure burghers, John Somerford and Jane Brerton, three and two years old respectively, were held in arms by adults who spoke the words of the ceremony for them. In another such espousal, John Rigmardon, aged three was coaxed by a priest to repeat the matrimonial vows aloud; halfway through, the child said he would do no more, to which the priest replied: 'You must speak a little more, and then go play.'[26]

If a girl could not bring social status to a marriage, then she especially needed a large dowry. A father with several daughters could become bankrupt trying to get them married. In the 15th century in Italy "a respectable dowry for a merchant's daughter amounted to about 1,000 florins . . . one could buy a female slave for 50 florins . . . With a dowry of 1,000 florins, a young man could buy a quarter interest in a silk or wool shop, on which he could earn 15 percent interest . . ."[27]

An engaged couple exchange rings in front of their parents. The main objective of a nobleman was to kill a stag and acquire a large dowry at marriage.

In Catholic countries fathers could still place their unmarried daughters in the remaining convents, but in Anglican England where the convents had been closed and unemployment was limited, marriage arrangements were extremely important and it was a mother's duty to get her daughter to agree to a marriage, beating her if necessary until her daughter complied.[28]

Because of the difficulties of getting girls married and the need for dowries, girl babies were not very welcome in families. In England, "by 1547 girl children could legally be placed in an enforced apprenticeship until the age of 15 or marriage, which amounted to *de facto* slavery."[29]

Carrying on the family name, which meant carrying on the name of the father, a practice that started in the 15th century [30] increased the desirability of having male children. As Alberti wrote of Italian women, "the first duty of women was to bear male offspring." And as Martin Luther said, "If women get tired and die of bearing, there is no harm in that; let her die as long as they bear; they are made for that."[31]

As at other times, women were expected to be virgins at marriage and faithful to their husbands in marriage, while men were expected "to be free to pursue sexual liasons outside marriage."[32] Bastards, that is, children of husbands by other women, were socially acceptable. Married men often persuaded their wives to raise their bastard children along with their own.

> Sexual license was dangerous for women, especially in Italy where a man's "point of honor" was involved. ". . . in the 16th century, the husband felt called upon to punish his wife's adultery with death, while preserving his pristine privileges unimpaired. The husband might desert his wife and still prosper; the deserted wife had no remedy except to reclaim her dowry, return to her relatives, and live a lonely life; she was not allowed to marry again."[33]

Nevertheless love and consideration did grow out of enforced marriages. Even in the rules of how an ideal wife should behave, as written by Alberti at the end of the 1400's, one can sense a certain tenderness.

After my wife had been settled in my house a few days, and after her first pangs of longing for her mother and family had begun to fade, I took her by the hand and showed her around the whole house. I explained that the loft was the place for grain and that the stores of wine and wood were kept in the cellar. I showed her where things needed for the table were kept, and so on, through the whole house. At the end there were no household goods of which my wife had not learned both the place and the purpose. Then we returned to my room, and, having locked the door, I showed her my treasures, silver, tapestry, garments, jewels, and where each thing had its place . . .

Only my books and records and those of my ancestors did I determine to keep well sealed . . . These my wife not only could not read, she could not even lay hands on them. I kept my records at all times . . . locked up and arranged in order in my study, almost like sacred and religious objects. I never gave my wife permission to enter that place, with me or alone. I also ordered her, if she ever came across any writing of mine, to give it over to my keeping at once. To take away any taste she might have for looking at my notes or prying into my private affairs, I often used to express my disapproval of bold and forward females who try too hard to know about things outside the house and about the concerns of their husbands and of men in general . . .

When my wife had seen and understood the place of everything in the house, I said to her, 'My dear wife . . . you have seen our treasures now, and thanks be to God they are such that we ought to be contented with them. If we know how to preserve them, these things will serve you and me and our children. It is up to you, therefore, my dear wife, to keep no less careful watch over them than I.'

. . . She said she would be happy to do conscientiously whatever she knew how to do, and had the skill to do, hoping it might please me. To this I said, 'Dear wife, listen to me. I shall be most pleased if you do just three things: first, my wife, see that you never want another man to share this bed but me. You understand.' She blushed and cast down her eyes. Still I repeated that she should never receive anyone into that room but myself. That was the first point. The second, I said, was that she should take care of the household, preside over it with modesty, serenity, tranquility, and peace. That was the second point. The third thing, I said, was that she should see that nothing went wrong in the house.

(Addressing the other interlocutors)

. . . I could not describe to you how reverently she replied to me. She said her mother had taught her only how to spin and sew, and how to be virtuous and obedient. Now she would gladly learn from me how to rule the family and whatever I might wish to teach her.

. . . Then she and I knelt down and prayed to God to give us the power to make good use of those possessions which he, in his mercy and kindness, had allowed us to enjoy. We also prayed . . . that he might grant us the grace to live together in peace and harmony for many happy years, and with many male children, and that he might grant to me riches, friendship, and honor, and to her, integrity, purity, and the character of a perfect mistress of the household. Then, when we had stood up, I said to her: 'My dear wife, to have prayed God for these things is not enough . . . I shall seek with all my powers to gain what we have asked of God. You, too, must set your whole will, all your mind, and all your modesty to work to make yourself a person whom God has heard . . . You should realize that in this regard nothing is so important for yourself, so acceptable to God, so pleasing to me, and precious in the sight of your children as your chastity. The woman's character is the jewel of her family; the mother's purity has always been a part of the dowry she passes on to her daughters; her purity has always far outweighed her beauty . . . Shun every sort of dishonor, my dear wife. Use every means to appear to all people as a highly respectable woman. To seem less would be to offend God, me, our children, and yourself.'

(Finally, turning to interlocutors again)

. . . Never, at any moment, did I choose to show in word or action even the least bit of self-surrender in front of my wife. I did not imagine for a moment that I could hope to win obedience from one to whom I had confessed myself a slave. Always, therefore, I showed myself virile and a real man.[34]

Alberti further advised husbands to control their wives, to "never letting her gain any point, and using her sometimes with spirit, sometimes with a delicate hand, just as one does a sparrow hawk, so that she does what you want. And make her love and honor you, and not resent your harshness."[35]

The attitude about ladies of the courts and castles was influenced in the Renaissance by an Italian nobleman, Baldassar Castiglione (1478-1529) who served in the courts of Milan and Mantua. He wrote a book entitled, *The Courtier*, which means, "the nobleman of the court." The book which was reprinted one hundred times and translated from Italian to Spanish, German, French, and English during the sixteenth century attempted to answer the questions, "What is a woman, her essence, her destiny?"

The author answers through his dialogue that "women were very imperfect creatures, inferior in every respect to man, . . . (and) since woman was all body, whoever possessed a woman's body was master of her mind."[36]

One of his speakers continues, saying

Learned men have written that, since nature always intends and plans to make things most perfect, she would constantly bring forth men if she could and that when a woman is born, it is a defect or mistake of nature . . . as is seen too in the case of one who is born blind, or lame, or with some other defect.[37]

Another speaker answers "that women can understand all the things men can understand," but the first person claims "all women without exception desire to be men, by a certain natural instinct that teaches them to desire their own perfection."[38]

The first person returns with,

That poor creatures do not desire to be men in order to become more perfect, but in order to gain freedom and to escape that rule over them which man has arrogated to himself by his own authority.[39]

The writer of this book, important at the time, gave women a role other than housewifery. It is almost a defense of women, urging their participation in intellectual life and praising their accomplishments.

. . . if you examine ancient histories (although men have always been very chary in writing praise of women) and modern histories, you will find that worth has constantly prevailed among women as among men; and that there have always been women who have undertaken wars and won glorious victories, governed kingdoms with the greatest prudence and justice, and done all that men have done.[40]

But the book, *The Courtier*, referred only to upper-class women and was read only by the upper classes. Efforts toward changing the attitudes about middle and lower-class women were non-existent. Education, which often can open doors for opportunities to raise one's status, was also virtually non-existent for girls in all but the upper-class.

In the Renaissance, with its emphasis on intellectualism, education did increase with the establishment of elementary schools. However, in most countries these were for boys. All except upper-class girls were educated at home.

Education in the Medieval period had been mainly for the purpose of training priests and students of religion. With the rise of universities, other subjects besides theology were taught, yet women in most countries were prohibited from attending universities because of the religious tradition. Women could not hold positions in the church so they, therefore, could not be educated for positions which they could not hold.

Nevertheless other things did enhance the possibility of women's education. The invention of the printing press provided more opportunities for both men and women to learn to read. And Protestantism, which emphasized the Scriptures, encouraged women to read. But it was the emphasis on "humanism" which helped women most.

When people looked back to their beginnings and studied their ancient cultures of Antiquity, they came to believe that the greatness of Antiquity was the result of education. They at least began to *talk* about the possibility of educating females.

In England there were few schools which girls could attend, and when the convents were closed after Henry VIII's break with the Catholic Church, there were practically no schools at all for females, though there was home tutoring for upper-class girls.[41]

Except in Spain and Italy, where women could attend universities, learning was a special class privilege of the nobility and well-to-do . . . it could only exist when tolerated—or encouraged—by men.[42]

The question of whether or not girls should be educated was the subject of considerable writing in the Renaissance. Agrippa D'Aubigne, (1552-1630) advised his daughters in this letter:

My daughters, your brother has brought . . . you my summary of Logic in French, 'Logic for girls,' . . . I am letting you have it on condition that you make use of it only for yourselves and not against your companions or superiors, as it is dangerous for women to use such things against their husbands. Moreover, I recommend that you conceal its art and terminology . . . whenever possible . . . I do not blame your eagerness to learn with your brothers, but I would be loath either to discourage or encourage you. Still, if anything, I would be more inclined to the former than the latter. [Proceeds to give an account of the learned women he has known or heard of: Queen Elizabeth, Margared of Navarre, Louise Labe, 'the Sappho of her time,' Mademoiselle de Gournay.] I have just given you my opinion of the advantages that women may derive from a superior education. However, I have nearly always found that such preparation turned out to be useless for women of middling rank like yourselves . . . There is the fact, moreover, that a disproportionate elevation of the mind is very apt to breed pride. I have seen two bad effects issue from this: (1) contempt for housekeeping, for poverty, and for a husband less clever than oneself, and (2) discord. And so I conclude that I would be most reluctant to encourage girls to pursue book learning unless they were princesses, obliged by their rank to assume the

231

responsibilities, knowledge, competence, administration, and authority of men. Then doubtless, as in the case of Queen Elizabeth, an education can stand girls in good stead.[43]

Erasmus, (1467-1536) a leading humanist, took a stronger position in favor of educating females, though he was writing only about noble and upper-class girls.

The distaff and spindle are in truth the tools of all women and suitable for avoiding idleness . . . Even people of wealth and birth train their daughters to weave tapestries or silken cloths . . . it would be better if they taught them to study, for study busies the whole soul . . . It is not only a weapon against idleness but also a means of impressing the best precepts upon a girl's mind and of leading her to virtue.[44]

The education of boys, especially noble and upper-class boys was an entirely different matter and was jealously guarded by men. When a boy turned seven he came under the authority of his father until he was fourteen when he should be ready for life. As soon as he was seven he was sent away to school, out of his mother's reach.

It was an axiom that boys must be subject to thoroughly masculine management, a life of birching, under the firm hand of the father; the father had a perfect right to forbid them to see their mother.

Nowhere was the battle against feminism fought more resolutely than on this ground. The adversaries of women may be almost infallibly recognized by this mark, that they insist above all things on keeping in their hands, the education of men, because they regard this as the direction in which the influence of women is most manifestly fatal.[45]

One of the leading educators of the sixteenth century, Juan Luis Vives, (1492-1540), was a tutor for Henry VIII's daughter, Princess Mary. When he opposed the king's divorce he lost his position in the English court and went to Belgium where he wrote at length about the philosophy of educating girls and claimed that he was the first person to write on this subject.

Vives' point of view was that

> girls should be taught to read in order to study holy books, but she should also learn the domestic arts, needlecraft, spinning and weaving, in order to better serve her parents and her husband. Though Vives believed that intelligent girls should go on to study he felt their field should be severely restricted.

> . . . because a woman is a frail thing, and of weak discretion, and that may lightly be deceived, . . . a woman should not teach lest when she hath taken a false opinion and belief of any thing, she spread it unto the hearers, by the authority of mastership and lightly bring others into the same error, for the learners commonly do after the teacher with a good will.'

> Good Christian women were to be secluded from the world for fear that they would develop a taste for misbehavior . . . they must not be allowed to read romances written by idle men, but . . . Vives seemed to believe that if a woman was left to herself she would instinctively read dangerous nonsense, and thus it was essential girls go to wise and learned men for guidance.[46]

It was generally felt that "allowing women to study Latin and Greek would encourage them to become too independent."[47] "Some of the male writers wondered if women should be taught to read at all since there were dangers in books."[48] And even those who felt it would be all right for them to read, suggested that their reading material be censored.

> The purpose of education for a lady was to ensure proficiency in domestic affairs, to give her moral and

religious training, to help her remain chaste, obedient, and run a well-managed household . . . the male was to develop to the utmost every power he had and direct every action to enhance his authority. Women were also urged to marry early in order to increase their chance of being virgins at marriage, but also to curtail their opportunities for education and to force them to turn to the problem of attending to children.[49]

Even with all these restrictions, many noble and upper-class women were educated, and it was these women who opened their homes for discussion groups of both men and women—discussions which led eventually to considerations years later about equality for *all* people of all classes. Women in these groups acted more as moderators, being careful not to assert themselves. King James I of England had urged the clergymen in his kingdom to scold self-assertive women, and women had taken heed.

The example of strong women rulers led other women to question why they needed to remain subordinate. Because Queen Elizabeth, if she married, would have had to turn over the rule of her kingdom to her husband, she chose not to marry, rather than subordinate herself. Women in all classes looked to these female rulers, and wondered how their sex could be considered defective and unworthy of education.

The rise of a merchant class throughout Europe decreased the power of craft and trade guilds, as work which had been done in the homes, supervised by the master and his wife, was moved into central buildings in the towns where more people worked together. The guilds, which had stood both as protectors of the rights of apprentices, journeymen and masters in the trades, and as overseers of the quality of the goods, could not serve this purpose in assembly-line manufacture of products. As the power of the guilds diminished, workers were left without protection. The employed men and women were required to work longer hours at low wages in a period of considerable job competition.

When employment became scarce, in the textile business for instance, "Men began to petition against women being given weaver's work, fearing competition . . ."[50]

Then, too, underneath the social strata of the working class throughout Europe there was a sea of slaves with whom the employed person must also compete. "In one ten-year period in the flourishing Venetian slave market, ten thousand slaves were sold."[51] One could buy a slave for a few florins and have him or her work for nothing. The wage earner had to keep his demands for wages low in order to make anything at all.

In better-off artisan homes, and increasingly in middle-class homes, women became unpaid domestic servants of their husbands as they left (or lost) their own employment opportunities.[52]

In England the effect of the Civil War was to leave women stranded, with their trade ruined and their husbands imprisoned. Thousands of women petitioned the House of Commons in protest, but were told to go home. When their numbers increased to five thousand they were "dispersed with bullets, swords, and bloodshed."[53]

Yet women persisted.

In 1647 the Maids of London petitioned parliament for protection against unreasonable working conditions . . . In the 1640's a brewer's wife, Anne Stagg, presented a petition on behalf of 'Gentlewomen, Tradesmen's wives, and many others of the female sex . . .' for protection against religious persecution. In 1651 the women were back again, petitioning for relief from imprisonment for debt . . . While men argued that women could not possibly understand the complexities of public affairs, due to weakness of intellect, these tradeswomen showed by word and deed that they understood not only what was going on, but what needed to be done about it.[54]

Though this was a period when women found some freedom in, for example, opening their homes for educated discussions, it was also the period when women restricted themselves severely in their clothing. This was the age when the corset came in vogue, which laced up a woman's waist to the point where she had difficulty breathing. "In general, prior to the 15th and 16th century, woman's costume had followed the natural configuration of the body with no artificial or confining shaping."[55] But in the Renaissance, women adopted full skirts with sometimes as much as 50 yards of material, padded and hooped, which couldn't help but restrict their movements. In addition, as beauty was very much admired in this period, elaborate hair styles monopolized upper-class women's time, with usually three hours a day devoted to creating a pleasing hair arrangement.

An upper-class woman being helped to her bath by her maid.

It was also a period when there was considerable writing devoted to what was called, "the debate about women." Many of the arguments about women's abilities were negative, but others, for the first time, spoke out for women.

The comments about educating females have already been mentioned. In addition to those, Henry Cornelius Agrippa von Nettesheim

> . . . published a defense of women in 1529 . . . Although he granted that women occupied a decidedly subordinate position in society, he said this subjection was not proof for the incapacity of women but rather the usurpation by men of women's natural right. Little more could be expected of women who were shut up in the house from the time they were born, given nothing serious or worthwhile to do, treated as if they were incapable of a real action, forced to make the needle and thread their sole occupation.[56]

Marguerite de Navarre whose writing was analyzed in 1612, wrote *Heptameron*, stating that women were the masterpieces of God.

> Because women had intuitive powers lacking to men they were also more intelligent and women should have been able to command more effectively because she was more willing to listen and was therefore more reasonable. In fact Marguerite held that women had originally commanded men until men usurped power, which made her an early advocate of the theory of matriarchy.[57]

Marie de Gournay (1565-1645) a leading intellectual in France, fought against the idea that women were inferior to men.

> She entered the battle for women's rights in 1594 and continued in it up to her death . . . She personally suffered . . . because of her refusal to follow the custom of submissiveness of women.[58]

Thomas Bacon, in the sixteenth century, "paid tribute to women's wisdom . . ." and Jeremy Taylor in the seventeenth century "went to some effort to disassociate himself from those . . . who deemed women unfit for man's friendship."[59]

Unlike earlier historical periods, women in the late Renaissance had possibilities other than marriage, convent life, or prostitution. With the opening of colonies, women could emigrate to America or they could become missionaries in other lands even as far away as Turkey, West Indies, or Russia.[60] Yet in spite of a new world which was opening up to women, and in spite of the great artistic and scientific knowledge explosion which took place in the Renaissance and the new idea of "humanism," which put man instead of religion at the center of thought, the status of women did not change. As Vern Bullough says

> In sum the sixteenth and seventeenth centuries, although many women were unhappy with their role, saw little effort to change. To be a good wife and mother was the end for which every young girl in the seventeenth century was carefully trained from early childhood . . . We might add that she was to be subordinate to her husband and to males in general.[61]

Morton Hunt writes that it is amazing that the split "in men's feelings about women appeared to be most extreme not in the Christian era nor in the Middle Ages, but in the golden Renaissance . . . , when women were glorified by great painters, courtiers, and burned at the stake on suspicion."[62]

Notable Renaissance Women

Joan of Arc, 1412-1431, is more often considered a woman of the Medieval period, but as this book sets the year 1400 as the approximate beginning of the Renaissance, her name is included in this period.

Joan was a religious French peasant girl who heard "voices" telling her to lead the French soldiers against the English, who were invading part of France. With the king's support, she led several successful battles against the English, fighting after she was wounded, and she was praised by her people.

When she lost a battle and was captured by the English, they put her on trial for witchcraft. Because she wore men's clothing into battle, her accusers said this kind of deviant behavior could only prove that she was a witch.

When she refused to say that the pope had more authority than the "voice" of God which she claimed she heard, she was judged guilty of heresy by 40 theologians and burned at the stake at the age of 19, in 1431. In 1456 the verdict was declared null and void, and in 1920 she was made a saint.[63]

Isabella of Castille, 1451-1504, known as "Isabella the Catholic," and Isabella the "crusading warrior queen," she was extremely religious and dreamed of uniting Spain under Catholicism. When she took the throne at the age of 17 she chose as her husband, Ferdinand of Aragon, so that the two territories could be combined, ensuring in the marriage contract that Ferdinand would have no ruling authority over Castille.

In her ruthless drive to unite Spain, "she personally directed major mattles against the Moors as well as supervised the extermination of Jews in Spain, and established the Inquisition.

"Isabel's success lay partly in the fact that she had the physical stamina to live on horseback. She frequently rode all night to be on the spot where something important was happening by morning. She had a miscarriage during one such wild night's ride, and nevertheless directed operations from horseback next morning for the reconquest of invaded territory. She had five children between 1470 and 1485 in spite of her activity level."[64]

Isabel was brighter, abler, stronger, and more ambitious than Ferdinand, and it is ironic that the history books tend to portray the reign as Ferdinands."[65]

Marguerite of Navarre, born in 1492, was a minor French queen who became known as a "peace queen" because she devoted herself to protecting Catholics against Protestants and vice versa. She was an educated woman, a writer, and a "model of peacemaking in the midst of the most virulent hatreds Europe had known."[66]

Jeanne of Navarre, Marguerite's daughter, became queen in 1555 after her mother died. When she announced her acceptance of Protestantism, Queen Elizabeth of England sent her a message of congratulations. Her country then became a "haven for Huguenots . . . She is said to be the only sovereign of the sixteenth century who put no one to death for religion . . . Like her mother, she led an embattled life as peacemaker and gave a lot of attention to local self-government in her little country."[67]

Elizabeth, Queen of England, 1558-1603, daughter of Henry VIII, she ruled England with a strong hand. As she would have had to turn her power over to her husband if she married, she chose not to marry. When she believed that religious groups outside the Anglican church were causing disturbances, she made them illegal, thereby persecuting religious freedom. However, laws helping working people and the poor were passed during her reign.

Queen Elizabeth was an example of independence and strong leadership. When she supported Sir Francis Drake who defeated the Spanish Armada, she "set the pattern for England as 'ruler of the waves.' The 'Elizabethan Age' is named after her.[68]

Catherine de Medici, 1519-1589, ruled in her own principality as regent. A Catholic, she "is considered to be the author of the massacre of St. Bartholomew. Yet she was also the architect afterward of peace with the Protestants, and was known equally as a skilled diplomat and a ruthless tactition. She has two major international treaties to her name . . ."[69]

Isabella d'Este was educated as a noble boy would have been. At 16 she married the Marquis of Mantua and when he was away she administered his lands. When her husband was taken prisoner she ruled Mantua and held it against the Venitians.[70]

"The heroines of the defense of Vienna in 1554 were a three thousand woman army which fought in three regiments." No women's names were recorded.[71]

Rullia d'Aragona, one of the 11,654 courtesans of Renaissance Venice whose "home was considered a second academy, and she considered herself very much with public affairs. She has been called the 'priestess of humanism.'"[72]

"She was received in Naples, Rome, Florence, and Ferrara like a visiting princess."[73]

Angela Merici, 1474-1540, founded the Ursulines, which is a Catholic women's religious order. She insisted that her followers not be cloistered, and not have to wear nun's habit, as they were to work as "apostles in the world." After she died, the Church forced her followers back to the old mode of convent living.

Marie de Gournay, 1565-1655, was a French feminist, intellectual and writer, who wrote about education and public affairs. She made a living writing. Her translations of Virgil, Ovid, Sallust, and Tacitus sold easily. She spoke out against unfair treatment of women in her two documents, *Equality of Men and Women*, and *Grief of Women*.

She said "the wonder was not that women had achieved so little, but that they had achieved anything at all given the lack of opportunity for education and development."[74]

"She entered the battle for women's rights in 1594 and continued in it up to her death . . . She personally suffered . . . because of her refusal to follow the custom of submissiveness of women."[75]

Anna Marie van Schurman, 1607-1678, was a Dutch artist and writer. "The best known woman of her time in Europe." Though women could not attend universities, the University of Utrecht allowed her to sit behind a special curtain at the university and listen to the lectures.[76]

Queen Christina, 1626-1689, was the daughter of the Swedish empire builder, King Gustavus Adolphus. She gave up her crown in order to leave the small and confining country of Sweden to settle in Rome where she could associate with the leading intellectuals of the period. "There she created not less than three academies, and supported many musicians, artists and a theatre troupe."[77]

She was one of the many "bluestockings" of the period, a term used to identify women intellectuals. This beginning trend of noble and upper-class women, supporting intellectuals, male and female, and providing meeting places in their homes, or salons, was to gain in importance in the Modern period.

Bianca Maria Visconti, "who in the absence of her husband, Francesco Sforza, governed Milan so capably that he used to say he had more confidence in her than in his whole army, and who was at the same time known for her 'piety, compassion, and beauty of person.' "[78]

Mme. de la Sabliere, astronomer who tried to "conceal her studies in astronomy. The word got out, however, and Boileau wrote a cutting satire on the woman who sat up nights studying the stars and ruining her complexion.[79]

Baroness de Beausoleil did "a major study of French mineral resources—a work widely recognized and used in her own time."[80]

"Maria Sibylla Marian of Frankfurt studied birds, insects, plants in Surinam . . . science has honored her by giving her name to new botanical discoveries."[81]

Josephine Kablick of Bohemia traveled widely to make botanical and paleontological collections for all the major schools, colleges, museums, and learned societies of Europe. She was happily married to a minerologist, and they managed 50 years of separate but coordinated field work.[82]

Amelia Deutsch, a botanical collector who got specimens from places "where no botanist had been before; she made many new botanical finds, and a number of plants bear her name. She was also happily married, to a fellow botanist."[83]

Maria Kirch, "Working as her husband Gottfriend's astronomer assistant, along with her three sisters-in-law, she discovered a comet which was not named after her because she was a woman . . ."[84]

Elizabeth Celleor, "a famed midwife . . . organized a corporation of midwives, and there is a document by her dated 1687 on this. She drew suspicion by visiting women prisoners in Newgate before prison visiting was conceived of. Having powerful enemies, she was imprisoned, pilloried, and fined a thousand pounds for supposedly plotting against Charles II."[85]

Margaret Fell. In England she established her home as the world center for Quakerism. "Missions to all continents went out from there. All correspondence and reports were sent there. Margaret Fell was not only the organizer, however; she was also a minister and interpreter of the faith. One of her tracts is entitled *Women's Speaking Justified*.[86]

Beatriz Galindo "founded schools, hospitals, and convents all over Spain."[87]

Catalina Mendoza founded a Jesuit college for women.[88]

Women's names are not listed in the art history books among the famous artists of the Renaissance. Nevertheless there were many, including:[89]

Caterine de Vigri, "patroness and painter of the aristocracy."

Properzia de Rossi, sculptor of Bologna, "who did not have the protection of being of the aristocracy, became so popular with the public that she roused the intense jealousy of her male colleagues. According to Clements they began to crusade against her so that her commissioned work was not mounted on the public building it was prepared for."

Anna Maria Ardian, "poet, artist, musician elected to the Academy of Arcadia.

Sophonisba of Cremona, "in demand all over Europe as a portrait painter."

Elisabetta Sirani of Bologna.

Lavinia Fontana of Bologna, "one of the most prolific and popular artists of the century (1552-1614)

Catharina van Hemessen (1528-1587) "celebrated as a portraitist both in Flanders and Spain."

Artemisia Gentileschi (1593-1652) "considered by many to be the greatest Italian woman artist. She worked in Rome, Florence, Genoa, Naples, and London and was a primary influence in the development of the Neopolitan School of Painting."

Leonia Teerling of Flanders, (1515-1576) "court painter of British royal family."

244

From the Lowlands: Anna and Marie Visscher, Anna Breughel, Judith Leyster, Maria Van Oosterwyck, Rachel Ruysch, Maria and Gezina Terburg, Maria Schalkers, Adriana Spilberg.

From England: Mary Beale, Anne Carlisle.

From Denmark: the daughters of Kings Christian IV and V; Anna Crabbe, "poet and painter of princes."

Women poets included:

Veronica Gambara

Vittoria Colonna, "who for a time was placed under the surveillance of the inquisition, and to be her friend was to risk indictment for heresy. Michelangelo took the risk, and developed for her an intense spiritual affection that never dared go beyond poetry . . . He was with her when she died."[90]

Tarquina Molza. So great was the esteem in which she was held that the senate of Rome conferred upon her the singular honor of Roman citizenship."[91]

Women Composers in Italy included:[92]

Vittoria Alcotti

Francesca Baglioncella

Orsini Vizzani

Barbara Strozzi

Cattarina Assandra

Mararita Cozzoloni

Cornelia Caligari

Lucrezia Vezzani

Women Composers in Germany included:

Madelka Bariona

Women Composers in Portugal included:
  Bernarda de Lacerda

Women writers:

  Oliva Sabuco de Nantes "at the age of twenty-five wrote the seven volume *Nueva Filosofia* (1587) the biology, pshchology, and anthropology of the day to medicine and agriculture."[93]

Women writing about the status of women:[94]

  Margaret Lucas, 1662 wrote "Female Orations Supposedly made by women who were deliberating on the possibility of combining to make themselves as 'free, happy and famous as men; . . .'"

  Mary Cary—a futurist who prophesied women's future roles.

  Lady Chudleigh wrote *The Ladies Defense*.

Chapter 5

MODERN—
1700 To The Present

Toward the end of the Renaissance many upper class women had opened their homes for discussion groups. In France these meetings took place in the luxurious sitting rooms of the rich. As the word for "room" in French is "salon," this movement became known as the "salon movement," important in history because it provided a place for sounding out new ideas.

In these French salons, Voltaire, Diderot, Rousseau and other great intellectuals of the period met and expounded their thoughts on the rights of people, including the growing sentiment that *all* people regardless of social class had certain natural rights. Voltaire argued that anyone should have the right to speak out without being punished, and Diderot added that all people should also have the right to knowledge.

Some of this talk about rights spilled over to discussions about women. Voltaire, for instance, "denounced the injustice of women's lot, and Diderot felt that women's inferiority had largely been made by society."[1] Rousseau, however, disagreed. He believed women should be taught

To please, to be useful to us, to make us love and esteem them, to educate us when young, and take care of us when grown up, to advise, to console us, to render our lives easy and agreeable: these are the duties of women at all times, and what they should be taught in infancy.[2]

Though the "woman question" was debated, the discussions of the salon movement revolved more about the concerns for the condition of France. Questions were raised about the all-inclusive rights which royalty had, when the masses of French men and women were repressed and lived in poverty.

The intellectuals in the French salon movement were undoubtedly influenced by the ideas of John Locke, an Englishman who had written his new ideas about representative government at the end of the 1600's. His writings were widely read and they greatly influenced the power shift in western civilization from monarchies to democracies.

A sensitive boy of seventeen when his English king, Charles I, was tried for treason and beheaded, Locke remembered how the English people had looked to Cromwell to rescue them from the tyranny of their king only to be tyrannized by Cromwell when he took over the English government. Those who had been tormented under Charles, became the tormenters under Cromwell. Locke came to believe that government should be representative and that a country ruled by one man was tyranny. These ideas were incorporated into the discussions in the French salon movement.

The king of France ruled under the theory that kings had divine rights, that is, god-given rights to rule as they wished. The French people might have gone along with this if other things had been all right. But by the end of the 1700's, unemployment had risen, the price of bread was outrageously high, there was a widening difference between the rich and the poor, and a growing uproar over the lavish spending of the king and queen, at the same time that taxes were very high and many people were starving.

The powerlessness of the masses, the insensitivity of the king and queen to the needs of the people, and the intellectuals' concern for human rights all added to the momentum that erupted into the French Revolution.

Women played a major role in the revolution. They had seen their infants starve when they had no money to buy food and they were anxious to set things right. Middle class, lower class, and working women organized, set up their strategies, and contributed to the success of the revolution. As in the American Revolution, women worked hard to achieve a greater equality for the populace, often putting their lives in jeopardy, but when the revolution was over, any equality gained was not extended to women.

In England a military revolution was avoided when Parliament increased representation and instituted reforms. England, however, gave birth to another revolution, the Industrial Revolution, which produced the greatest change in the way people lived since the Age of Cultivation began around 10,000 BC.

Before the factory system, the home was the factory, so-to-speak. Crafts were manufactured by hand. Women produced material for clothing by spinning wool and cotton into thread and then weaving the threads into cloth for the family's clothing, or to sell in the market. Often a middleman would supply the raw materials and the family would produce the desired goods, whether it was iron goods made on the family forge, or glass, or ale brewed in the family kitchen. These goods would be picked up by the middleman for distribution and sale.

But with the invention of the steam engine in 1712, the home began to lose out as the source for manufactured goods. Human power could not compete with steam power. Another device was invented which could spin six spools of thread at a time on a machine. This Spinning Jenny, invented in 1764, began to close down the home as the supplier of textiles. The additional inven-

Women and children were especially valued in the important coal mining industry because of their small size.

tion of the cotton gin in 1792 forced women to abandon the home textile industry which they had controlled. Working women had to move into town to work in the factories along with their husbands and their children. Factory wages were so low that it was necessary for all members of a lower class family to work in order to survive, and that at a poverty level. It was estimated that in the 1700's 75 per cent of the population in England lived in or near poverty.[3] The husband of a working woman in the lower classes not only depended on his wife's wages but he could legally claim them as his own.

This unskilled worker earned a few shillings a week. Many families lived in worse conditions than this.

Children went to work in the mines and textile mills when they were 5 or 6 years old. All factory workers, children and adult, worked six days a week, and from 14 to 16 hours a day. They went to work before the sun came up and returned after dark to their slum dwellings which had been built around the factories. On Sunday they could see daylight, though many slept most of that day.

The steam engines which needed coal to operate, created a surging demand for coal. Women and children worked alongside men deep in the coal mines. Women were harnessed to carts on tracks to pull the coal up out of the pits, crouched over to pass through the shallow passageways. This was said to be particularly difficult for pregnant women.

The Industrial Revolution, in addition to moving people off their lands, and out of their homes into towns to work in factories, created an expanded middle class made up of factory foremen, bankers, exporters and importers, and other merchants. The upper class, which had always looked down on work, lent money, or bought factories which other people operated, and the upper class grew richer.

The city of Leeds, 1885, with row houses and factory. Life expectancy in Leeds was nineteen years.

Middle class wives of factory foremen, or bankers, or merchants imitated upper class women, hiring numerous servants at low wages and rendered themselves useless. A merchant would point with pride to a wife who lived in genteel idleness: it was a mark of a husband's social status. The idea that a man's manhood was lessened if his wife worked, came from the Industrial Revolution.

The first occupations to move into the factories were those that women had controlled—textiles, brewing, baking, and preserving foods. Henceforth these industries would be controlled by men.

Moving the production of goods from the home to the factory decreased a wife's economic value. A middle class woman who had previously been her husband's business associate when goods were made at home, could not go out to work and still be socially acceptable. It is at this time that the family as we know it, makes its appearance in history.

In the medieval period the concept of a family was unknown. It was an institution developed to pass on a name and an estate.[4] But with the Industrial Revolution, the family became a different kind of institution.

Instead of working in his home, the middle class husband left his home to go to work. His wife remained at home, no longer associated with his work. As Toffler in his book, *The Third Wave*, suggests, the wife was left in the past as her husband stepped into the future. The apprentices in her home, who were often under the direction of the middle class wife, were replaced by servants. She could not with respectability do her own housework because that was something the servants did. In the British class system one was what one did.

The system was based on inferiors and superiors. It was important to keep inferiors in their place. But it was also important to keep superiors in *their* place. What would happen to the status of superiors if upper or middle class began to do manual work? A woman in those classes would not do anything her servants did, without risking losing her social position. Consequently maids attended to her clothing, her children, her shopping, cooking, housekeeping, and, with her upper class sisters, the middle class woman also became a dependent.

In a society where women's work was not valued, where more emphasis was put on their youth and beauty, things beyond their control, there was a frenzy to marry off the daughters of this class. The alternative was to become a spinster, a female who was known as "surplus woman." When girls depended on marriage as their major avenue to respectability, and for most, their economic survival, they were taught to defer to men. As Dr. Gregory wrote his daughter

> Be ever cautious in displaying your good sense. It will be thought you assume a superiority over the rest of the company. But, if you happen to have any learning, keep it a profound secret, especially from the men . . .[5]

A girl's education might jeopardize her opportunity for marriage, but there was little chance that she would be educated anyway. Most education was paid for by the parents, and the higher the social class, the better the education—except for girls. Even girls from the very rich were not permitted to enter professional schools.

Cambridge University students protest granting degrees to women by lowering a female effigy on a bicycle.

For most children there was little education until the 1900's. In England it was not until 1870 that elementary education was free and child labor was stopped, at least officially if not actually.

Secondary education was for children of middle and upper class, and higher education was for gentlemen's sons. Women had to fight for their own education, both because of the stigma surrounding an educated female, and because as a class women had no rights.

They had no legal rights to their own earnings, nor could they own property, make wills, testify in court, serve on juries, own a bank account, obtain a divorce before 1857 except by order of Parliament, or retain custody of their children if a divorce were granted.

Some women suffered under these injustices and spoke out against them and worked for reform. Mary Wollstonecraft, a mother raising a child by herself, experienced frequent humiliating discrimination and in 1791 she wrote her book, *Vindication for the Rights of Women*, wherein she protested that "it is time to restore women to their lost dignity and to make them part of the human race."[6] The modern women's rights movement is said to date from the publication of *Vindication* which was widely read in Europe and America.

Mary Wollstonecraft's statement was supported by a popular British philosopher, David Hume. He "held that the subordination of women was a sign of a barbarous society." John Stuart Mill championed the cause of fair treatment for women when he wrote in 1860 in his essay, *On the Subjection of Women*,

> All apparent differences between men and women 'especially those which imply inferiority in the female' are the result of the social demands of men on women. There remain no legal slaves (anywhere in the British Empire)—except for the woman in every man's home."[7]

For defending women, John Stuart Mill was treated by the male establishment as a traitor to his sex and to society. Dr. Samuel Johnson, England's leading writer in the

1700's was no such champion. He said he would not welcome home a daughter who had married beneath her class. ". . . it is our duty to maintain the subordination of civilized society and when there is a gross and shameful deviation from rank, it should be punished so as to deter others from the same perversion."[8] He also believed that illegitimate children should be penalized from birth, "because the chastity of women being of the utmost importance, as all property depends on it . . ."[9]

The property laws and child custody laws might have gone unchanged for more years had not Caroline Norton, a middle class woman and a writer, decided to take her three children and leave her husband because he had taken to beating her.

> She found she owned nothing, not even the clothes on her back. She found she could earn nothing. The copyrights on her books legally belonged to her husband, and any profits from her writing were his. Worst of all, she found she had no right to her children. . . . After a nasty and scandalous court case, the three little ones were taken from her and sent off to live with her ex-husband's relatives.[10]

Caroline Norton began campaigning in 1836 for improved child custody laws, and later, she and other women helped gain other reforms. By 1870 married women owned their own earnings. The Divorce Bill made divorce easier, especially for the upper class. It provided, however, that a man could divorce an adulterous wife, but added that for a wife to divorce an adulterous husband she had to prove also that he was sexually perverted, or cruel, or had deserted her.[11]

Many middle class women developed a social conscience about the conditions for working people in their country. They became outraged at the hours, the wages, the health, and living conditions of the working class. Middle class women and men persuaded Parliament to enact laws to improve conditions. The working class had no time to try to improve their condition; they needed all their energies simply to survive. The reform efforts of women campaigning to improve human conditions began to pay off. The Mines and Collieries Act of 1842 prevented women and children from working underground, though that did not prevent their being overworked in other trades.

Women formed organizations to campaign for health and safety laws for all workers, and to gain equality for themselves. The writings of Mary Wollstonecraft and John Stuart Mill bolstered their efforts. Known as feminism, the struggle for equal rights began with the middle class women who had the time and the resources to print pamphlets, arouse concern, and contact legislators.

Eventually the strongest efforts for equal rights were aimed at getting the vote for women. But the demand for the vote was a more serious threat to the establishment than their other demands had been. The idea of women voting was said to be "a dangerous, irreligious, immoral idea."[12] Social feelings ran high against a change in political place.

Because the vote is referred to as "suffrage," the women campaigning for the vote called themselves suffragettes. In spite of ridicule and family disapproval they organized suffrage meetings beginning in London in 1866.

In their plea for equality in voting, other discrepancies in the treatment of women and men were pointed to.

Under laws before 1869, a man was entitled to great physical control over his wife. Wife beating was winked at, and a man could confine his wife to their home to make her obedient. If she left him, he was entitled to bring her back by force, if necessary. Through a court decree for what was called 'restitution of conjugal rights,' a man could present his wife with the choice of returning to his home or of going off to jail.[13]

Women's efforts to stop this cruelty to women paid off in a court decision in 1891, and in the revision of the Matrimonial Causes Act.

The cruelties that came to light in testimonies brought further interest to the feminist cause for equality. British men put the subject to a vote in Parliament several times. Invariably it failed. Most legislators believed

> It was all right for women to be used in campaigning and in helping male candidates. That was a proper female role. It was all right for women to have a hand in local government. Such areas as education, social welfare, and local problems were extentions of women's role in the home.[14]

Parliament was not about to give full and equal political rights to women.

> After years of slow, steady, unspectacular work, the British suffrage struggle was to explode into violence, brutality, and destruction. The quiet, ladylike reformers of the 19th century died. They were replaced by bands of fanatically determined women who felt they had a right to use confrontation, vandalism, and arson as tools.[15]

Beginning in 1905, Emmeline Pankhurst led the suffrage movement joined by her three daughters. With a large following they demonstrated, made speeches, and were at times brutally attacked by police and jailed. In prison the suffragettes went on hunger strikes and were forced fed.

Year after year Parliament failed to bring a vote for women. The suffragettes turned to violence and arson. They were jailed and the forced feeding began again. In 1913 Emily Davison threw herself in front of the king's race horse to dramatize the suffragette cause. She was killed and became a martyr for the cause. At the time of her funeral, which thousands of people came to watch, there were 200 suffragettes in prison. The public was becoming aware of the seriousness of the cause. But when the First World War began in 1915, the suffrage movement had to take a back seat while Britain made itself ready for war.

As in any war, women play an important part. In World War I, 65 million men from 30 countries went to war, and huge numbers of women went to work. The Woolwich Arsenal in England by 1916 was employing 50,000 women. In munitions work, there were three women to every man. The women munitions workers earned about $2.80 a week, replacing men who had earned $15.00 a week.[16] Men were greatly concerned, not that the women earned so little compared to what they had earned, but that when the men returned they might have to work for what the women were paid. The government assured the men that they would be reinstated at "men's wages."

Disregarding the low wages and the dangers in war work, women flocked to this employment, for the wages were considerably higher than what women had earned as servants or in the pre-war factories. Middle and upper class women joined the military service corps, worked in hospitals, some even going behind enemy trenches in Belgium. Two women doctors, suffragettes Dr. Flora Murray and Dr. Louisa Garrett Anderson ran the largest woman-run hospital in London, with a staff of about 180, mostly women. And a new women's organization, the National Federation of Working Women, headed by Mary Macarthur, represented two million women. When the war was over Mary Macarthur attempted to decrease the number of women who were thrown out of work by returning men.

In peacetime, middle class women were urged to stay home and be ladylike, but when war came, barriers against their working broke down. And at least for a time the work that women did was valued and women were respected for their work. It would have been unthinkable for Parliament to turn down their new demands for the vote.

On January 10, 1918, the suffrage battle ended in England. Women thirty years old and over were given the right to vote. Men voted at age twenty-one, but the thirty-year requirement for women was written into the law to prevent a female majority. Ten years later, 1928, the voting age for women was lowered to twenty-one. It took women in England fifty-two years, from 1866, to get partial voting equality with men and another ten years to gain full voting equality.

In England, since the end of the Renaissance which saw the beginning of the Industrial Revolution, women's status changed for the better in property, education, marriage, divorce, child custody, and voting rights. Every gain was a hard-fought and sometimes bloody battle. But as Trecker says, ". . . total equality of the sexes still seems far off."[17]

The United States

The first people to come to North America from England were men, but it soon became obvious that England could not colonize any place unless there were women. Consequently the London businessmen who saw the Virginia Colony as a business venture encouraged women to go to America.

> Ninety came on one ship alone in 1619. 'Agreeable persons, young and incorrupt . . . sold with their own consent to settlers as wives, the price to be the cost of their own transportation.'[18]

Thus the first women to arrive in America were purchased brides.

A year later, the Mayflower headed for Virginia but lost its course and landed in Massachusetts. Of the 101 passengers, mostly Puritans escaping religious persecution in England, 18 were married women. The severe winter in Massachusetts with sickness and danger took its toll. By spring, only 4 of the 18 women were left.

But other ships brought more settlers, the children of the first arrivals grew up, and new colonies were developed all along the Eastern coast.

Many women came as wives of settlers and many as indentured servants, promising, or bonding, to work for a master for a definite period, anywhere from 5 to 7 years, in return for the cost of transportation. Men and women were kidnapped off the streets of London, or sold out of prison to become indentured servants in America.[19] "To be a bondsman or bondswoman was to be, for the time specified, little better than a slave."[20]

Many hands were needed to build the colonies and Black slaves were imported to do the most menial work. Unlike indentured servants who would be freed in seven years if they survived, the Black slave had no such future to look forward to. And the first thing to survive was the trip to America.

It is impossible to compute accurately the numbers taken from Africa over several centuries; estimates run as high as 20,000,000. Nor is there agreement as to the proportion— somewhere between one-half and one-third—who lived to reach their final destination. For, after the warlike raids on the villages in upland plain or jungle, after the breaking-up of tribes and separation of families, the march through equatorial heat and rain for hundreds of miles, the slave pens on the coast, the branding and the chains, came the Middle Passage.

The 4,000 mile crossing was made at first in ships even smaller than the Mayflower, and the passenger lists were longer. There are records of one-hundred-ton vessels carrying five hundred, even seven hundred and fifty men and women; usually the small ships carried between two and three hundred. Only a small space was reserved for the crew and supplies; the rest was filled with 'cargo,' chained in pairs to platforms of benches which occupied most of the floor space, sometimes with as little as eighteen inches between the 'floor' and the 'ceiling.' Each tier had its complement of manacled bodies chained side by side; occasionally they would have to double up their legs, with no room to move them. There, except for brief periods to relieve themselves or go on deck, they remained during a five or six weeks' voyage.

Approximately one third of the cargo was usually women. The only concession to their sex was that they were chained in a separate room; 'packed spoon-fashion, they often gave birth to children in the scalding perspiration from the human cargo.' . . .

Although the slave trade was formally abolished by both Great Britain and the United States in 1808, illicit trading by American ships continued. When a patrol ship came in view, the best guarantee for trader and crew was to dump the manacled cargo overboard, where it quickly sank from sight or was disposed of by the sharks.

The slaves themselves left no chronicle of the Middle Passage; coming from many tribes, they often could not communicate with each other.[21]

White women coming to America were spared the degradation which accompanied the Black slaves, though many were purchased as they landed on dock.

. . . groups of women were shipped to most of the colonies and purchased by the men on landing. Some men paid only the passage money for the brides; others paid the market price, whatever it was.[22]

Unlike girls in England, the girl in America needed no dowry to get married. As time went on, the wealthier parents selected partners for their children, but there were alternatives for the boy or girl who did not want to marry his parents' choice. With all the free land available they could strike out for themselves into the seemingly endless frontier.

Marriage was early and it was often. Life was dangerous and short. Women who had been previously married were in demand because they were experienced housekeepers, gardeners, and child raisers.

Once married, a woman's freedom ceased. The laws of England were the laws of the early colonists. Until 1860, for women, marriage was a "civil death." A married woman could own nothing. Even the clothes she wore were her husband's. And she was "not responsible for her actions . . . and had almost no right of divorce regardless of cause."[23]

Religion, which was the hope and the inspiration for many colonists, was restrictive, especially the Puritan religion which forbid dancing, adornment of clothing, jewelry, and women speaking out. The Quakers were the only religious group which allowed women to speak in church. All others followed the dictates of St. Paul, that had been used against Anne Hutchinson, a colonist who had arrived with her husband in 1634. She had gathered women together for Bible studies, but St. Paul's words, "Let your women keep silent in the churches for it is not permitted unto them to speak," were used against her when she was condemned and banished from Boston.

The Salem witch-hunts further restricted women. Any person of deviant behavior could be accused of being a witch, and the witch-hunts "centered on women and seriously affected their position, not only in Salem, Massachusetts, but to some extent in all colonies."[24]

In spite of restrictions on women within their marriage, in the law, and in religion, and in spite of severe hardships and dangers which all people were exposed to, free white women in the early colonial years of North America were still able to make significant contributions. They founded the first schools, established orphanages, acted as doctors developing medicines and salves, and they became missionaries among the Indians. All this at the same time that they also worked side-by-side with their husbands as they established industries.

Among the colonists, all people needed to work in order for the group to survive, and, at least in the first years, there was no place for the British class system. Whether one was male or female, indentured servant or slave, craftsman or noble born, all people worked. But when the English factory system was transported across the Atlantic Ocean, the social structure of the upper, middle, and lower classes became more obvious.

In the early factory, most workers were women and children. The textile factories opened with a 14-hour work day. Women were unskilled and therefore their wages were low; because they were considered inferior they could receive no training. It took women one week to make as much as men made in one day.[25]

Women textile workers.

If the industrial revolution had a beginning in the United States, it began in 1798 when Samuel Slater opened the first American textile factory in Pawtucket, with a labor force of 9 children, girls and boys all under the age of 12. By 1820, half of all workers were girls and boys ten years of age and younger . . .[26]

The typical factory working day lasted from sunup to sundown . . . The hours ran from 12 to 15 or 16 a day. In Paterson, New Jersey, women and children had to be at work at 4:30 A.M., and work as long as they

264

could see, with time off for breakfast and dinner, until a strike in 1835 cut the working day to twelve hours.

Women's wages, always lower than those of men on similar work, ranged from $1.00 to $3.00 a week, out of which they had to pay $1.50 or $1.75 for board in company-owned or leased boarding houses.[27]

Yet, no matter how small a wage a woman earned,

she could be compelled to hand over every penny of her wages to a drunkard husband, even if she was left with nothing for her own subsistence or the maintenance of her children, and even if the husband was known to be making no provision for them. If she sought to divorce such a husband, he might, irrespective of the kind of father he was, be legally entitled to sole guardianship of the children.[28]

When it came time for America to break its ties with England, women joined in that Revolutionary War effort as they had done in the French Revolution, but when it was all over they learned that women had helped men in America to achieve representation in their own government but they had not achieved representation for themselves. Abigail Adams, in 1789, pleaded with her husband, John Adams, who was away helping to write the Constitution of the United States. Hers is the famous, "Remember the Ladies," letter.

. . . I long to hear that you have declared an independency—and by the way, in the new Code of Laws which I suppose it will be necessary for you to make I desire you would Remember the Ladies, and be more generous and favourable to them . . . Do not put such unlimited powers into the hands of the Husbands. Remember all Men would be tyrants if they could.

If particular care and attention is not paid to the Ladies we are determined to foment a Rebellion, and will not hold ourselves bound by any Laws in which we have no voice or Representation.[29]

But the ladies were not mentioned in the Constitution. The American Revolution, the French Revolution, and the Industrial Revolution—three revolutions which changed the world, did not change the status of women. And women were not yet ready to work for representation. Instead they turned their attentions to the moral issue of slavery.

The Black slave woman was often used by her white male master for sexual purposes, which humiliated both the slave and the master's wife.

It is not the slave who alone suffers . . . but the wronged and dishonored wife and daughters who are deeply injured and weep in secret places.[30]

The slave woman was both a worker and a reproducer, and her children became the property of her master. Yet, "It mattered little to the slaveholder who did the actual impregnating since the 'increase' belonged to him by law . . . The female was often arbitrarily assigned a sexual partner or 'husband' and ordered to mate," and scolded or whipped if she produced no children for her master.[31] A good breeder promised a steady supply of slave children who were put to work when they were six or eight years old.

In-country breeding was crucial to the planter economy after the African slave trade was banned in 1807, and the slave woman's value increased in accordance with her ability to produce healthy offspring. Domestic production of slave babies for sale to other slave states became a small industry in the fertile upper South.

Field laborer, house servant and breeder woman were the principal economic roles of the female slave but she was also used by her white owner for his own sexual-recreational pleasure, a privilege that spilled over to his neighbors.[32]

Some white women began to speak out against the injustice they saw committed against the slaves. "Margaret Douglass, a Southern white woman who was convicted and jailed in Virginia for teaching black children to read, wrote from prison in 1853:

White mothers and daughters of the South have suffered under this custom for years; they have seen their dearest affections trampled upon, their hopes of domestic happiness destroyed . . . They know the facts, and their hearts bleed under its knowledge . . .[33]

Two sisters, Angelina and Sarah Grimke, with Angelina's husband, Theodore Weld, in 1839, compiled testimony about slavery into a publication, *American Slavery As It Is: Testimony to a Thousand Witnesses*, arousing moral indignation among religious groups against slavery.

The Grimke sisters had been born in a South Carolina slaveholding plantation. They abhorred slavery, appealed to Christian women in the South to speak out about it, traveled around in the north, speaking against slavery to groups, became Quakers, and were denounced by the church Congregationalist Ministers in Massachusetts as being unchristian because they spoke out in public.

The Grimkes and other women created the American Anti-Slavery Society, and Lucretia Mott as its leader, setting up the Underground Railroad, a system of getting slaves out of the south and into the north where they could be free. Thus began the abolition movement—the movement to abolish slavery, which took about thirty years to accomplish its goal.

The abolition movement and the women's rights efforts were linked together. Women lectured wherever they could on the moral corruption of slavery and on the morality of the inequality of women. Women speaking on any subject was a new event in history. As Page Smith writes in his *Daughters of the Promised Land*,

> Thousands of people of both sexes came, like visitors to a zoo, simply to *see* a woman stand on a platform and talk like a man about politics and social injustice and a better human order, and above all, about a new kind of relationship between men and women . . .[34]

> Something must be said about what was perhaps the most remarkable phenomenon of the antislavery—women's rights movement—the speaking of women to large and responsive audiences. Hearing a woman speak in public in the early years of the nineteenth century was at once a shocking and exciting novelty.

> How can the success of women lecturers in the first half of the nineteenth century be explained? It must be said first of all that women were speaking of the two most fundamental of all human relationships—those between the sexes and those between races . . .[35]

In 1840, an American delegation represented by Lucretia Mott and Elizabeth Cady Stanton, sailed across the Atlantic Ocean to the World-Wide Anti-Slavery Convention in London. Before the convention opened the women witnessed a debate among the men about whether or not to allow women the right to vote at the convention. After heated arguments, the men voted against the women. The women who had been instrumental in starting the abolition movement in America had to watch the convention from the balcony as the men decided on issues which women had brought to their attention.

When Lucretia Mott and Elizabeth Cady Stanton returned to America they discussed the powerlessness of women. Without the vote, women were hampered in their efforts to free the slaves. And even if slave women were freed, without being able to vote, they would still be limited. These two women with three others, all Quakers, decided to hold a women's rights convention for the social, civil, and religious rights of women. Referred to in history as the Seneca Falls Convention because it was held at Seneca Falls in New York, this gathering launched the Women's Rights movement in America in 1848. Its goals were to get property and voting rights for women.

As a platform, Elizabeth Cady Stanton paraphrased the Declaration of Independence of the United States. Instead of King George's tyranny over the colonists, the Seneca Falls Declaration related to the tyranny of men over women.

Partial text of the Seneca Falls Declaration of Sentiments and Resolutions, July 19, 1848

. . . We hold these truths to be self-evident; that all men and women are created equal; . . .

The history of mankind is a history of repeated injuries and usurpations on the part of man toward woman, having in direct object the establishment of an absolute tyranny over her. To prove this, let facts be submitted to a candid world.

He has never permitted her to exercise her inalienable right to the elective franchise (vote).

He has compelled her to submit to laws in the formation of which she had no voice.

He has withheld from her rights which are given to the most ignorant and degraded men—both natives and foreigners.

Having deprived her of this first right of a citizen, the elected franchise, thereby leaving her without representation in the halls of legislation, he has oppressed her on all sides.

He has made her, if married, in the eyes of the law, civilly dead.

He has taken from her all rights in property, even to the wages she earns . . .

He has monopolized nearly all the profitable employments and from those she is permitted to follow, she receives but a scanty remuneration. He closes against her all the avenues to wealth and distinction which he considers most honorable to himself. As a teacher of theology, medicine, or law, she is not known.

He has denied her the facilities for obtaining a thorough education, all colleges being closed against her.

He allows her in Church, as well as State, but a subordinate position, claiming Apostolic authority for her exclusion from the ministry, and, with some exceptions from any public participation in the affairs of the Church . . .

Now, in view of this entire disenfranchisement of one-half of the people of this country, in view of their social and religious degradation, in view of the unjust laws above mentioned, and because women do feel themselves aggrieved, oppressed, and fraudulently deprived of their most sacred rights, we insist that they have immediate admission to all the rights and privileges which belong to them as citizens of the United States . . .[36]

Over the next ten years other women's conventions were held, attended and supported by influential men as well as women, and derided and ridiculed by others, especially the press. The *New York Herald* commented,

What *do* the leaders of the women's rights convention want? They want to vote and hustle with the rowdies at the pools . . . They want to fill all other posts which men are ambitious to occupy, to be lawyers, doctors, captains of vessels, and generals in the field. How funny it would sound in the newspapers that Lucy Stone, pleading a cause, took suddenly ill in the pains of parturition and perhaps gave birth to a fine bouncing boy in court! . . . A similar event might happen on the floor of Congress, in a storm at sea or in the raging tempest of battle, and then what is to become of the woman legislator?[37]

Though the press ridiculed them, and "the church was largely hostile,"[38] women continued to work for their equality. They discussed other problems besides the suffrage problem, including property rights, divorce equity, and opportunity for education and employment. But it was Susan B. Anthony another Quaker, who recognized that unless women got the vote, whatever rights they had gained could be taken from them. She also believed that

Susan B. Anthony

in order for women to be heard in the legislatures they had to bring in petitions with thousands of signatures to the state capitols and to Congress.

After years of tramping the streets from door to door with her volunteers, literally over miles of snow in county after county, after years of insults and at least one failure before the New York legislature, Susan B. Anthony's work paid off when her co-worker, Elizabeth Cady Stanton, addressed the New York legislature in 1860. At that time women were given the right to own their own property, to receive their own wages, and to sue in a court of law. It was a landmark event for women, and they believed they could see the vote in their near future.

But the Civil War interrupted efforts to gain woman's suffrage. Men and women went into war, one way or another. The women became involved in nursing the wounded. Women like "mother Bicherdyke and Clara Barton, saw the possibility of saving many lives by following closely after battle lines."[39]

The issue of slavery was more immediately important than the issue of women's suffrage, and when the war was over the Fourteenth Amendment to the Constitution, ratified in July 1868, abolished slavery. Six months later the Fifteenth Amendment was introduced. It read, "The right of citizens of the United States to vote shall not be denied or abridged by the United States nor any state, on account of race, color, or previous servitude." The suffragists urged that the word "sex" be included in the proposed amendment. But it was feared by many that the women's vote would destroy the home, the church, and the government. It would be another fifty-two years.

In the meantime, more middle class women were being employed. The typewriter and the telephone had been invented and women proved to be capable employees who could be hired at lower wages than men. Women had been working in the expanding factory system in the United States. In 1850 they had accounted for twenty-four per cent of the employees in manufacturing.[40] These were women who needed to work in order to support themselves as single women, or who were supporting themselves and their children, or adding to the inadequate wages paid to their husbands.

The women's suffrage movement was brought back to life by two women. One was a young Quaker, Alice Paul, who had gone to study in England, had helped in England's women's suffrage ordeal in 1907, was jailed, went on a hunger strike, and was forcibly fed. When she returned home she completed her Ph.D. at the University of Pennsylvania and she also began working with the American suffragist. The other woman was Carrie Chapman Catt, who became the organizing head of the National American Woman Suffrage Association. Once again women rallied to the cause behind their leaders. They picketed the White House, were jailed, and denied legal counsel. And when it seemed that the suffragists were getting the public's attention, the country, once again, went to war. During World War I, the suffragists and other women responded to the country's needs by entering industry and public service jobs in large numbers. In World War I women substituted for men in jobs.

. . . in blast furnaces, in the manufacture of steel plate, high explosives, armaments, machine tools, agricultural implements, electrical apparatus, railway, automobile and airplane parts; they worked in brass and copper smelting and refining, in foundries, in oil refining, in the production of chemicals, fertilizers, and leather goods.[41]

When the war was over, suffragists argued once again that it was time that they be given the vote. As had happened in England, the legislators could not deny the great contribution women had made to the war effort as fully participating citizens of their country. On January 10, 1918, the Nineteenth Amendment, known as the Anthony Amendment, was proposed in the House of Representatives. It took another year and a half to pass the Senate and another fourteen months on its precarious route through the state legislatures for final ratification in 1920. It had taken seventy-two years, from the time of the Seneca Falls Convention in 1848, for women to get the vote.

The heroines in America were not limited to those women breaking down the barriers to getting the vote. There were also heroines in the struggle to break down educational barriers for females. One of these women was Emma Willard, a teacher who sat in on the examinations for boys at a nearby university so she could return to her classroom to teach the girls the subjects previously taught only to boys, like mathematics and science.

Almost all free education after elementary school was for boys. It wasn't until after the Civil War that free high schools had been opened for girls.[42] Any schooling for girls beyond elementary had to be paid for by their parents. Consequently only the rich girls were educated. But Emma Willard felt that education should not be a well-to-do privilege. Because she lived in a time when women were not considered ladylike if they gave speeches, she persuaded others to speak for her, providing them with

Emma Willard

274

her arguments for educating girls beyond the elementary years. In 1821, as a result of her work and her convincing arguments that girls could and should learn equally with boys, the Troy Female Seminary opened for girls. The money for her school was paid for by the town of Troy, New York, and from private individuals who "endowed" the school with money. It was the first "endowed" girls' school. The parents of the girls attending did not have to pay for their daughters' education.

One of the many heroines of the education of Black students, who had to overcome the double discrimination of being both Black and a woman, was Mary Bethune, a teacher from a poverty family who graduated from college and later raised money for her college for Black women by selling sweet potato pies she and her students baked each night. As her college grew she became a symbol of achievement for the Blacks, standing up to racial slurs with pride and calm, intelligent responses. She was the first of her race to become the head of a federal agency, the Division of Negro Affairs of the National Youth Administration.[43] The Bethune Cookman College now graduates about one thousand students each year.

As more schools opened for both boys and girls, more teachers were needed, teacher-training schools were opened, and women began to fill the demand both as teachers in the training schools, and as teachers in the schools themselves.

As teachers, even as late as 1922, women were restricted in their activities outside the classroom. The following contract, for seventy-five dollars a month outlines the do's and don'ts for a female teacher in Pennsylvania:[44]

Miss _____ agrees:

1. Not to get married. This contract becomes null and void immediately if the teacher marries.

2. Not to have company with men.

3. To be at home between the hours of 8:00 p.m. and 6:00 a.m. unless in attendance at a school function.

4. Not to loiter downtown in ice cream stores.

5. Not to leave town at any time without the permission of the Chairman of the Trustees.

6. Not to smoke cigarettes. The contract becomes null and void immediately if the teacher is found smoking.

7. Not to drink beer, wine or whiskey. This contract becomes null and void immediately if the teacher is found drinking beer, wine or whiskey.

8. Not to ride in a carriage or automobile with any man except her brother or father.

9. Not to dress in bright colors.

10. Not to dye her hair.

11. To wear at least two petticoats.

12. Not to wear dresses more than two inches above the ankles.

13. To keep the schoolroom clean:

    a. To sweep the classroom floor at least once daily.

    b. To scrub the classroom floor at least once weekly with soap and hot water.

    c. To clean the blackboard at least once daily.

    d. To start the fire 7:00 a.m. so that the room will be warm at 8:00 a.m. when the children arrive.

14. Not to wear face powder, mascara or to paint the lips.

Women also responded to the call of the church. Not that they could be ministers, but that they could be missionaries. Like other reform movements of the time, women were the forerunners. The missionary movement filled the need for women to do Christian work which as missionaries they could do on near equality with men.

Missionaries were sent out to the Christians of the Ottoman Empire—the Armenians, Greeks, Bulgarians, Syrians—starting in 1820 and the same year a few brave souls carried mission activity to the Turkish, Arab, and Persian Muslims . . . The hardships they endured are perhaps best suggested by the fact that in the early year of the missions, especially in India and in the Middle East, missionaries died faster than they could be replaced. For a time the life expectancy of a missionary was less than five years.[45]

"By 1910 there were 10,000 women divided almost equally between married and unmarried, in seventeen mission fields: three hundred thirty-two were doctors."[46]

Women in the missionary movement "wrote books, started printing presses and founded colleges, kindergartens, training schools, hospitals and orphanages. Yet as far as academic history is concerned it is as if all of this had not happened."[47] Women missionaries, traveling to convert the Indians to Christianity, were among the pioneers who moved West across the plains and over the mountains in their covered wagons.

Many pioneer women set out enthusiastically for this new adventure. But there were thousands who reluctantly left the comfort of their eastern homes, their friends and relatives and approached the journey with fear of the unknown.

Women pioneers, who were among the shock troops of the western migration, died on the trail along with men, from dysentery, fever, cholera, and Indian attacks. Childbirth was accommodated by only a one-day stop on the trail. In the urgency to cover fifteen to twenty miles a day, most of the wagons were driven from daybreak to sundown each day of the week. For women the migration was probably a more serious uprooting than it was for men.

Clinging to a few treasured heirlooms as reminders of a kinder life, they accompanied their husbands across the continent, suffering the most desperate physical hardships as well as a desolatiing sense of loneliness. More place-bound than men, more dependent on the company of other women, on the forms of settled social life, they grew old and died before their time, on the trail, in a sod hut or a rude cabin pierced by icy winds . . . When Eastern ladies were fainting at a coarse word or vulgar sight, their Western sisters fought off Indians, ran cattle, made homes and raised children in the wilderness.[48]

The hard life of a frontier's woman.

When the wagon train arrived at its destination, whether it was Nebraska, California, Oregon or any other western state, the work for both women and men was physically demanding, and women did almost every job that a man did. In the new West there was no lack of employment.

Though women missed the niceties of the East, and though with many women there was a great longing for Eastern friends and relatives, there were some letters sent back home that said the women would not return even if they could. The women wrote that they could make more money in the West than they could in the East, and they could also get free land by homesteading. Women were the shock-troops of the westward expansion, paving the way for others to follow.[49]

Pioneer women making a home on the frontier.

The frontiersmen were anxious to marry because a wife and children would lighten the work load on the land. Unlike the city-dweller, the frontiersman was as dependent on his wife as she was on him.[50]

The dangers of settling a new territory followed the pioneers across the country and also accompanied their settled life. They needed to protect themselves against the weather, against animals and sometimes against Indians who could burn them out and even carry off the women as captives. Actually the number of white women captured by Indians was small, but the nation was outraged whenever this happened.

Perhaps . . . it was in the area of higher education that the difference between Eastern and Western attitudes toward women were most dramatically revealed. Not only did Antioch admit women (and Negroes) soon after it was founded (the first woman graduated in 1841), but most Midwestern and Western state universities opened their doors as coeducational institutions.[51]

Though the Indian woman was considered an inferior, the expedition that opened up the West owes its success to a young Shoshone woman, Sacajawea. Captured from the Shoshone by the Hidatsa tribe, Sacajawea was sold to a Frenchman, a member of the Lewis and Clark Expedition which was to open up the West. Lewis and Clark were persuaded to take Sacajawea with them as a guide and interpreter to help them get through hostile Indian territory. On April 7, 1805 this sixteen-year-old girl strapped her new-born son into his cradleback where she carried him as she guided the expedition from Missouri to the Oregon coast. By her presence she smoothed the way for the expedition to negotiate with the various tribes and to reach Oregon six months later, crossing the Rocky Mountains with her baby on her back. She had "procured for the white men food and horses from the Indians and prevailed over her brother's determination to destroy the whites . . ."[52] One hundred years later a statue was dedicated to her in Portland, Oregon.

Many other Native American women and other minority women should have statues dedicated to them to commemorate their deeds. Unfortunately little is as yet recorded in history of minority women, including Hispanic women in their early years in America.

Mexican women have been in this country since about 1528 when the Spaniards came into what is now the southwest United States, bringing Mexican guides and servants. Years later, after they had established themselves in California, Texas, Arizona and New Mexico, the Mexicans were conquered in 1848 when much of their territory was claimed for the United States. Today both male and female Mexican Americans share a poor wage scale. Many women have taken leading roles in the labor movement to improve their condition for their families.[53]

The Chinese immigration to America was different than others because the women for the most part, stayed in China. The men came to earn money and intended to send for their wives or to return to China. Then in the 1880's all Chinese were excluded from coming to America by the immigration laws. The men who were here could stay, but their wives could not join them. This had a devastating effect on the morale of Chinese men as many could not afford to return to China and they died in the United States without an heir, an important traditional responsibility for them.

Early in the 1800's Chinese "coolie" labor was needed in the West. They worked in poor conditions and for very little money. But when more white men were available, and needing jobs, discrimination against Chinese, Mexicans, Filipinos, and other minorities was severe.

This is the same employment pattern that occurs for women. When labor was sorely needed in World War I and II, women moved into the labor market and worked for less than what men had made. It didn't matter, then, that middle class housewives worked in shipbuilding plants and steel mills. Women were praised for their contribution. As in the Colonial or frontier times, the previously defined clear-cut roles of what was woman's work and what was man's were changed by the demand for her labor. In the absence of definite roles, women were everything from mule drivers to hospital administrators. But after each war they were nudged to go back home, more so after the Second World War because for the first time in United States history women made up a sizable proportion of the labor market and the prospects that men might have to compete with women in the labor market frightened many men.

The government made a concerted effort with posters and other propaganda to get the women out of the labor market. The woman doing "man's" work was no longer a popular symbol. Women were told to go home and take care of their children, though many were single and had no children.

Nevertheless, women responded. In droves they left employment, married, moved out to the suburbs, purchased houses with their husbands, aided by low-interest veterans loans, had large families, and created a baby boom.

Twenty years later the babies grew up to become part of the college campuses Protest Movement, and the Civil Rights Movement in the South. Many of the Civil Rights workers were women who risked their lives going into the southern states to apprise Blacks of their rights and to help them get registered to vote.

Concerned about the lack of rights for Blacks, the women looked at their own lack of rights—their unequal treatment in employment, marriage, credit, and education, and they realized that most women were not permitted to develop their potential as fully as most men were able to do.

At about this time, Betty Friedan's book *The Feminine Mystique*, was published, (1963). It touched a nerve in suburban housewives when she wrote of the discontent women felt in leading unfulfilled lives dedicated to household and child care duties with little opportunity for expanding their vision beyond the endless filling and refilling of the dishwasher and washer-dryer.

Once again it was middle class women who picked up the struggle for equality and started the most recent women's movement. Many of these were women who had been involved either directly or indirectly in the Civil Rights Movement of the Sixties, or women on college campuses disturbed by national politics, or housewives who reacted to Betty Friedan's, *The Feminine Mystique*, who felt there should be something in addition to keeping house to make women's lives more worthwhile.

Women campaigned for reform and helped enact the Civil Rights Act, the Equal Pay Act of 1963, the 1964 Credit Law giving credit more equitable to women, Title IX of the

Education Omnibus Act of 1972, which prohibits sex discrimination in schools. And they reintroduced the Equal Rights Amendment which was initially introduced by Alice Paul in 1923. The proposal to amend the Constitution passed both the houses of Congress in 1972. It failed by three states to be ratified before June 30, 1982, and did not become law. It has been reintroduced in Congress but has not as yet come up for a vote. It reads:

Section 1. Equality of rights under the law shall not be denied or abridged by the United States or by any State on account of sex.

Secton 2. The Congress shall have the power to enforce, by appropriate legislation, the provisions of this article.

Section 3. This amendment shall take effect two years after the date of ratification.

Certainly the Equal Rights Amendment is controversial. Arguments, pro and con, are filled with emotion, as are all issues dealing with women. As a current issue this is discussed further in the last chapter.

Notable American Women

In the modern period the history of many more lives is recorded than in all the previous historical periods combined. It would be impossible to list all the notable women. The new *Notable American Women*, published in 1980 by Harvard University Press, summarizes the lives and accomplishments of 442 women. In comparison the list here is very short and limited by space to only those women who have worked for the betterment of humanity, and, of course, not all of those. In order not to burden the reader, the list is also limited to American women, though innumerable women in America and around the world have worked to improve the lot of humankind.

Anne Hutchinson was born in England in 1591 and came to Boston in 1634. Groups of people, mostly women, gathered in her home to hear her religious theories that every individual could establish communication with God. This outraged the community dominated by strict Calvinist Puritans. Her "speaking out" was threatening to the religious and governmental leaders. She was brought to trial for speaking on religion and she was banished from Boston. She left with her family for Rhode Island, traveling with 35 families who joined her. All of them went into what was at that time a dangerous wilderness. She and all in her household, except for a ten-year-old daughter were killed by Indians. The Dutch ransomed her daughter in 1651.

Molly Pitcher (1754-1832) joined her husband during the Revolutionary War at the Battle of Monmouth, June 27, 1778. She brought water to the men in the battalion, earning the name "Molly Pitcher" though her name was Molly Hays. When her husband collapsed, she took over the firing of the canon. In 1833 the government of Pennsylvania awarded her a pension of $40.00 a year.

Emma Willard (1787-1870), concerned that girls were not educated equally with boys, she introduced subjects into their curriculum that it had been thought unwise to teach females, such as science and mathematics. She opened a school for secondary education for girls, the first such school, in Troy, New York. She also helped establish a school for training women teachers in Greece in 1830. She was the first to establish teacher-training schools for men. She traveled and lectured, promoting higher education for women and wrote textbooks which were widely distributed and translated. In 1905 she was elected to the Hall of Fame for Great Americans at New York University.

Sojourner Truth (c. 1790-1882) was a Black slave in New York for 40 years. She was sold many times and saw her sisters, brothers and children sold. After slavery was outlawed in New York she was freed in 1827. In 1843 she decided she was going to travel and to preach. Though her real name was Bell, she called herself Sojourner because she traveled, and Truth because she would tell the truth.

She spoke out about the inhumanity of slavery, and she operated an underground railroad station at Battle Creek, Michigan, and was a nurse during the Civil War. Her famous speech occurred in Akron, Ohio in 1851 at a Women's Rights Convention. When the men in the audience had protested that men were superior because Christ was a man, and that Eve, the first mother, had sinned, Sojourner slowly rose and said,

> That man over there says women need to be helped into carriages and lifted over ditches, and to have the best place everywhere. Nobody ever helps me into carriages or over puddles, or gives me the best place—and ain't I a woman?

> Look at me. Look at my arm! I have ploughed and planted and gathered into barns, and no man could head me—and ain't I a woman? I could work as much and eat as much as a man—when I could get it—and bear the lash as well! And ain't I a woman? I have born thirteen children and seen most of 'em sold into slavery, and when I cried out with my mother's grief, none but Jesus heard me—and ain't I a woman?

> Then that little man in black there, he say women can't have as much rights as men, 'cause Christ warn't a woman. Where did your Christ come from? . . . From God and a woman. Man had nothing to do with him. If the first woman God ever made was strong enough to turn the world upside down, all alone, these women here ought to be able to turn it back and get it right side up again, and now they are asking to do it and the men better let 'em.

Dorothea Dix (1802-1887) began teaching school at age 14 and started teaching Sunday School in a prison. She was disturbed by the prison conditions. She began investigating other institutions, insane asylums, prisons, poorhouses. She wrote about the terrible conditions and as a result improvements were made and she was encouraged to visit asylums in every state.

She was instrumental in getting humane treatment for the mentally ill and for getting at least 30 asylums started. Her work took her to Canada, England, and on to the European continent. During the Civil War she was a superintendent of nurses.

Angelina and Sara Grimke (Sara 1792-1827; Angelina 1805-1879) were sisters raised on a southern plantation who hated slavery. "When Sara Grimke had tried to teach her slave maid to read, she did so behind a locked bedroom door. She was soon discovered and the lessons stopped."[55]

They traveled and lectured against slavery, becoming leaders in the abolition movement. They spoke in churches, in lecture halls, and in private homes, eventually denounced by the ministers for such activity. In 1836 Angelina wrote, "An Appeal to the Christian Women of the South," urging them to speak out on behalf of the slave. When they inherited slaves as part of their estate, they immediately freed them.

Lucretia Mott (1793-1880), a Quaker and founder of the Female Anti-Slavery Society. With Elizabeth Cady Stanton she founded the Women's Rights Convention in Seneca Falls in 1848, some years after they had been refused voting rights at the World Anti-Slavery Convention in London.

Margaret Fuller (1810-1850) was a very well-educated feminist who conversed with equality with the most learned men of the period in Massachusetts and in Europe. She wrote literary criticism for the *Tribune* and became known as one of the best literary critics in America. In 1845 she wrote *Woman in the Nineteenth Century*, arguing for the full development of women.

Harriet Beecher Stowe (1811-1896) was the daughter of a preacher and a teacher who wrote numerous stories and articles. Her most famous was *Uncle Tom's Cabin*, a story attacking slavery, published in book form in 1852. It was printed in many editions and in many languages and became the most controversial document of the abolitionist movement, awakening a social conscience to the moral issue of slavery. When President Lincoln met her he said "So this is the little lady who started the Civil War."

Clara Barton (1821-1912) founded the American Red Cross. In the beginning of the Civil War she became a volunteer nurse and was in the midst of several battles. President Lincoln put her in charge of searching for missing men.

During the Franco-Prussian War, 1870, she set up military hospitals and was given the Iron Cross of Merit from Germany. She was the first president of the American Red Cross, 1881, and in 1888 was made superintendent of Women's Reformatory Prison at Sherborn, Massachusetts. At her suggestion the Red Cross would relieve distress, not only in war, but in other calamities. With the Red Cross she brought relief to flood victims in Pennsylvania, famine sufferers in Russia, victims in Armenian massacres, in Turkey.

Lucy Stone (1818-1893) an abolitionist who spoke out against taxation of women without representation. She graduated from college prepared to speak out for the oppressed. She gave regular lectures against slavery and for women's rights. With Susan B. Anthony and Elizabeth Cady Stanton, she worked tirelessly for women's vote at the same time that she carried out the household duties of a wife.

Susan B. Anthony (1820-1906) was a Quaker abolitionist and suffragist and one of the first to recognize that signatures on a petition were necessary in order to get the men in government to hear the grievances of women. The petitions she and her "captains" collected led to the New York legislature in 1854 giving women the right to their own property. When Susan Anthony tried to vote she was imprisoned. However, after 72 years of struggle, the 19th Amendment, in 1920, gave women the right to vote, It is called the Anthony Amendment.

Elizabeth Cady Stanton (1815-1902) was as well educated as a girl could be in those days; she attended Emma Willard's school in Troy. She was a Quaker abolitionist and suffragist and as a delegate to the World Anti-Slavery Convention in London, in 1840 was banished to the galleries because women couldn't vote. Years later she and Lucretia Mott initiated the Women's Rights Convention in Seneca Falls, New York. She paraphrased the United States Declaration of Independence to include women, and to point out the injustices to women, endeavoring to secure equal rights to a free education, equal pay for equal work, freedom to enter all fields of endeavor, the right to own property, and be guardians of their own children, the right to speak out, and the right to vote. She was married to an abolitionist and the mother of many children. She worked for fifty years to help women achieve the vote and other equal benefits.

Harriet Tubman (c. 1821-1913) worked in the fields as a Black slave and escaped to the North. She spent her life after that helping other slaves escape, often putting her own life in danger. "During a period of ten years she made nineteen journeys into slave territory."[56] Referred to as "Moses," she is credited with helping 300 slaves to freedom. The Quakers helped her get back into the South to collect slaves and encourage them to leave. Owners of slaves offered a reward of $40,000 for her capture, a huge sum in those days. But she evaded her pursuers and never lost a slave she was bringing North.

She could neither read nor write, but she spoke at many anti-slavery meetings. During the Civil War she worked as a cook, a nurse, and a spy for the North behind the southern lines. Her work did not end when the Blacks were freed. She established a home in Auburn, New York, for needy Black freedmen and women. After she died, the citizens erected a monument to her and maintained the home she had established as the Harriet Tubman Home for needy Blacks.

Elizabeth Blackwell (1821-1910) was the first woman doctor in the United States. She had applied and was denied admittance to 29 medical schools. Geneva College in New York accepted her "as a lark," and though she suffered ridicule, she graduated at the head of her class. But once graduated, no private patients came to her and she was not permitted to work in the city hospitals. Other doctors shunned her. A woman doctor was considered a monstrosity.

After a while she opened a small office in the slums and later raised funds to rent a house for a forty-bed hospital. On May 12, 1857, the New York Infirmary, with an all-woman staff under her direction, opened. She initiated a medical school for training women doctors in 1868 and changed the teaching of medicine from strictly a lecture course to actual work with patients. In the Civil War the hospital trained nurses for the Union Army, which gained sympathy for their hospital. She later went to England and helped to establish the London School of Medicine for Women where she was a professor for 32 years.

"Mother" Mary Jones (1830-1920) became a full-time labor organizer at the age of 60. She organized "from the coal towns of West Virginia and Pennsylvania all the way west to the copper mines of Colorado."[57] She campaigned against child labor in the South. Many governors called on the state militia when she came to town, though her only weapons were a hat pin and an umbrella. When asked is she had a permit to speak on the streets she said she had, given to her by Patrick Henry, Thomas Jefferson, and John Addams. When she was ninety-three she worked with the West Virginia coal miners to help them gain a living wage. She was called "Mother Jones," and

her words she lived by "pray for the dead, but fight like hell for the living," are remembered today among union organizers.

Ida Wells (c1850?-1910) was the daughter of a slave who became a journalist, campaigning against lynching. In partnership she owned the newspaper, *Memphis Free Speech*, and wrote about racial discrimination in the South. When, in 1892, she attacked the white community of Memphis for the lynching of three Black men, her newspaper was destroyed and her life was threatened. Because it was estimated that between 1865 and 1919 over 3300 Black men had been lynched, Ida Well's campaign helped to make Americans aware of this crime and attempt to reduce it.

In 1895 she wrote *A Red Record*, "the first authentic account of lynching ever compiled. It gave full details of three years of lynching in the United States. To ensure its authenticity, Ida took all her data from white sources . . . In an era when Blacks and even sympathetic whites were reluctant to speak out against this injustice, one woman had the courage to stir the country's conscience.[58]

Mary McLeod Bethune (1875-1955) the first free Black person born in her family. She became an educator, creating from almost nothing the Bethune-Cookman College, and establishing the National Council for Negro Women. She believed the worth of a race was in the character of its womanhood.

She was the first Black woman in this country to hold a federal office, appointed by President Franklin Roosevelt as Director of the Division of Negro Affairs of the National Youth Administration. She wrote:

> For I am my mother's daughter and the drums of Africa still beat in my heart. They will not let me rest while there is a single Negro boy or girl without a chance to prove his worth.

Carrie Chapman Catt (1859-1947) graduated from Iowa State College in 1880 and studied law, and then became principal of a school and later was the first woman superintendent of her school district. She was president of the International Woman Suffrage Alliance and the National American Woman Suffrage Association. She lectured on women's suffrage, and in 1919 she founded the National League of Women Voters. She was especially capable of organizational work and very important in getting the 19th Amendment passed, stressing that votes for women would be votes for social welfare and reform.

Jane Addams (1860-1935). A major fighter for the rights of poor people, she founded Hull House in Chicago in 1889 where middle and upper class women settled to work closely with the poor. This started what became known as the Settlement Movement. Numerous Settlement Houses were created in the cities' slums where young, educated women moved in order to help slum residents. Jane Addams believed that the best place for saving a city was in its slums. Women, especially college women, moved into the Settlement Houses, in the midst of the slums with the express purpose of helping women and children. Though she is best known for her establishment of Hull House, Jane Addams also worked with the Women's International League for Peace and Freedom and the National Council for Social Work.

Catherine Booth, with her husband, William, founded the Salvation Army in 1895. The Booths were concerned with helping the poor in the slums by providing the necessities of life—food, clothing, and shelter. While the Salvation Army has a religious basis, it has maintained that helping people is more important to their organization than preaching.

Margaret Sanger (1883-1966) as a nurse, worked in the New York slums and was distressed at the number of women who were either overburdened with too-large families which were not adequately fed, or women who were mutilated by clumsy and unsanitary abortions they had sought, not wanting to bring more infants into poverty. Margaret Sanger worked to help women control pregnancy, distributing contraceptive information to poor women. She was arrested for doing so and fled to England and France where she learned more about birth control methods. She wrote that, "A woman's body belongs to herself," and believed no other gains women made would amount to anything if they could not plan their families.

She returned from Europe, the government dropped their case against her, she opened a birth control clinic in Brooklyn in 1916, was arrested and jailed. She was released; the law which forbid the dissemination of birth control information was changed, and she opened clinics in spite of persistent Catholic Church opposition.

By the late 1930's there were over 300 of them (Birth Control Clinics) in the United States and a survey made in 1940 showed that over nine tenths of upper-middle-class protestant couples and nearly as many Catholic ones were making at least some efforts to regulate their own parenthood.[59]

Eleanor Roosevelt, (1884-1962) wife of President Franklin Roosevelt, worked tirelessly as Ambassador to the United Nations. She traveled all around the world in her work to help the poor and to bring their condition to the attention of the United Nations. She was the victim of many cruel jokes, as women have been when they attempt to change either their own status or the status of the poor or minorities. Her primary goals were in working for equality and peace.

Alice Paul (1885-1976). A Quaker and a graduate of Swarthmore College, she studied in London, returned to get her Ph.D., helped working women organize into trade unions, organized a suffrage march of 5000 women in Washington to coincide with President Wilson's inaugural procession. After the 19th Amendment was passed, the Woman's Party, under her leadership, introduced the Equal Rights Amendment to Congress in 1923.

Chapter 6

LINKING THE PAST
WITH THE PRESENT

Studying the past is valuable for more than just the information it provided; it can also provide insight into understanding the present. Currently in the United States there are several issues centering around male/female relationships such as abortion, the Equal Rights Amendment, comparable worth in the labor market and violence against women. It may be that at least some of these issues are similar to problems in the past and can be understood better if they are looked at from the perspective of history.

There seem to be several major trends in male/female relationships which appear periodically. Some of these may be presently apparent and some may not. One of these historical trends is that many activities developed by women were taken over by men. In prehistory it was women who were the first cultivators of the land, the first animal breeders, pottery makers, and house builders—activities which men took over and controlled. In the Industrial Revolution it was women's work, that is, textile manufacture, beer-making, and food preservation, which men first mechanized in their factories.

Another trend is women's involvement in major social changes which leaves women at the end of their experience with no place in the administration of the organization which they helped to create. Some examples of this are in early Christianity, in the development of minor Protestant religions, in the French Revolution, in colonization of America. In these efforts, women at the outset worked equally with men and participated fully in decisions, organization, and action. As long as the experience was new, and roles between men and women had not yet been clearly defined, both sexes worked and shared equally. This was true also when a country was in an emergency, as in war, when the roles were blurred and women defended Medieval castles, or later became ambulance drivers or welders. But when the wars came to an end, or when social movements progressed from the innovation of the idea to the acceptance by society in general, women found themselves with no important place in the structure of the institution.

Some would say that the reason women are in at the beginning, and out when the desired goal has been reached, is because women are the child-bearers and need to be at home. Yet when they have been involved in major social changes, women have also raised families and maintained homes. Those roles have not kept women from being called to the forefront when they have been needed, but the roles have been used as an excuse to keep them from sharing in the rewards of the efforts.

As the lessons of history have shown, it is probably more likely that women have been left out of the institutions which they helped create because as they have been consciously taught to defer to men, females were not apt to cause a disturbance when men took over. As long as the main thrust of a girl's life had been to get married, her survival had depended on the approval of men. As a multitude of historical records reveals, a girl was consistently conditioned to believe that unless she were passive and pleasing to men, she would not attract a future husband.

Another trend in history is that whenever there were more choices open to women in a society, women were blamed for the ills of society. Apparently the people in power became fearful of the choices of the less powerful, and they tended to restrict and punish subservients. For instance, Aristotle in Ancient Athens said that the reason Sparta fell was because it gave too much freedom to women, justifying the continued seclusion of women in Athens. When Rome began to crumble, women were blamed for the Fall of Rome, because it was said they had become too free. In the Renaissance, when women were beginning to educate themselves, the massive witch-hunts began. Today it is said that because of "women's lib.," the divorce rate, and female employment, women are destroying the family. Women who seek independence do so at risk of punishment. As Margaret Mead has said, society rewards conformity and punishes those who step out of line. Joan of Arc, who wore men's clothing into battle and insisted on following the direction of the voices she heard in her attempts to save France, was burned at the stake as a witch. The witch-hunts, violence directed mainly against women who were somewhat independent or different, tended to keep all women under control.

There were trends in education in which slaves and females were purposefully not educated because it was believed they might get ideas their superiors did not want them to have. Only a truly democratic society risks educating all its citizens equally.

In war-like countries population trends appear, in for instance, Ancient Assyria and Rome, and again during World War II in Italy and Nazi Germany when soldiers were needed, mothers were honored for having many children, and abortion became a crime against the country. Under Hitler, women who had miscarried had to prove that they had not tried to abort.

Historically, in the area of employment, poor and lower class women have always had to work regardless of how often it is said that women's place is in the home. Women have had the added job of raising children and managing a household and they have always also earned less money than men on the job and were the first to be fired in a production slow-down.

The reader is challenged to try to link these trends, and an understanding of what he or she has learned from this history book, to the following social issues: abortion, education, employment, the Equal Rights Amendment, exclusion of women, violence against women, the changing family, and women in the ministry.

Abortion

To invalidate the 1973 Supreme Court decision that made abortion a constitutional right, anti-abortionists are attempting to introduce an Amendment to the United States Constitution which could make abortion, except possibly for rape or incest, a crime related to murder. The anti-abortionists claim that life begins at conception and that unborn life has rights.

The pro-choice groups claim that children born to parents who don't want them or can't afford to raise them don't have a good life before them. They also believe that a woman should have the right to control her own body, and that denied legal abortion, women will endanger their lives having abortions anyway in unsanitary conditions with unskilled technicians.

Education

Females and minorities are still under-represented in textbooks. As mentioned in the Introduction to this book, among 12 popular United States History textbooks, in 1974 there was one page about women to 700 pages about men. By 1979 this had improved to only 14 pages about women, to men's 700 pages. These are books which students are required to read in required classes.

Minorities are seldom shown in textbooks though they represent a large percentage of the school population in this country. The director of the Council on Interracial Books for Children has stated that "public schools have no right to purchase with public funds and to require children to read texts which in any way belittle the worth of females or minorities, or stereotype them."[1]

Employment

Ever since World War II the number of women in employment has increased. Women make up 45 per cent of the work force and there are now more women working outside the home than women working inside the home.[2] It is no longer generally believed that a man's masculinity is diminished if his wife works. She does so to buy the refrigerator, or help him buy his boat, or to supplement a salary which is inadequate for the family's subsistence. As one wage analyst reported, "if the ratio of women in the labor force weren't so high—we simply couldn't maintain the two trillion dollar gross national product the country enjoys." The country depends on women's employment, and most women who work do so because it keeps them alive, not because they are earning money for frills.

Yet the statistics for employment point out that in spite of affirmative action, women earn 57 cents for every dollar earned by men. California Labor Commissioner said

"that the pay gap between men and women has widened, rather than narrowed, in the 17 years since federal equal pay laws were enacted. Women's wages average 57 per cent of men's now, compared with 63 per cent then."[3]

When Mary Wolfe was in the Women's Bureau of the United States department of Labor she was quoted:

Young women still believe that they can find some man to marry who will take them out of the work force. But the majority of women who work are doing so to put food on the table. We have to disabuse ourselves of the Cinderella myth. When I talk to young women I tell them Prince Charming doesn't come riding a white horse anymore; he comes with a Honda and he needs help with the payments.

Whenever a woman moves into a male construction job there is a lot of publicity, yet the Department of Labor reported that women represented only 2 per cent of all registered craft apprentices, the equivalent of the earlier guilds. It is only in recent years that women have been admitted to apprenticeship jobs. Yet in San Francisco, for instance, when a plumber's beginning salary is about $33,000 year, and a nurse's top-of-the-scale salary is about $22,000, it is obvious why women desire entry into craft aprenticeships rather than stereotyped female jobs.

The United States Census study reported that even when girls are educated equally, college women earned a median salary of $12,600, for a full year of employment, while the same college degree earned $20,600 for men. The report concluded that "discrimination in hiring, promotions, hours of work and pay cannot be ruled out as contributing to the difference in pay."[4]

Minority women are discriminated against even further. For full time work, for every dollar the white male earns, the black man earns 69 cents; the white woman 57 cents; and the black woman 48 cents.[5]

Women are clustered in lower paying jobs though their responsibilities, training, and skills may exceed men's. A male custodian or shipping clerk invariably earns more than a secretary. Yet the wage scales for typical male work is higher than the wage scales for typical female work. Unions and women's groups for the past ten years have been attempting to work out a fair and equitable job description system so that wages will be based on what is becoming known as "comparable worth." Under the concept of comparable worth, nurses in Denver filed suit because they were being paid less than sign painters. They argued that their worth was at least equal.

"If traditionally female jobs continue to be viewed as less valuable, then 80 per cent of all women must continue to be discriminated in the work place."[6] The comparable worth issue is a major point in wage discussions. Also, women's groups will be ready to speak out against eliminating affirmative action and lowering the minimum wage, which they believe will hurt women and minorities the most.

The Equal Rights Amendment

As a *Reader's Digest* article stated, "ERA is not just a zany 'women's lib.' idea. First introduced in Congress in 1923 it's been around for 54 years."[7]

Though the ERA was defeated, many states have enacted their own Equal Rights Amendments. Those people who were against the ERA say that an amendment is not the way to insure equality, yet many states have discriminatory laws, while others do not. The ERA would give all women in the United States equal protection.

In Georgia a couple's home belongs only to the husband even if the wife earns wages, supports her spouse, and pays for the place they live. The husband can do anything he wishes with the property without consulting his wife, and she has no legal recourse . . . In Florida, widows who inherit property they co-owned must pay an inheritance tax, while widowers do not.[8]

Equal ownership of property by husband and wife accumulated during a marriage is a legal right in only eight states. Wisconsin is one of these states, passing the Marital Property Act becoming effective January, 1986.

The ERA has been reintroduced in Congress though it is uncertain when it will come up for a vote. Opponents of the ERA were concerned that if it passed women would be drafted into the armed services. The Supreme Court, however, made that a mute question when it voted that women could not be drafted. Many women feel that if men have to be drafted that it is only fair that women should be too. After all, they say, it is their country too.

As history has shown, women have not faulted when their country has needed them.

Exclusion of Women

Women do not have equal access to valuable business and professional contacts which are made in all-male clubs. The federal government, recognizing this inequality, has refused to grant income tax deductions for expense account items paid to discriminatory organizations. President Carter's attorney general of the United States, Griffith Bell, resigned from his all-white club in the South before taking office, saying that the attorney general's office should be a symbol of equality. Ronald Reagan's first attorney general, William French Smith, said he sees no reason why he should resign from the all-male Bohemian Club, or the all-male California Club which has been picketed by civil rights and women's groups.

Women claim that men's clubs help to maintain the "old boy network" which funnels men into important jobs as they become available. The exclusion of women limits their opportunities for advancement.

Violence Against Women

Each day the newspaper, it seems, reports one or more rapes of women. No female is immune from attack, rich or poor, young or old, ugly or beautiful, in good physical condition or blind or crippled. True, more rapes are being reported than were reported before, especially as rape laws are passed aimed at preventing the humiliation of the victims. Even though many rapes still go unreported, the statistics rise.

The statistics on wife-beating are also rising. "At least 1.8 million women are known to suffer from wife-beating each year—a statistic stunning in itself but representing only the *reported* physical attacks."[9]

Wife-beating, which occurs in all social classes. may be more under-reported among the upper class where wives risk their lives not wanting to hurt their husbands' careers. Some government money is being spent on battered wives shelters set up by women in the community to receive battered women and their children where their whereabouts remain unknown to their husbands. Counseling and other services are provided for wives to help them determine the future course of their lives.

Some men have claimed that they have been beaten by their wives, and some claim that they have been raped. Not denying that that may be so, the incidence of men who have been beaten or raped by women is infinitesimal compared to these acts against women.

Violence against women is also visible photographically. Time Magazine reported, Despite the rise of feminism—or perhaps because of it—images of women being physically abused are becoming increasingly common. In record album photos, fashion and men's magazine layouts, and even a few department store windows and billboards, women are shown bound, gagged, beaten, whipped, chained or as victims of murder or gang rape. 'Men are feeling guilty or sexually threatened,' says Cambridge, Massachusetts teacher, Jean Kilbourne, who lectures on the influence of the communications industry. 'The image of the abused woman is a logical extension of putting the uppity woman in her place.' Many psychiatrists agree that the trend reflects the emotional problems of males. Says Manhattan psychoanalyst, Lawrence Hatterer, 'Men's angry and hostile and impotent feelings are surfacing in all these ways because men don't know where to go with these feelings . . .'[10]

In movies too, there is "a disturbing major trend portraying violence against women," as movie critics Roger Ebert and Gene Siskel reported on P.B.C. They see a trend where women who are scantily dressed and independent are decapitated or stabbed all over their bodies. In these movies the camera zooms in on the destruction of the females in such a way that the audience becomes identified with the killer. The audience, according to these two critics, rejoices "in these sadistic acts against helpless females . . . systematically demeaning half the human race."

Ebert and Siskel believe that these movies are a response to the women's movement. Men are saying "get back." "They can't deal with the women's movement so they destroy women. As soon as the woman in the film begins to act independent you know she's going to get killed . . . it's behavior that if a man were doing it would be okay. The film is a coalesced dream. The filmmakers have hit on men's anger at women."

The Home and the Family

The "typical" family evolved with the Industrial Revolution and the growth of the middle class. The typical family was composed of a wage-earning husband, a wife who stayed home, and their children. The poor families included both parents who worked and their children who also worked, beginning when they were five or six years old.

The family of today, often referred to as the "nuclear," "traditional," or "typical" family, is the middle class family. But the family with a father who is a wage earner, a wife who stays home, and their children, no longer is typical. It no longer represents the majority of families. The Bureau of Labor Statistics reported, "The old fashioned 'typical American family' with a husband breadwinner, a homemaker wife, and children now makes up only seven per cent of the nation's families."[11]

The family combination that outnumbered the rest was a childless couple with both husband and wife working. Also, the number of families headed by women was the fastest growing lifestyle in the 1970's, according to the Census Bureau and the latest figures available. From 1970 to 1979 this classification grew by 51 per cent. These families headed by women have the least income.[12]

Families at the poverty level are most often those headed by women or minorities, the National Advisory

Council on Economic Opportunity reports. "Almost one female-headed family in 3 is poor, about one in 18 families headed by a man is poor. The Council speaks of "feminization of poverty" and predicts that "the poverty population will be composed solely of women and their children by about the year 2000."[13]

Based on a survey of the Census Bureau taken March 1979, "the proportion of family households maintained by a woman with no husband in the home is 8 per cent for whites, 16 per cent for Hispanics, and 29 per cent for Blacks."

The so-called typical, nuclear family or traditional family was the predominant family type from about 1750 to about 1960, or for only about 200 years of the 5000 years of history. As all institutions, in order to survive, must change as society changes, the institution of the family is changing, and it is surviving. Though there are many divorces today, there are more marriages than divorces.

The age at which young people marry is later than it was 20 years ago, and couples are postponing having children until they have been married several years, or they are deciding not to have children. The family is not the same as it was at the beginning of the Industrial Revolution, but then neither is any other surviving institution.

Women and Physical Endurance

During the prehistoric period women were said to have the same strength as men. Because they did the heavy work their bodies developed to meet that challenge. As times changed and upper and lower class societies developed it was not considered "ladylike" to do hard work. Upper and middle class women's bodies were corseted, they wore high heels and long dresses, their feet were even bound, as in China.

Only with the most recent women's movement since the 1960's have women related their political freedom with freedom of bodily movement and therefore freedom of their clothing. Their athletic performances have won them a distinguished place in the Olympics and their

Tennis costume (1888).

endurance and skill is nearly equivalent to men. The gap between the times for swimming and running competitions of men and women is narrowing, with women now running the mile in four minutes sixteen seconds. Not too long ago the world exclaimed when a man ran the mile in four minutes.

Women are only recently gaining access to training activities that men have always enjoyed. As James Peterson, the former United States Military Academy fitness director said, "Equality comes from equal expectations and treatment. A lot of the biological differences between the sexes may be in our minds."

Women in the Ministry

The struggle to permit more women to the upper hierarchy of religion, to become priests and ministers, will no doubt continue. And so will the hostility to the idea.

Some of the concerns about the woman preacher go back to the idea that menstruating women are polluters. The fear is that women will be menstruating when they are preaching. And of course a great deal of discrimination is related to the Biblical admonition that forbids women to speak in church.

In 1984 the Church of England's general synod voted to draft legislation to allow women to become priests. If the motion is approved by the diocese and British Parliament, women may be ordained by about 1990.

In the meantime there are efforts to revise the sexist language of the Bible, not to change the content but to refer to both sexes, and to females when possible. Sister Ann Patrick Ware, Associate Director, Commission on Faith and Order of the National Council of Church of Christ wrote

> The scriptures are unredeemably sexist. Even though here and there women may appear in a favorable light, the overwhelming stance of writers toward women is that they are inferior to men, weak, needing protection and foolish. To say this portrayal reflects the cultural condition of the age in which the books were written in no way solves the problem.[15]

There are those who would have Catholic nuns, for instance, put their habits back on and be quiet. But the historical fact is that women were ordained up to the fifth century, and the abbesses of Las Huelgas served as bishops even up to 1874.

In Conclusion

Women's status and achievements are relative to those of men. If women at one time had a higher status than men, their status has not been even equal to men in the past 5000 years. In spite of the lack of equal education and other opportunities, women's achievements have been remarkable. However a recent report, "Women: A World Survey," sponsored by the Carnegie, Ford, and Rockefeller foundations, states, "There is no major field of activity and no country where women have attained equality with men."

The United Nations Decade for Women Conference was held in Nairobi, Africa, 1985. Some improvements in women's conditions over the past decade were noted, especially in the area of equal pay. Ninety countries now have equal pay laws compared to only twenty-eight countries in 1978. But the United Nations statistics revealed that women do two-thirds of the work of the world, yet their wages bring them only one-tenth of the income. And women own only about one hundredth of the world's property. Women's struggle for equality is hampered by traditions in the culture, and by traditions in religion.

This book nevertheless ends with the same kind of optimism women have demonstrated through history. Just think what women will be able to accomplish for future generations when they have equal opportunities with men to make decisions in society's social institutions—religion, industry, education, and government!

Rep. Shirley Chisolm.
Nominated for President
of the United States.

NOTES

INTRODUCTION

1. Jensen, Marj. "Council Challenges Racist/Sexist Textbooks," *National NOW Times,* January, 1980, p. i.
2. Davis, Elizabeth Gould, *The First Sex,* Maryland: Penguin Books, Inc., 1973.

CHAPTER I

PREHISTORIC PEOPLES AND TODAY'S HUNTERS AND GATHERERS

1. Brain, Robert, *The Last Primitive Peoples,* New York: Crown Publishers, Inc., 1976, p. 45.
2. Boulding, Elise, *The Underside of History, a View of Women Through Time,* Colorado: Westview Press, 1976, pp. 119-31; Darlington, C.D., *The Evolution of Man and Society,* New York: Simon and Schuster, 1969, p. 89.
3. Benedict, Ruth, *Patterns of Culture,* New York: New American Library, 1934, p. 32.
4. Lee, Richard B., and Devore, Irwen, eds. *Man the Hunter,* Chicago: Aldine Publishing Company, 1968, . 5.
5. Boulding, *op. cit.,* p. 84.
6. Muller-Lyer, F., *History of Social Development,* New York, 1921, pp. 24-27.
7. Neumann, Erich, *The Great Mother,* tr. R. Manheim, New York: Princeton University Press, 1955, pp. 94-5.
8. Lee and Devore, *op. cit.,* p. 7.
9. Evans-Pritchard, Sir Edward, Supervisory Editor of the Series, 20 vols., *Peoples of theEarth,* Verona: The Danbury Press, 1973, Vol. 6, p. 35.
10. Evans-Pritchard, *op. cit.,* Vol. 2, p. 104.
11. *Ibid.,* Vol. 9, p. 113.
12. *Ibid., Vol. 1, p. 104.*
13. *Evans-Pritchard, op. cit.,* Vol. I, p. 84.
14. Evans-Pritchard, *op. cit.,* Vol. 6, p. 26.
15. Durant, Will, *The Story of Civilization,* 10 vols. New York: Simon and Schuster, 1954-1967, Vol. I, p. 49.

16. Hoebel, E. Adamson, *Man in the Primitive World*, New York: McGraw-Hill, 1949, p. 233.
17. Durant, *op. cit.*, I, pp. 30-1.
18. Lee and Devore, *op. cit.*, p. 7.
19. Muller-Lyer, F., *The Family*, New York, 1931, p. 232.
20. Devore, Irven, quoted in *Christian Science Monitor*, June 3, 1969.
21. Hoebel, *op. cit.*, p. 105.
22. Lee and Devore, *op. cit.*, p. 33.
23. Reed, Evelyn, *Woman's Evolution*, New York: Pathfinder Press, 1975, p. 153.
24. Durant, *op. cit.*, I, p. 33.
25. Mead, Margaret, *Male and Female*, New York: New American Library, 1949.
26. "Goodbye to the Stone Age.", *National Geographic*, Vol. 147, No. 2, February, 1975, p. 278.
27. Hays, H.R., *In the Beginnings, Early Man and His Gods*, New York: G.P. Putnam's Sons, 1963, p. 321.
28. Evans-Pritchard, *op. cit.*, Vol. 9, p. 113.
29. Webster, Hutton, *Primitive Secret Societies*, New York: Macmillen Publishing Co., Inc., 1908, p. 74.
30. Langdon, Davies, John, *A Short History of Women*, London: Watts & Co., 1928, pp. 63-4.
31. Mead, *op. cit.*, p. 58.
32. Evans-Pritchard, *op. cit.*, Vol. 6, p. 49.
33. *Ibid.*, Vol. 9, p. 58.
34. Hays, *op. cit.*, p. 292.
35. Reed, *op. cit.*, p. 23.
36. Evans-Pritchard, *op. cit.*, Vol. I, p. 84.
38. Reed, *op. cit.*, pp. 83-4.
39. Malinowski, Bronislaw, *The Sexual Life of Savages*, New York: Harcourt, Brace and World, Inc., 1929, p. 75.
40. Briffault, Robert, *The Mothers: The Matriarchal Theory of Social Origins*, (abridged ed. in 1 vol.), New York: Macmillan Publishing Col, Incl, 1931, pp. 386-87.
41. Mead, *op cit.*, p. 129.
42. Briffault, *op. cit.*, p. 386-7.
43. Davis, *op. cit.*, p. 90.
44. Tyler, E.B., *Anthropology*, abridged ed., Ann Arbor: University of Michigan Press, 1960, p. 132.
45. Benedict, *op. cit.*, p. 42.
46. Evans-Pritchard, *op. cit.*, Vol. 7, p. 49.
47. Kroeber, A.L., and Waterman, T.T., eds. *Source Book in Anthropology*, New York: Harcourt, Brace and World, 1931, p. 278-9.
48. Briffault, *op. cit.*, pp. 259-60.
49. Hoebel, *op. cit.*, p. 243.
50. Durant, *op. cit.*, Vol. I, p. 47.

51. Lowie, Robert, *Primitive Society*, New York: Harper, 1961, p. 127.
52. Durant, Vol. I, p. 45.
53. Tannahill, Reay, *Sex in History*, New York: Stein and Day, 1980, p. 40.
54. Deckard, Barbara, *The Women's Movement*, New York: Harper & Row, 1975, p. 186.
55. McGowan, Kenneth and Hester, Joseph Jr., *Early Man in the New World*, Doubleday, Anchor Books, The National History Library, 1962, pp. 38-39.
56. Reed, *op. cit.*, pp. 127-8.
57. Durant, *op. cit.*, Vol. I, pp. 33-4.
58. Boulding, *op. cit.*, p. 131.
59. Tannahill, *op. cit.*, p. 40.
60. *Ibid*.
61. Leavitt, Ruby quoting Gornick, Vivian and Moran, Barbara, *Women in Sexist Society*, New York: Signet Books, 1971, p. 396.
62. Deckard, Barbara, *op. Cit.*, p. 186.
63. Briffault, *op. cit.*, Vol. I, p. 207.
64. Tannahill, *op. cit.*, pp. 47-8.
65. Langdon-Davies, *op. cit.*, p. 32.
66. Durant, *op. cit.*, Vol. I, p. 19.
67. Briffault, *op. cit.*, Vol. I, p. 328.
68. Boulding, *op. cit.*, p. 146.
69. Langdon-Davies, *op. cit.*, p. 16.
70. Briffault, *op. cit.*, Vol. II, pp. 443-4.
71. Boulding, *op. cit.*
72. Tannahill, *op. cit.*, p. 47.
73. Durant, *op. cit.*, Vol. I, pp. 46-7.
73A. Briffault, *op. cit.*, p. 178.
74. Evans-Pritchard, *op. cit.*, Vol. 7, p. 42.
75. Langdon-Davies, *op. cit.*, quoted on p. 235.
76. Diner, Helen, *Mothers and Amazons*, New York: Doubleday, 1973, pp. 19-20.
77. Darlington, *op. cit.*, p. 49.
78. Briffault, *op. cit.*, p. 169.
79. Reed, *op. cit.*, p. 304.
80. Briffault, *op. cit.* pp. 72-3.
82. Benedict, *op. cit.*, p. 124.
83. Reed, *op. cit.*, p. 312.
84. Evans-Pritchard, *op. cit.*, Vol. 9, p. 117.
85. Lowie, *op. cit.*, pp. 57-8.
86. Evans-Pritchard, *op. cit.*, Vol. 6, p. 27.

87. Briffault, *op. cit.*, Vol. I, pp. 198-201.
88. *Ibid.*, Vol. II, p. 218.
89. *Ibid.*, p. 110.
90. Durant, *op. cit.*, Vol. I, pp. 42-3.
91. Evans-Pritchard, *op.cit.*, Vol. I, p. 86.
92. Cotlow, L., *Twilight of the Primitive*, New York: Ballantine, 1971, p. 76.
93. Hoebel, *op. cit.*, p. 209.
94. *Ibid.*, p. 208.
95. Boulding, *op. cit.*, p. 52.
96. Diner, *op. cit.*, p. 32.
97. Briffault, *op. cit.*, Vol. II, pp. 280-81.
98. Neumann, *op. cit.*, p. 94.
99. de Riencourt, Amaury, *Sex and Power in History*, New York: David McKay Co., Inc., 1974, p. 24.
100. Briffault, *op. cit.*, p. 377.
101. *Ibid.*, p. 35.
102. Dobell, Elizabeth, "God and Woman, the Hidden History," *Redbook Magazine*, March, 1978, pp. 27-44.
103. Briffault, *op. cit.*, p. 35.
104. *Ibid.*, p. 287.
105. *Ibid.*, p. 40.
106. de Riencourt, *op. cit.*, p. 40.
107. Reed, *op. cit.*, p. 148.
108. Singer, June, *Androgeny*, New York: Doubleday, 1976, p. 60.
109. Davis, *op. cit.*, p. 76 quoting Campbell.
110. *Ibid.*, p. 76, quoting from Fromm, Erich, *The Forgotten Language*, p. 210.
111. *Ibid.*, quoting from Campbell.
112. Diner, *op. cit.*, p. iii.
113. *Ibid.*, p. 20.
114. Davis, *op. cit.*, quoting James Mellaart.
115. Darlington, *op cit.*, p. 79, quoting in Boulding, *op. cit.*, p. 127.
116. Reed, *op. cit.*, p. 133.
117. Pomeroy, Sarah, *Goddess, Whores, Wives, and Slaves; Women in Classical Antiquity*, New York: Schocken Books, 1976, p. 15.
118. Deckard, *op. cit.*, p. 189.
119. *Ibid.*, p. 189, referring to Childe.
120. *Ibid.*, p. 190, referring to Leacock.
121. *Ibid.*, referring to Childe.
122. *Ibid.*, p. 191.
123. de Riencourt, *op. cit.*, p. 34.

CHAPTER II

ANTIQUITY

1. Durant, *op. cit.*, Vol. I, p. 127.
2. Woolley, C. Leonard, *The Sumerians*, London, 1928, p. 106.
3. *Ibid.*, pp. 40, 43-54.
4. Durant, *op. cit.*, Vol. I, p. 125.
5. Durant, *op. cit.*, Vol. I, p. 130.
6. Boulding, *op. cit.*, pp. 79-80.
7. Saggs, H.W.F., *The Greatness That Was Babylon*, New York: Mentor, 1968, p. 13.
8. Bullough, Vern L., *TheSubordinate Sex, a History of Attitudes Toward Women*, Maryland, Penguin Books, Inc., 1974, p. 27.
9. *Ibid.*,
10. *Ibid.*,
11. Dobel, *op. cit.*, p. 41.
12. Weidenfeld, George and Nicolson, Ltd., *Milestones in History*, New York: W. W. Norton and Company, Inc., 1971, p. 22.
13. Durant, *op. cit.*, Vol.I, p. 234, quoting CAH i, pp. 529-32.
14. Boulding, *op. cit.*, p. 220.
15. Durant, *op. cit.*, Vol. I, p. 245, quoting Herodutus, I, 199; Strabo, XVI, i, 20.
16. Langdon-Davies, *op. cit.*, pp. 86-7.
17. Sumner, W.G., *Folkways, A Study of the Sociological Importance of Usages, Manners, Customs, mores, and Morals*, Boston: Ginn, 1906, p. 387.
19. Bullough, *op. cit.*, p. 23.
20. Harper, R.F., ed.,: *The Code of Hammurabi*, Chicago: The University of Chicago Press, 1904, XL, p. viii.
21. Seltman, Charles, *Women in Antiquity*, New York: St. Martin's Press, 1955, p. 32.
22. Maspero, Gaston, *The Dawn of Civilization, Egypt and Chaldaea*, London, 1897, p. 739.
23. *Ibid.*, p. 735.
24. Boulding, *op. cit.*, p. 221.
25. Stone, Merlin, *When God Was a Woman*, New York: Dial Press, 1976, 1976, pp. 42-3.
26. Durant, *op. cit.*, Vol. I, p. 266.
27. *Ibid.*, p. 267.
28. *Ibid.*
29. *Cambridge Ancient History*, iii, p. 107.
30. Boulding, *op. cit.*, p. 221.
31. *Ibid.*, p. 225; Durant, *op. cit.*, I, 267.

32. *Ibid.*, 227.
33. Durant, *op. cit.*, p. 218.
34. *Ibid.*, p. 299.
35. *Ibid.*, pp. 300-1.
36. Moscati, Sabatino, *Ancient Semetic Civilizations*, New York: G.P. Putnam's Sons, 1957, p. 127.
37. *Ibid.*, p. 129.
38. *Ibid.*, p. 130.
39. Durant, *op. cit.*, I, p. 321.
40. Moscati, *op. cit.*, p. 137.
41. Bullough, *op. cit.*, p. 40.
42. Boulding, *op. cit.*, p. 236.
43. *Ibid.*
44. Quoted in Stone, *op. cit.*, p. 55.
45. Bullough, *op. cit.*, pp. 40-2.
46. *Ibid.*
47. Briffault, *op. cit.*, p. 223.
48. Agonito, Rosemary, Ed., *History of Ideas on Women*, New York: G.P. Putnam's Sons, 1977, pp. 17-18.
49. Sanger, Wm., *History of Prostitution*, New York 1910, p. 36.
50. Lev. xx, 10; Deut. xxii, 22.
51. Briffault, *op. cit.*, p. 223.
52. *Ibid.*
53. Stone, *op. cit.*, pp. 59-60.
54. *Ibid.*
55. *Ibid.*
56. Casson, Lionel, *Daily Life in Ancient Egypt*, New York: American Heritage publishing Co., Inc., p. 90.
57. Quoted in Patrick, Richard, *Egyptian Mythology*, London: Octopus Books, 1972, p. 5.
58.*Ibid.*, *pp. 31-56.*
59. *Ibid.*, *p. 54.*
60. *Langdon-Davies, op. cit.*, pp. 84-5.
61. Reed, *op. cit.*, p. 339.
62. Briffault, *op. cit.*, pp. 83-4.
63. Stone, *op. cit.*, p. 38.
64. Briffault, *op. cit.*, pp. 32-4.
65. Langdon-Davies, *op. cit.*, pp. 87-8.
66. Diner, *op. cit.*, p. 171.
67. Briffault, *op. cit.*, pp. 83-4.
68. *Ibid.*,
69. Diner, *op. cit.*, p. 171.
70. Diodorus Siculus, *Library of History*, Loeb Classical Library, Vol. I, New York, 1933, p. lxxxvii.
71. Bullough, *op. cit.*, p. 33.
72. Durant, *op. cit.*, Vol. I, p. 164.

73. Bullough, *op. cit.*, p. 33; Durant, *op. cit.*, Vol. I, p. 16; Casson, *op. cit.*, p. 33.
74. Diner, *op. cit.*, p. 173.
75. Bullough, *op. cit.*, p. 40.
76. Casson, Lionel, *op. cit.*, p.31.
77. Briffault, *op. cit.*, p. 384.
78. Boulding, *op. cit.*, p. 235.
79. Patrick, *op. cit.*, p. 51.
80. *Ibid.*, p. 58.
81. Dudley, Lavinia P., Ed. in Chief, *Encyclopedia Americana*, 30 vols., New York: Americana Corp., 1961, Vol. 10, p. 12.
82. Casson, *Ancient Egypt, op. cit.*, p. 29f.
83. Boulding, *op. cit.*, p. 229.
84. Bullough, *op. cit.*, p. 35.
85. Casson, *Daily Life in Ancient Egypt, op. cit.*, p. 100.
86. Durant, *op. cit.*, Vol. II, p. 39.
87. *Ibid.*, pp. 11, 2, 66, 244, 458, 555.
88. Wells, H.G., *The Outline of History*, 2 Vols. New York: Macmillen Publishing Co., Inc., 1921, Vol. I, p. 304.
89. *Ibid.*, pp. 309-10.
90. Durant, *op. cit.*, Vol. II, p. 439.
91. *Ibid.*, p. 441.
92. *Ibid.*, p. 558.
93. *Ibid.*, p. 175.
94. Stone, *op. cit.*, p. 46.
95. *Ibid.*, p. 5.
96. Durant, *op. cit.*, Vol. II, p. 180.
97. Stone, *op. cit.*, p. 31.
98. Spretnak, Charlene, *Lost Goddesses of Early Greece, A Collection of Pre-Hellenic Myths*, Berkeley: Moon Books, 1978, Boston: Beacon Press, p. 18.
99. Bullough, *op. cit.*, pp. 56-7.
100. Pomeroy, *op. cit.*, p. 2.
101. *Ibid.*, p. 4.
102. *Ibid.*, p. 8.
103. *Ibid.*
104. Spretnak, *op. cit.*, p. 19.
105. Durant, *op. cit.*, Vol. II, p. 50.
106. *Ibid.*, p. 51.
107. Lippert, Julius, *The Evolution of Culture*, New York: Macmillan Publishing Co., Inc., 1931, pp. 308-12.
108. Donaldson, James Longmans, *Woman; Her Position and Influence in Ancient Greece and Rome and Among the Early Christians*, New York: Green and Co., 1907, p. 50.
109. Deckard, *op. cit.*, p. 191.
110. Briffault, *op. cit.*, p. 233.

111. Bullough, *op. cit.*, p. 66.

112. Donaldson, *op. cit.*, p. 51.

113. Durant, *op. cit.*, Vol. II, p. 287.

114. *Ibid.*, p. 302.

115. Pomeroy, *op. cit.*, p. 72.

116. *Ibid.*, p. 86.

117. Bullough, *op. cit.*, p. 67.

118. Donaldson, *Op. cit.*, p. 51.

119. Bullough, *op. cit.*, p. 66.

120. Briffault, *op. cit.*, p. 228.

121. Pomeroy, *op. cit.*, p. 62.

122. *Ibid.*, p. 63.

123. Bullough, *op. cit.*, pp. 67-8.

124. Diner, *op. cit.*, p. 115.

125. Plato, Symposium, 180 f.

126. Durant, *op. cit.*, Vol. II, p. 320.

127. Pomeroy, *op. cit.*, p. 74.

128. Durant, *op. cit.*, Vol. II, p. 259; Pomeroy, *Ibid.*, p. 73.

129. Briffault, *op. cit.*, p. 405.

130. Wells, *op. cit.*, Vol. I, p. 309.

131. Durant, *op. cit.*, Vol. II, p. 306.

132. Agonito, *op. cit.*, P. 41.

133. Eripedes, *Medea*, trs. Rex Warner in Grene and Lattimore, *Complete Greed Tragedies*, vol. 3, p. 67, II, 231-151.

134. Durant, *op. cit.*, Vol. II, p. 305.

135. Langdon-Davies, *op. cit.*, p. 89.

136. Durant, *op. cit.*, Vol. II, p. 77.

137. Seltman, *op. cit.*, p. 7.

138. Langdon-Davies, *op. cit.*, p. 100.

139. Donaldson, *op. cit.*, p. 81.

140. *Ibid.*, p. 28.

141. Aristotle, *Politics*, II, 6, 1269 B-1270A, 5-11.

142. Bullough, *op. cit.*, p. 69.

143. Carroll, A., *Greek Women*, Philadelphia, 1908, p. 102.

144. Durant, *op. cit.*, Vol. II, p. 163.

145. Boulding, *op. cit.*, p. 261.

146. Foster, Jeannette, *Sex Variant Women in Literature*, London: Muller, 1958, pp. 17-24.

147. Boulding, *op. cit.*, p. 262.

148. IIbid.

149. *Ibid.*, pp. 262-3.

150. *Ibid.*, p. 263.

151. *Ibid.*, p. 262.

152. *Ibid.*, p. 263.

153. Mannix Daniel, *Those About to Die*, New York: Ballentine Books, New York, 1958, p. i.

154. Casson, Lionel, *Daily Life in Ancient Rome*, New York: American Heritage Publishing Co., Inc., p. 100.
155. Durant, *op. cit.*, Vol. III, p. 7.
156. Durant, *op. cit.*, Vol. III, pp. 7-8.
157. Casson, *op. cit.*, p. 79.
158. Boulding, *op. cit.*, p. 350.
158A.Pomeroy, *op. cit.*, p. 213.
159. Durant, *op. cit.*, Vol. III, p. 63.
160. Boulding, *op. cit.*, p. 350.
161. Pomeroy, *op. cit.*, p. 211.
162. Durant, *op. cit.*, Vol. III, p. 64.
163. *Ibid.*, p. 97.
164. Stone, *op. cit.*, p. 146.
165. Casson, *op. cit.*, p. 80.
166. Boulding, *op. cit.*, p. 350.
167. Casson, *op. cit.*, p. 87.
168. *Ibid.*, p. 90.
169. Barrow, R.H., *The Romans*, Chicago, Aldine Publishing Co. 1949, p. 175.
170. Durant, *op. cit.*, Vol. III, p. 647.
171. *Ibid.*, p. 664.
172. *Ibid.*, p. 7.
173. Bullough, *op. cit.*, p. 82.
174. *Ibid.*, p. 84.
175. Donaldson, *op. cit.*, p. 79.
176. Durant, *op. cit.*, Vol. III, p. 57; Bullough, *op. cit.*, p. 83.
177. Reed, *op. cit.*, p. 393.
178. Donaldson, *op. cit.*, p. 87.
179. Quoted in Durant, *op. cit.*, Vol. III, p. 89.
180. *Ibid.*, p. 395.
181. Donaldson, *op. cit.*, p. 114.
182. *Ibid.*, p. 142.
183. *Ibid.*
184. Pomeroy, *op. cit.*, p. 160.
185. *Ibid.*
186. Durant, *op. cit.*, Vol. III, p. 146.
187. Donaldson, *op. cit.*, p. 146.
188. Pomeroy, *op. cit.*, p. 201.
189. Bello, Nino Lo, "The Gladiator Girls of Ancient Rome," This World, *San Francisco Chronicle*, January 19, 1975.
190. Boulding, *op. cit.*, p. 360.
191. Pomeroy, *op. cit.*, pp. 192-96.
192. *Ibid.*, p. 189.
193. *Ibid.*
194. Bullough, *op. cit.*, p. 82.
195. *Ibid.*, p. 86.

196. Boulding, *op. cit.*, p. 351-52.
197. Durant, *op. cit.*, Vol. III, p. 117.
198. Pomeroy, *op. cit.*, pp. 175-76.
199. Boulding, *op. cit.*, p. 352.
200. Langdon-Davies, *op. cit.*, p. 110.
201. Pomeroy, *op. cit.*, p. 161.
202. Boulding, *op. cit.*, p. 354.
203. *Ibid.*, p. 357.
204. *Ibid.*, pp. 260-61.
205. *Ibid.*, p. 360.
206. Dietrick, 1879; 42, quoted in Boulding, *op. cit.*, p. 360.
207. Durant, *op. cit.*, Vol. III, p. 564.
208. Agonito, *op. cit.*, p. 67.
209. Ruether, Rosemary, Ed., *Religion and Sexism*, New York: Simon and Schuster, 1974, p. 138.
210. Barrow, *op. cit.*, p. 177.
211. Durant, *op. cit.*, Vol. III, p. 578.
212. Barrow, *op. cit.*, p. 177.
213. *Ibid.*, p. 572.
214. Durant, *op. cit.*, Vol. III, p. 646.
215. *Ibid.*, p. 616.
216. Ruether, *op. cit.*, p. 123.
217. *Ibid.*, pp. 136-37.
218. Boulding, *op. cit.*, p. 361.
219. Ruether, *op. cit.*, pp. 276-78.
220. *Ibid.*, p. 273.
221. Evans-Pritchard, *op. cit.*, Vol. 6, p. 617.
222. Hunt, Morton, *The Natural History of Love*, New York: Knopf, 1967, p. 103.
223. Durant, *op. cit.*, Vol. III, 588.
224. *Ibid.*, p. 596.
225. Agonito, *op. cit.*, p. 68.
226. Bullough, *op. cit.*, p. 115.
227. Durant, *op. cit.*, Vol. III, p. 612.
228. Durant, *op. cit.*, Vol. III, p. 613.
229. Evans-Pritchard, *op. cit.*, Vol. 6, p. 617.
230. Seltman, *op. cit.*, p. 198.
231. Wells, *op. cit.*, Vol. I, p. 605.
232. Davis, *op. cit.*, p. 273.
233. Hunt, *op. cit.*, p. 111.
234. Boulding, *op. cit.*, p. 367.
235. *Ibid.*, p. 372.
236. *Ibid.*, p. 370.
237. *Ibid.*
238. *Ibid.*, p. 371.
239. *Ibid.*
240. *Ibid.*

CHAPTER III

THE MEDIEVAL PERIOD

1. Durant, *op. cit.*, Vol. II, pp. 22-43.
2. Wells, *op. cit.*, Vol. I, pp. 608-09.
3. Durant, *op. cit.*, Vol. IV, p. 92.
4. Durant, *op. cit.*, Vol. II, p. 31.
5. Durant, *op. cit.*, Vol. IV, p. 107.
6. *Ibid.*, p. 111.
7. *Ibid.*, p. 113.
8. *Ibid.*, p. 117.
9. *Ibid.*, p. 45.
10. Block, Marc, *Feudal Society*, 2 v. tr. L.A. Manyon, Chicago: University of Chicago Press, 1961, p. 41.
11. *Ibid.*, p. 40.
12. Durant, *op. cit.*, Vol. IV, p. 462.
13. Bloch, *op. cit.*, p. 16.
14. *Ibid.*, p. 17.
15. *Ibid.* 16. *Ibid.*, pp. 12-13.
17. *Ibid.*, p. 32.
18. *Ibid.*, p. 148.
19. Durant, *op. cit.*, Vol. IV, pp. 555-56.
20. Bloch, *op. cit.*, p. 151.
21. Durant, *op. cit.*, Vol. IV, p. 574.
22. Bloch, *op. cit.*, p. 225.
23. *Ibid.*, p. 224.
24. *Ibid.*, p. 222.
25. Hunt, *op. cit.*, pp. 132-39.
26. Durant, *op. cit.*, Vol. IV, p. 8.
27. James, E.O. *TheCult of the Mother Goddess*, New York: Praeger, 1959, p. 181.
28. Durant, *op. cit.*, Vol. IV, p. 765.
29. *Ibid.*, p. 766.
30. Heer, Friedrich, *The Medieval World, Europe 1100-1350*, Cleveland and New York: World Publishing Co., 1961, p. 402.
31. Durant, *op. cit.*, Vol. IV. p. 611.
32. Wells, *op. cit.*, Vol. II, p. 84.
33. Durant, *op. cit.*, Vol. IV, pp. 612-13.
34. Davis, *op. cit.*, p. 244.
35. Durant, *op. cit.*, Vol.IV, p. 746.
36. *Ibid.*
37. Bullough, *op. cit.*, p. 171.
38. *Ibid.*, pp. 171-72.

39. Ruether, *op. cit.*, p. 246.

40. Durant, *op. cit.*, Vol. IV, p. 782.

41. *Ibid.*, p. 777.

42. Heer, *op. cit.*, p. 174.

43. Durant, *op. cit.*, Vol. IV, pp. 773-75.

44. Heer, *op. cit.*, p. 172.

45. *Ibid.*, p. 163.

46. Durant, *op. cit.*, Vol. IV, p. 784.

47. *Ibid.*, pp. 212-13.

48. *Ibid.*, p. 783.

49. Davis, *op. cit.*, p. 257.

50. Boulding, *op. cit.*, p. 427.

51. DAvis, *op. cit.*, p. 257.

52. *Ibid.*

53. Durant, *op. cit.*, Vol. VI, pp. 85-6.

54. *Ibid.*, p. 233.

55. *Ibid.*, Vol. IV, p. 88.

56. O'Faolain, Julia, and Martines, Lauro, eds., *Not in God's Image, Women in History From the Greeks to the Victorians*, New York: Harper & Row Publishers, Inc., 1973, p. 96.

57. Durant, *op. cit.*, Vol. IV, p. 90.

58. Bullough,*op. cit.*, p. 154.

59. O'Faolain and Martines, *op. cit.*, p. 96.

60. *Ibid.*, p. 101.

61. *The Burgundian Code* as quoted in O'Faolain and Martines, *op. cit.*, p. 102.

62. O'Faolain and Martines, *op. cit.*, p. 103.

63. *Leges Visigothorum* quoted in O'Faolain and Martines, *op. cit.*, p. 100.

64. *Leges Saxonum und Les Thuringorum* as quoted in O'Faolain and Martines, *op. cit.*, p. 97.

65. *Leges Saxonum* as quoted in O'Faolain and Martines, p. 98.

66. Durant, *op. cit.*, Vol. IV, p. 505.

67. *Ibid.*, p. 825.

68. Davis, *op. cit.*, p. 238.

69. O'Faolain and Martines,*op. cit.*, p. 131.

70. Wells, *op. cit.*, Vol. I, p. 309.

71. Paraphrased from *Summa Theologica* in Reuther, *op. cit.*, p. 217, in an article by McLaughlin, "Equality of Souls, Inequality of Sexes: Woman in Medieval Theology."

72. O'Faolain and Martines,*op. cit.*, p. 120.

73. *Oeuvres de Galen* quoted in O'Faolain and Martines, p. 120.

74. Power, E.E., *Medieval Women*, Cambridge, N.Y.: Cambridge University Press, 1975, p. 39.

75. *Ibid.*, pp. 39-40.

76. Winston, Clara and Richard, *Daily Life in the Middle Ages*, New York: American Heritage Publishing Co., 1975, p. 86.

77. Bloch, *op. cit.*, p. 227.
78. Durant, *op. cit.*, Vol. IV, p. 826.
79. Power, *op. cit.*, pp. 16-19.
80. Davis, *op. cit.*, p. 254, quoting *Geoffrey de la Tour de Landry, Book of the Knight Tower*, 1371.
81. *Coutumes de Beauvaises* quoted in O'Faolain and Martines, *op. cit.*, p. 175.
82. Durant, *op. cit.*, Vol. IV, p. 826.
83. Taylor, G. Rattray, *Sex in History*, New York: Harper and Row, 1970, p. 63.
84. Durant, *op. cit.*, Vol. IV, p. 556.
85. Quoted from Gene Brucker, ed., *The Memoirs of Renaissance Florence*, in O'Faolain and Martines, *op. cit.*, pp. 170-72.
86. Bloch, *op. cit.*, p. 138.
87. *The Lawes Resolutions of Womens Rights* quoted in O'Faolain and Martines, *op. cit.*, p. 147.
88. A. Pertile, *Storia del diritto italiano*, quoted in O'Faolain and Martines, *op. cit.*, p. 148.
89. Bloch, *op. cit.*, p. 201.
90. Boulding, *op. cit.*, p. 485.
91. Power, *op. cit.*, p. 76.
92. Boulding, *op. cit.*, p. 209.
93. Power, *op. cit.*, p. 80.
94. *Ibid.*
95. France, Thirteenth Century, Phillippe de Navarre,*Les Quatre Ages de l'Homme*, as quoted in O'Faolain and Martines,*op. cit.*, p. 167.
96. Power, *op. cit.*, p. 86.
97. *Ibid.*, p. 80.
98. *Ibid.*, p. 84.
99. *Essays in the History of Medicine*, Sing and Sigerist, ed., quoted in Postan, *Ibid.*, p. 86.
100. Bullough, *op. cit.*, p. 209.
101. Durant, *op. cit.*, Vol. IV, p. 806.
102. Ruether, *op. cit.*, p. 237.
103. Boulding, *op. cit.*, p. 254.
104. *Ibid.*, p. 455.
105. Hilpish quoted in Boulding, p. 456.
106. Boulding, *op. cit.*, p. 456.
107. Hentsch, Alice, *De la litterature didactique du moyenage s'dressant specialement aux femmes*, referred to in Ruether, *op. cit.*, p. 244.
108. Boulding, *op. cit.*, p. 445.
109. *Ibid.*, pp. 446-48.
109. *Ibid.*, pp. 446-48.
110. Boulding, *op. cit.*, p. 446.
111. Heer, *op. cit.*, pp. 264-65.
112. Power, *op. cit.*, p. 99.

113. Boulding, *op. cit.*, pp. 397-98.

114. *Ibid.*, p. 443.

115. *Ibid.*, p. 439.

116. Bullough, *op. cit.*, p. 180.

117. Power, *op. cit.*, p. 45.

118. *Ibid.*, pp. 45-46.

119. Boulding, *op. cit.*, p. 481.

120. Power, *op. cit.*, p. 74.

121. Boulding, *op. cit.*, p. 491.

122. Toileau, Etienne, *Livres des Metiers*, ed. by G.B. Depping, Paris, 1837, pp. 68-69, 73, 79, quoted in O'Faolain and Martines, *op. cit.*, p. 156.

123. O'Faolain and Martines, *op. cit.*, p. 157.

124. Power, *op. cit.*, p. 53.

125. *Ibid.*, pp. 59-60.

126. Boulding,*op. cit.*, p. 486.

127. *Ibid.*, p. 487.

128. *Ibid.*, p. 490.

129. *Ibid.*, pp. 500-501.

130. Power, *op. cit.*, p. 60.

131. Boulding, *op. cit.*, p. 503.

132. *Ibid.*, p. 423.

133. Heer, *op. cit.*, p. 265.

134. Boulding, *op. cit.*, p. 398.

135. *Ibid.*, p. 379; Durant,*op. cit.*, Vol. IV, p. 103.

136. Boulding, *op. cit.*, p. 380.

137. Durant, *op. cit.*, Vol IV, p. 136.

138. *Ibid.*, p. 427.

139. *Ibid.*

140. *Ibid.*; Boulding, *op. cit.*, p. 381.

141. Durant, *op. cit.*, Vol. IV, p. 427; Boulding, *op. cit.*, p. 380.

142. Boulding, *op. cit.*, p. 382.

143. Durant, *op. cit.*, Vol. IV, p. 430.

144. Boulding, *op. cit.*, p. 472; Durant, op. cit., Vol. IV, p. 650.

145. Boulding, *op. cit.*, p. 414; Durant, *op. cit.*, Vol. IV, p. 37.

146. Boulding, *op. cit.*, p. 394.

147. *Ibid.*, p. 380.

148. Davis, *op. cit.*, p. 221; Durant, *op. cit.*, Vol. IV, p. 84.

149. Boulding, *op. cit.*, p. 464.

150. *Ibid.*, p. 441.

151. *Ibid.*, Durant, *op. cit.*, Vol. IV, p. 810.

152. Boulding, *op. cit.*, p. 376.

153. *Ibid.*, p. 397.

154. *Ibid.*, p. 396.

155. *Ibid.*, p. 377;Durant, *op. cit.*, Vol. IV, p. 515.

156. Boulding, *op. cit.*, p. 458-60; Durant, *op. cit.*, p. 809; Heer, *op. cit.*, p. 264.

157. Boulding, *op. cit.*, p. 460.
158. *Ibid.*, p. 396.
159. *Ibid.*, pp. 466-68; Durant, *op. cit.*, Vol. IV, pp. 805-6.
160. Boulding,*op. cit.*, p. 465-66.
161. *Ibid.*, p. 473.
162. *Ibid.*, p. 376.
163. *Ibid.*, p. 377.
164. *Ibid.*, p. 396.
165. Boulding, *op. cit.*, p. 440; Durant, *op. cit.*,Vol. IV, pp. 672-74; Heer, *op. cit.*, pp. 130-34.
166. Heer, *op. cit.*, p. 262.
167. *Ibid.*, pp. 109, 262.
168. Boulding, *op. cit.*, p. 475.
170. O'Faolain and Martines, *op. cit.*, p. 182.
171. Heer, *op. cit.*, pp. 262-63.

CHAPTER IV

THE RENAISSANCE

1. *Durant, op. cit.*, Vol. IV, p. 376.
2. Boulding, *op. cit.*, p. 199.
3. Hunt, *op. cit.*, pp. 226-27.
4. Bullough,*op. cit.*, p. 200.
5. *Ibid.*, . 203.
6. Quoted in Bullough, *Ibid.*, p. 205, from Daly, Mary, *The Church and the Second Sex*, New York: Harper and Row, 1968, p. 56.
7. Quoted in Bullough,*Ibid.*, p. 205, fromDaly,*Ibid.*, p. 57.
8. Boulding, *op. cit.*, p. 548.
9. Bullough,*op. cit.*, pp. 204-5.
10. Boulding, *op. cit.*, p. 562.
11. Dudley, *op. cit.*, Vol. 12, p. 106.
12. Hunt, *op. cit.*, p. 195.
13. *Ibid.*, pp. 195-97.
14. O'Faolain and Martines, *op. cit.*, p. 211.
15. Friedrich von Spee, *The Witch Persecutions*, ed. by G.L. Burr, *Translations and Reprints from the Original Sources of European History*, Vol. III, 4, Philadelphia, 1897, pp. 31, 33, 35 quoted in O'Faolain and Martines, *op. cit.*, pp. 212-13.
16. From the canon of Linden, *Gesta Trevirorum*, inBurr, *Ibid.*, *The Witch Persecutions*, pp. 13-14, quoted in O'Faolain and Martines, *op. cit.*, p. 215.
17. Bullough, *op. cit.*, p. 224.

18. Boulding, *op. cit.*, p. 554.
19. O'Faolain and Martines, *op. cit.*, p. 217.
20. Langdon-Davies,*op. cit.*, p. 194.
21. Bullough, *op. cit.*, p. 224.
22. *Ibid.*, p. 208.
23. Durant, *op. cit.*, Vol. VI, 578.
24. de Maulde le Caviere, *The Women of the Renaissance*, tr. by George Herbert Ely, New York: G.P. Putnam's Sons, 1901, pp. 109-10.
25. Hunt, *op. cit.*, p. 188.
26. *Ibid.*, pp. 188-89.
27. Mee, Charles L. Jr., *Daily Life in Renaissance Italy*, New York: American Heritage Publishing Co., Inc., 1975, p. 20.
28. Boulding, *op. cit.*, p. 552.
29. *Ibid.*, p. 553.
30. Durant, *op. cit.*, Vol.VI, p. 303.
30A. Mee, *op. cit.*, p. 19.
31. Durant, *op. cit.*, Vol. V, p. 416.
32. Mee, *op. cit.*, p. 23.
33. Durant, *op. cit.*, Vol. V, p. 579.
34. Leon Battistata Alberti, *The Family in Renaissance Florence*, Renee Neu Watkins, trans, (Columbia: University of South Carolina press, 1969), pp. 208-17. Copyright 1969 by Renee Neu Watkins.
35. Mee. *op. cit.*, p. 19.
36. Bullough, *op. cit.*, p. 215.
37. Mee, *op. cit.*, p. 65.
38. *Ibid.*
39. *Ibid.*
40. O'Faolain and Martines, *op. cit.*, pp. 192-93.
41. Boulding, *op. cit.*, p. 545.
42. *Ibid.*, p. 546.
43. Aubigne,*Oeuvres Completes*, ed. by E. Reaume and F. de Caussade, Paris, 1873, I, pp. 445 ff., as quoted in O'Faolain and Martines, *op. cit.*, p. 186.
44. Erasmuc, *Christiani matrimonii institutio*, Basel, 1526, Ch. 17, unpag, as quoted in O'Faolain and Martines, *op. cit.*, p. 182.
45. de Maulde de Claviere, *op. cit.*, p. 76.
46. Bullough, *op. cit.*, pp. 212-13.
47. *Ibid.*, p. 213.
48. *Ibid.*, p. 214.
49. *Ibid.*, pp. 214-15.
50. Boulding, *op. cit.*, p. 555.
51. Mee, *op. cit.*, p. 15.
52. Boulding, *op. cit.*, p. 555.
53. Boulding, *Ibid.*, p. 560.
54. *Ibid.*, p. 561.
55. Bullough, *op. cit.*, p. 226.

56. *Ibid.*, p. 217.
57. *Ibid.*, p. 218.
58. *Ibid.*
59. *Ibid.*, p. 203.
60. Boulding, *op. cit.*, p. 563.
61. Bullough, *op. cit.*, p. 229.
62. Hunt, *op. cit.*, p. 177.
63. Durant, *op. cit.*, Vol. VI, pp. 81-6.
64. Boulding, *op. cit.* p. 536.
65. *Ibid.*
66. *Ibid.*, p. 538.
67. *Ibid.*
68. *Ibid.*, p. 540.
69. *Ibid.*, p. 539.
70. Mee, *op. cit.*, pp. 70-2.
71. Boulding, *op. cit.*, p. 443.
72. *Ibid.*, p. 542.
73. Durant, *op. cit.*, Vol. V, p. 577.
74. Boulding, *op. cit.*, p. 545.
75. Bullough, *op. cit.*, p. 218.
76. Boulding, *op. cit.*, p. 572.
77. *Ibid.*, p. 571.
78. Durant, *op. cit.*, Vol. V, p. 584.
79. Boulding, *op. cit.*, p. 575.
80. *Ibid.*
81. *Ibid.*
82. *Ibid.*
83. *Ibid.*
84. *Ibid.*, p. 576.
85. *Ibid.*
86. *Ibid.*, p. 563.
87. *Ibid.* p. 343.
88. *Ibid.*
89. *Ibid.*, pp. 342, 574.
90. Durant, *op. cit.*, Vol. V, pp. 585, 718.
91. Boulding, *op. cit.*, p. 541.
92. *Ibid.*, p. 574.
93. *Ibid.*, p. 543.
94. *Ibid.*, p. 559.

CHAPTER V

THE MODERN PERIOD

1. Bullough, *op. cit.*, pp. 268-69.
2. Quoted in Langdon-Davies, *op. cit.*, p. 227.
3. Trecker, Janice Law, *Women on the Move, Struggles for Equal Rights in England*, New York: MacMillan Publishiing Co., Inc., 1975, p. 2.
4. Aries, Philippe,*Centuries of Childhood, a Social History of Family Life*, tr. Robert Baldick, New York: Random House, 1962, p. 353.
5. Quoted in Langdon-Davies, *op. cit.*, p. 220.
6. Wollstonecraft, Mary, *A Vindication of the Rights of Women*, New York: Norton, 1967, p.84.
7. Mill, John Stuart, *On the Subjection of Women*, London: Oxford University Press, 1912, pp. 518, 522.
8. Langdon-Davies, *op. cit.*, pp. 235-36.
9. *Ibid.*
10. Trecker, *op. cit.*, p. 46.
11. *Ibid.*, p. 50.
12. *Ibid.*, p. 52.
13. *Ibid.*, p. 58.
14. *Ibid.*, p. 64.
15. *Ibid.*, p. 65.
16. *Ibid.*, p. 89.
17. *Ibid.*, p. 96.
18. Quoted from Charles and Mary Beard, *The Rise of American Civilization*, New York, 1930, I, 44, in Flexner, Eleanor, *Centuries of Struggle*, New York: Atheneum, 1972, p. 3.
19. Flexner,*Ibid.*, p. 18.
20. *Ibid.* p. 5.
21. *Ibid.*, pp. 18-19.
22. Dexter, E.A., *Colonial Women*, Boston: Houghton-Mifflin Co., 1924, p. 28.
23. *Ibid.*, p. 29.
24. *Ibid.* p. 40.
25. Flexner, *op. cit.*, p. 53.
26. Boulding, *op. cit.*, p. 638.
27. Flexner, *op. cit.*, p. 54.
28. Dexter, *op. cit.*, p. 26.
29. Quoted in Hecht, Marie, *et.al. The Women, Yes!* New York: Holt, Rinehart and Winston, Inc., 1973, p. 63-4.
30. Quoted in Flexner, *op. cit.*, p. 21, from *The Letters of Theodore Weld, Angelina Grimke Weld and SarahGrimke, 1822-1844* New York: 1934.
31. Brownmiller, Susan, *Against Our Will, Men, Women and Rape*, New York: Simon and Schuster, 1978, p. 156.

32. *Ibid.*, pp. 154, 157.
33. *Ibid.*, pp. 160-61.
34. Smith, Page, *Daughters of the Promised Land*, Boston: Little,Brown & Co., 1970, p. 121.
35. *Ibid.*, p. 123.
36. Quoted in Hecht,*op. cit.*, pp. 65-8.
37. Quoted in Flexner,*op. cit.*, pp. 81-2.
38. *Ibid.*, p. 83.
39. *Ibid.*, p. 106.
40. *Ibid.*, p. 78.
41. *Ibid.*, p. 288.
42. *Ibid.*, p. 28.
43. Lerner, Gerda, *The Woman in American History*, California: Addison-Wesley Publishing Company, 1971, p. 122.
44. Reprinted from "President's Notes," a publication of the Pennsylvania State Education Association—from CTA, Human Relations Department, Nov. 15, 1974.
45. Smith, *op. cit.*, p. 181.
46. *Ibid.*, p. 195.
47. *Ibid.*, p. 201.
48. *Ibid.*, pp. 223-24.
49. *Ibid.*, p. 223.
50. *Ibid.*
51. *Ibid.*, pp. 223-224.
52. Dudley, Lavinia, Ed. in Chief,*Encyclopedia Americana, op. cit.*, Vol, 24, p. 86.
53. Cotera, Martha, *Diosa y Hembra, History and Heritage of the Chicanas in the U.S.*, Texas: Stateline Printing, 1976.
54. Salper, Roberta, ed., *Female Liberation*, New York: Alfred A. Knopf, 1972, p. 79; Flexner,*op. cit.*, p.79.
55. Flexner, *op. cit.*, p. 37.
56. *Ibid.*, p. 96.
57. Merriam, Eve, ed. *Growing up Female in America*, New York: Doubleday & Company, Inc., 1971, p. 183.
58. Truman, Margaret, *Women of Courage*, New York: William Morrow and Company, Inc., 1976, p. 108-9.
59. Hunt, *op. cit.*, p. 348.

CHAPTER VI

LINKING THE PAST WITH THE PRESENT

1. Jensen, *op. cit.*,
2. *Wall Street Journal*, August 8, 1978.
3. Rannels, Jackson, "Job Laws Needed, Bay Area Women Say," *San Francisco Chronicle*, Jan. 28, 1981.
4. *Napa Register*, April 9, 1980.
5. Bonk, Kathy, "The Wage Gap," *National Now News*, Aug. 1, 1980.
6. Fox, Susan, "Comparable Worth is Studied at D.C. Conference, *Women's Political Times*, Dec. 1980, p. 17.
7. D'Aulaire, Emily and Paul, "Equal Rights Amendment: What's it all About?" *Readers Digest*, February, 1977.
8. Holtz, Jean, "Housewives Not 'Protected' By Most State Laws," *National NOW Times*, Dec. 1977.
9. Porter, Sylvia, "Plight of Battered Women," *San Francisco Chronicle*, November 1, 1979.
10. "Really Socking it to Women," *Time*, Feb. 7, 1977.
11. "The New 'Typical' Family," *San Francisco Chronicle*, March 8, 1977.
12. "Families Led by Women Increasing," *San Francisco Chronicle*, December 3, 1980.
13. "The American Poor: Report Says More and More are Women, Minorities," *San Francisco Chronicle*, Oct. 19, 1980.
14. *San Francisco Chronicle*, Dec. 10, 1980.

BIBLIOGRAPHY

Agonito, Rosemary, ed., *History of Ideas on Women*, New York: G.P. Putnam's Sons, 1977

Aries, Philipe, *Centuries of Childhood, A Social History of Family Life*, tr. Robert Baldick, New York: Random House, Inc., 1962

"The American Poor: Report Says More and More Are Women, Minorities," *San Francisco Chronicle*, October 19, 1980

Bachofen, J.J., *Myth, Religion and Mother-Right*, tr. by Ralph Manheim, New Jersey: Princeton University Press, 1967

Barrow, R.H., *The Romans*, Chicago: Aldine Publishing Company, 1949

Bello, Nino Lo, "The Gladiator Girls of Ancient Rome," This World, *San Francisco Chronicle*, January 19, 1975

Benedict, Ruth, *Patterns of Culture*, New York: New American Library, 1934

Bloch, Marc, *Feudal Society*, 2 v. tr. L.A. Manyon, Chicago: University ofChicago Press, 1961

Bonk, Cathy, "The Wage Gap," *National NOW News, August 1, 1980*

Boulding, Elise, *The Underside of History, A View of Women Through Time*, Colorado: Westview press, 1976

Briffault, Robert, *The Mothers: The Matriarchal Theory of Social Origins* (abridged ed. in 1 vol.). New York: Macmillan Publishing Company, Inc., 1931

Brownmiller, Susan, *Against Our Will, Men, Women and Rape*, New York: Simon and Schuster, 1978

Bullough, Vern L., *The Subordinate Sex. A History of Attitudes Toward Women*, Maryland: Penguin Books, Inc. 1974

Cambridge Ancient History, Vols., I-VI, New York, 1924

Campbell, Joseph, *The Masks of God: Primitive Mythology*, New York: Viking Press, Inc., 1959

Carroll, A., *Greek Women*, Philadelphia: 1908

Casson, Lionel, *Daily Life in Ancient Egypt*, New York: American Heritage Publishing Co., Inc., 1975 —*Daily Life in AncientRome*, New York: American Heritage Publishing Co., Inc., 1975

Castiglione, Baldesar, *The Book of the Courtier*, tr. C.S. Singleton, New York: Anchor Books, 1959

Chafe, William, *The American Woman*, New York & Oxford: Oxford University Press, 1972

Cotera, Martha, *Diosa y Hembra, History and Heritage of the Chicanas in the U.S.*, Texas: Stateline Printing, 1976

Cotlow, L., *The Twilight of the Primitive*, New York, Ballantine Books, 1971

Croft, Peter, *Roman Mythology*, London: Octopus Books, 1974

Daly, Mary, *The Church and the Second Sex*, New York: Harper & Row Publishers, Inc., 1968

Darlington, D.C., *The Evolution of Man and Society*, New York: Simon and Schuster, 1969

D'Aulaire, Emily and Paul, "Equal Rights Amendment: What's It All About?" *Readers Digest*, February, 1977

Davis, Elizabeth Gould, *The First Sex*, Maryland: Penguin Books, Inc. 1973

Deckard, Barbara, *The Women's Movement*, New York: Harper and Row, Publishers, Inc., 1975

de Maulde le Caviere, *The Women of the Renaissance*, tr. by George Herbert Ely, New York: G. Putnam's Sons, 1901

Demond, Clark J., "Studies of Hunters-Gatherers as an Aid to Interpretation of Prehistoric Societies," from *Man the Hunter*, ed. by Richard B. Lee and Irven de Vore, ed. Chicago: Aldine Publishing Co., 1968

de Riencourt, Amaury, *Sex and Power inHistory*, New York: David McKay Co., Inc., 1974

Dexter, E.A., *Colonial Women*, Boston: Houghton Mifflin Co., 1924

Diner, Helen, *Mothers and Amazons*, New York: Doubleday and Co., Inc., 1973

Dobell, Elizabeth Rodgers, "God and Woman, The Hidden History," *Redbook Magazine*, March, 1978, pp. 27-44

Donaldson, James Longmans, *Woman, Her Position and Influence in Ancient Greece and Rome and Among the Early Christians*, New York: Green and Co., 1907

Driver, G.R., and Miles, John C., *The Assyrian Laws*, Oxford: Clarendon Press, 1955

Dudley, Lavinia P., ed. in chief, *Encyclopedia Americana*, 30 vols., New York: Americana Corp., 1961

Durant, Will, *The Story of Civilization*, 10 vols., New York: Simon and Schuster, 1954-1967

Ehrenreich, Barbara and Deirdre, English,*Witches, Midwives and Nurses, A History of Women Healers*, New York: The Feminist Press, 1973

Equal Rights Amendment Project of the California Commission on the Status of Women, *Impact, ERA, Limitations and Possibility*, California, Les Femmes Publishing, 1976

Evans-Pritchard, Sir Edward, Supervisory Editor of the Series, 20 vols., *Peoples of the Earth*, Verona: The Danbury Press, 1973

Flexner, Eleanor, *Century of Struggle*, New York: Atheneum Publishers, Inc., 1972

Friedan, Betty, *The Feminine Mystique*, New York: Dell Publishing Co., Inc., 1963

Foster, Jeannette, *Sex Variant Women in Literature*, London: Muller, 1958

Fox, Susan, "Comparable Worth is Studied at D.C. Conference," *Women's Political Times*, December, 1980

Frazer, Sir James, *Totemism and Exogamy*, 4 vols. London and New York: Macmillan Publishing Co., Inc., 1910

Gibbon, Edward, *The Decline and Fall of the Roman Empire*, (Portable) New York: The Viking Press, Inc., 1952

Giest Frances and Joseph, *Women in the Middle Ages*, New York: Crowell Publishers, 1978

Graves, Robert, *The Greek Myths*, 2 vols., Baltimore: Penguin Books, 1955

Gray, Dorothy, *Women of the West*, California: Les Femmes Publishing Co., 1976

Gurko, Mirian, *The Ladies of Seneca Falls*, New York: Macmillan Publishing Co., Ind. 1974

Harper, R.F., ed., *The Code of Hammurabi*, The University of Chicago Press, 1904

Harrison, J.F.C., *The Early Victorians, 1832-1851*, London: Weidenfeld and Nicolson, 1971

Hastings, James, ed., Encyclopedia of Religion and Ethics, 12 vols., Edinburgh: Clark; New York: Scribner's, 1908-21

Hays, H.R., *In the Beginnings, Early Man and His Gods*, New York: G.P.Putnam's Sons, 1963

Hecht, Marie; Berbrich, Joan D.; Healey, Sally; Cooper, Clare, *The Women, Yes*, New York: Holt, Rinehart and Winston, Inc., 1973

Heer, Friedrich, *The Medieval World, Europe 1100-1350*, Cleveland and New York: World Publlishing Co., 1961

Hibbert, Christopher, *Daily Life in Victorian England*, New York: American Heritage Publishing Co., Inc. 1975

Hoebel, E. Adamson, *Man in the Primitive World; an Introduction to Anthropology*, London and New York: McGraw-Hill Book Co., 1949

Holtz, Jean, "Housewives Not 'Protected' by Most State Laws," National NOW Times, December, 1977

Hornblower, Margot, "Legislating a 'New Dawn' for the American Family," *Washington Post*, August 10, 1980

Howells, Wm. W., *Man in the Beginning*, London: Bell, 1956 —*Mankind in the Making: The Story of Human Evolution*, Garden City, New York: Doubleday & Co., Inc., 1959 —*Mankind So Far*, American Museum of Natural History Science series, Garden City, New York: Doubleday & Co. Inc., 1944

Hunt, Morton, *The Natural History of Love*, New York, Alfred A. Knopf, Inc., 1967

James, E.O., *The Cult of the Mother Goddess*, New York: Praeger, 1959

Jastrow, Morris, Jr., *The Civilization of Babylonia and Assyria*, Philadelphia: 1915

Jensen, Marj. "Council Challenges Racist/Sexist Textbooks," *National NOW Times*, January, 1980

"Jump in U.S. "Non-Family' Households," *San Francisco Chronicle*, November 26, 1979

Kramer, Samuel, *History Begins at Sumer*, Garden City, New York: Doubleday & Co., Inc., 1959

Kroeber, A.L., and Waterman, T.T., eds. *Source Book in Anthropology*, New York: Harcourt, Brace, 1931

Langdon-Davies, John, *A Short History of Women*, London: Watts & Co., 1928

Lee, Richard B., and Devore, Irven, eds., *Man the Hunter*, Chicago: Aldine Publishing Co., 1968

Lerner, Gerda, *The Woman in American History*, California: Addison-Westley Publishing Company, 1971

Levi-Strauss, Claude, *Totemism*, Boston: Beacon Press, 1962

Lowie, Robert, *Primitive Society*, New York: Harper and Row Publishers, Inc., 1961

Malinowski, Bronislaw, *The Sexual Life of Savages*, New York: Harcourt, Brace & World, Inc., 1929

Mannix, Daniel P., *Those About to Die*, New York: Ballentine Books, 1958

Maspero, Gaston, *The Dawn of Civilization: Egypt and Chaldaea*, London: 1897

McGowan, Kenneth and Hester, Joseph Jr., *Early Man in the New World*, Doubleday, Anchor Books, The Natural History Library, 1962

Mead, Margaret, *Male and Female*, New York: The New American Library, 1949

Mee, Charles L. Jr., *Daily Life in Renaissance Italy*, New York: Heritage Publishing Co., Inc., 1975

Merriam, Eve., ed., *Growing up Female in America*, New York: Doubleday and Company, Inc., 1971

Mill, John Stuart, *On the Subjection of Women*, London: Oxford University Press, 1912

Morgan, Lewis H., *Ancient Society*, Chicago: Kerr, 1877

Moscati, Sabatino, *Ancient Semitic Civilizations*, New York: G.P. Putnam's Sons, 1957

Muller-Lyer, Franz C., *Social Development*, New York: AMS Press, Inc., 1921 —*The Family*, New York: AMS Press, Inc. 1931

Neumann, Erich, *The Great Mother*, tr. R. Manheim, New Jersey: Princeton University Press, 1955

O'Faolain, J., and Martines, L., eds., *Not in God's Image, Women in History From the Greeks to the Victorians*, New York: Harper and Row Publishers, Inc., 1973

O'Neill, William, *Everyone Was Brave*, Chicago: Quadrangle Books, 1971

Patrick, Richard, *Egyptian Mythology*, London: Octopus Books, 1972

Petrie, Sir W. Flinders, *Social Life in Ancient Egypt*, Boston: Houghton Mifflin Co., 1923

Pomeroy, Sarah, *Goddess, Whores, Wives, and Slaves; Women in Classical Antiquity*, New York: Schocken Books, 1976

Porter, Sylvia, "Plight of Battered Women," *San Francisco Chronicle*, November 1, 1979

Power, Eileen Edna, ed. by M.M. Postan, *Medieval Women*, Cambridge; New York: Cambridge University Press, 1975

Rannalls, Jackson, "Job Laws Needed, Bay Area Women Say," *San Francisco Chronicle*, January 28, 1981

"Really Socking it to Women," *Time*, February 7, 1977

Reed, Evelyn, *Woman's Evolution*, New York: Pathfinder, 1975

Ruether, Rosemary Radford, ed., *Religion and Sexism*, New York: Simon and Schuster, 1974

Saggs, H.W.F., *The Greatness That Was Babylon*, New York: The New American Library, 1968

Salper, Roberta, ed., *Female Liberation*, New York: Alfred A. Knopf, Inc., 1972

Seltman, Charles, *Women in Antiquity*, New York: St. Martin's Press, 1955

Sewall, Sam, *Legal Conditions of Women in Massachusetts*, Boston: C.K. Whipple, 1869

Siculus, Diodorus, ed. & tr. by C.H. Oldfather, *Library of History*, London: Heineman, 1933

Simons, Gerald, *Barbarian Europe*, New York: Time-Life Book, 1968

Sinclair, T.A., *Hesiod, Works and Days*, Hildesheim, Georg Olms, 1966

Singer, June, *Androgeny*, New York: Doubleday and Co., Inc., 1976

Smith, Page, *Daughters of the Promised Land*, Boston: Little, Brown & Co., 1970

Stone, Merlin, *When God Was a Woman*, New York: Dial Press, 1976

Spretnak, Charlene, *Lost Goddesses of Early Greece, A Collection of Pre-Hellenic Myths*, Berkeley: Moon Books 1978; Boston: Beacon Press, 1981

Sumner, William Graham, *Folkways: A Study of the Sociological Importance of Usages, Manners, Customs, Mores, and Morals*, Boston: Ginn and Co., 1906

Tannahill, Reah, *Sex in History*, New York: Stein & Day, 1980

Taylor, G. Rattray, *Sex in History*, New York: Harper & Row, 1970

Terrell, John and Donna, *Indian Women of the Western Morning*, New York: Dial Press, 1974

Toffler, Alvin, *The Third Wave*, New York: William Morrow and Company, Inc., 1980

Trecker, Janice Law, *Women on the Move, Struggles for Equal Rights in England*, New York: Macmillan Publishing Co., Inc., 1975

Treece, Henry, *The Crusades*, New York: Random House, Inc., 1962

Truman, Margaret, *Women of Courage*, New York: William Morrow and Company, Inc., 1976

Webster, Hutton, *Primitive Secret Societies*, New York: Macmillen Publishing Co., Inc. 1908

Weidenfeld, George and Nicolson, Ltd., *Milestones in History*, New York: W.W. Norton and Company, 1971

Weld, Theodore,*The Letters of Angelina Grimke-Weld and Sarah Grimke, 1822-1844*, New York: Appleton-Century Crofts and The American Historical Association, 1934

Wells, H.G., *The Outline of History*, 2 vols., New York: Macmillan Publishing Co., Inc., 1921

West, M.L., ed. *Hesiod*, Theogeny, Oxford: Clarendon Press, 1966

Westermarck, W., *History of Human Marriage*, London: Macmillan Publishing Co., Inc., 1903

Winston, Clara and Richard, *Daily Life in the Middle Ages*, New York, American Heritage Publishing Co., 1975

Wollstonecraft, Mary, *A Vindication of the Rights of Women*, New York: Norton Co., Inc., 1967

Woolley, C. Leonard, *The Sumerians*, Oxford, 1928

Wyse, William, ed., *Speeches*, Isaeus, Hildesheim, George Olms, 1967

INDEX

Notable women of each time period are listed at the end of each chapter and are therefore not repeated here.